GINGERBOY

TEAGE EZARD   CHRIS DONNELLAN

Creative Street Food

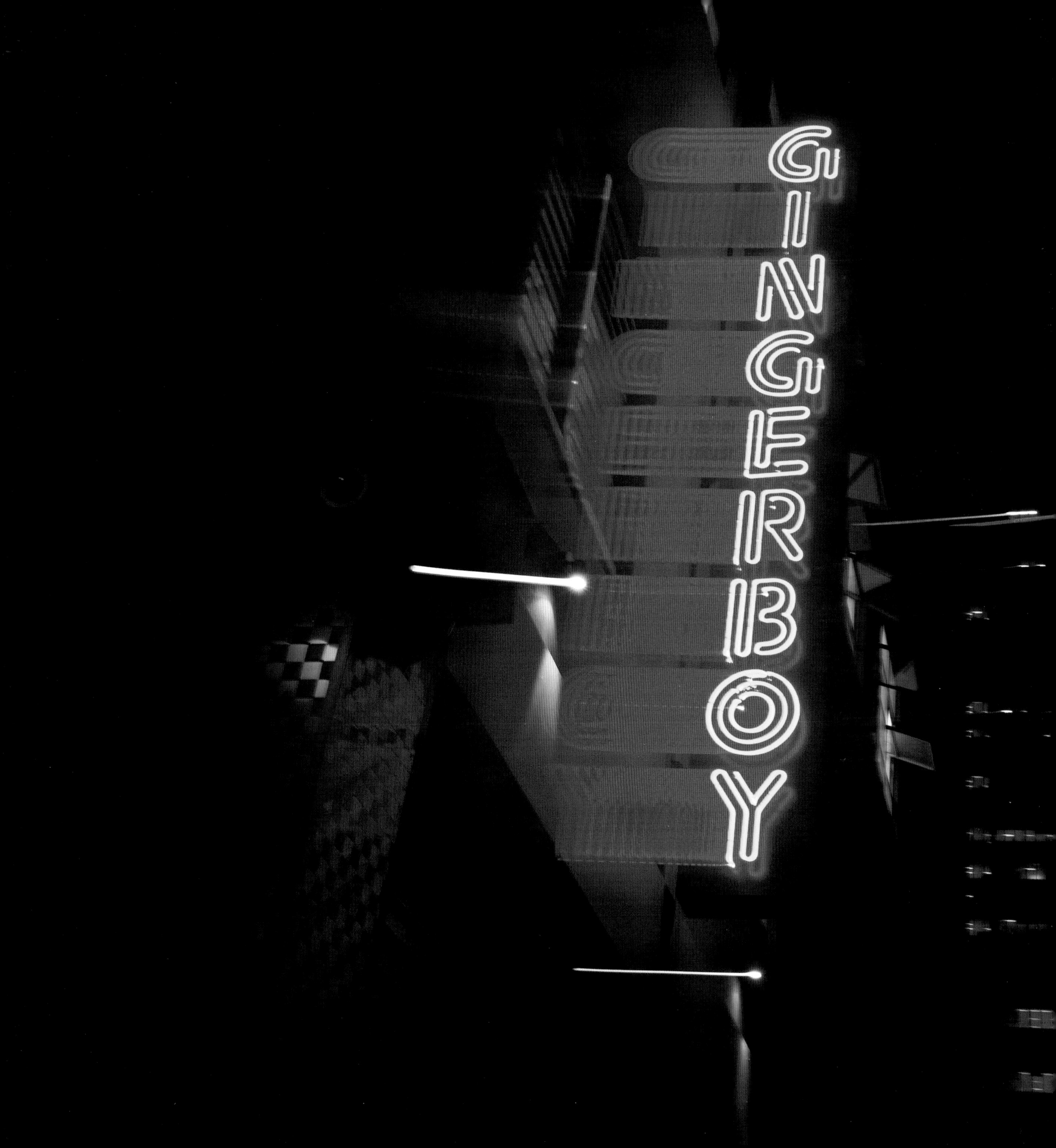
GINGERBOY

This book is for all of the street stall vendors across
Southeast Asia who inspired us to write it.

CONTENTS

INTRODUCTION

We decided to write this book as an expression of our love and passion for Asian food. In our travels through Asia, we have both developed a deep respect for its culture and a deep understanding of the many different cuisines each country has to offer. Gingerboy is a modern interpretation of the much-loved street vendor food found through Kuala Lumpur, Singapore, Hong Kong and Bangkok. Each one of these beautiful cities brings us a new food experience and new food stories, making them so interesting.

The dining experience we aim for at gingerboy is centred on a modern Australian adaption of the Asian hawker-style street market food. The restaurant's hustle and bustle, its fast-paced, youthful and dynamic environment is influenced not only by the dining culture of Southeast Asia but also by buzzing Asian marketplaces and an Asian sense of colour and fun.

The style of food we have decided to include in this book is designed to be cooked and shared in a fun way by groups of four or more – it's all about sharing. Shared food and communal dining with close friends and family is very much the way of the Asian community, and this is a major inspiration for the gingerboy experience. We suggest selecting four to six recipes to be cooked and shared as a banquet. Asian food also allows you to break the rules and to push more boundaries, which is a great breeding ground for creativity. Many of the dishes are Asian classics while some are new, developed by us through cooking Australian seasonal produce using Asian methods. The recipes in this book are the sort of foods that we should eat every day: well balanced and bursting with flavour and interesting textures.

We hope that you enjoy the flavours in this book as much as we do.

PHILOSOPHY

To understand the philosophy of Asian cooking is to understand first of all the components used to create a masterpiece of flavour and texture – the balance of hot, sweet, sour and salty flavours with exciting underlying textures.

This form of artistry relies on all five senses: sight, hearing, smell, touch and taste. We always encourage our chefs to cook with the senses; they're the heart and soul of cooking. Our chefs, too, have a sixth sense that is developed through experience, cooking every dish time and time again. It is essential each chef also takes an experimental approach, using knowledge of the seasons and how each ingredient can vary in its nature from one month to the next, to develop new dishes.

Magic is created in each dish by understanding not only flavour combinations but also textures, colours and cooking methods. Success comes from combining fried and steamed food – pairing crisp with soft, hot with sour, and sweet with salt.

Menus at gingerboy are written according to the seasons. The approach over the colder months is to braise, steam, and cook curries and clay pots; using subtle, deep flavours, while cooking in the warmer climate brings cool, refreshing, crisp, clean and more vibrant flavours to the menu. We use each ingredient at the height of its flavour, colour, appearance and quality. This approach in our philosophy is the most significant, as it delivers consistently great dishes.

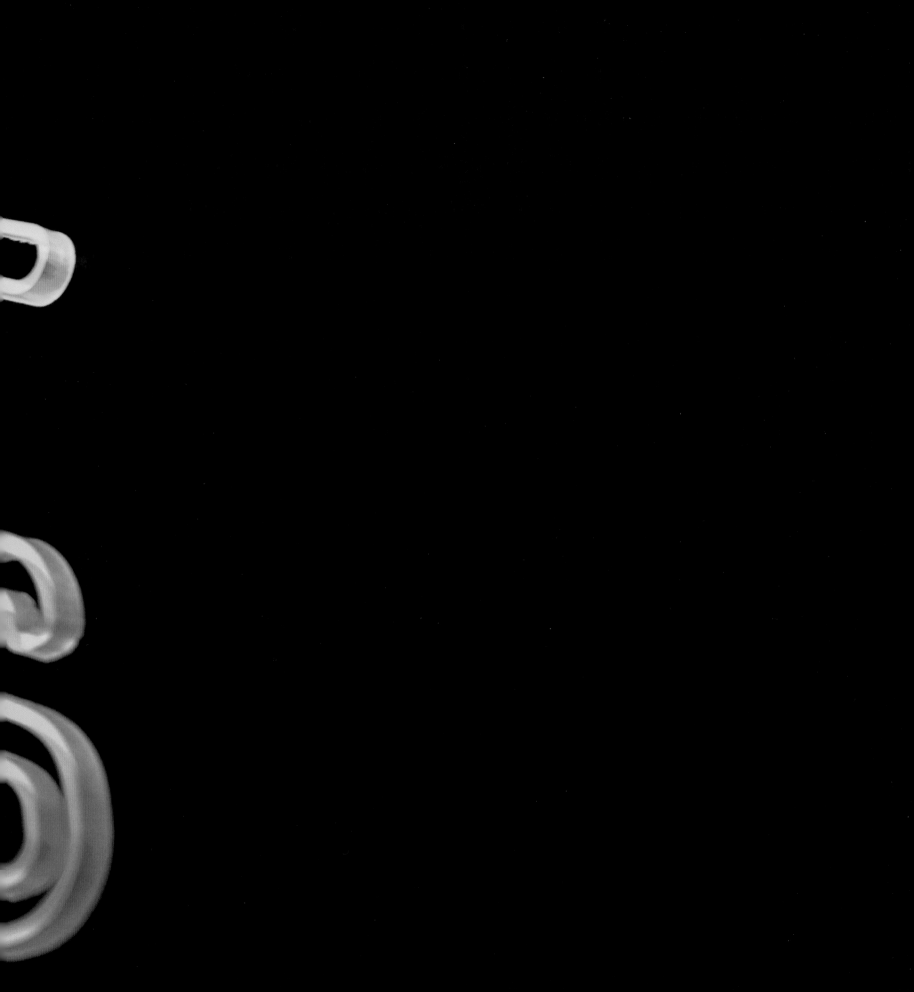

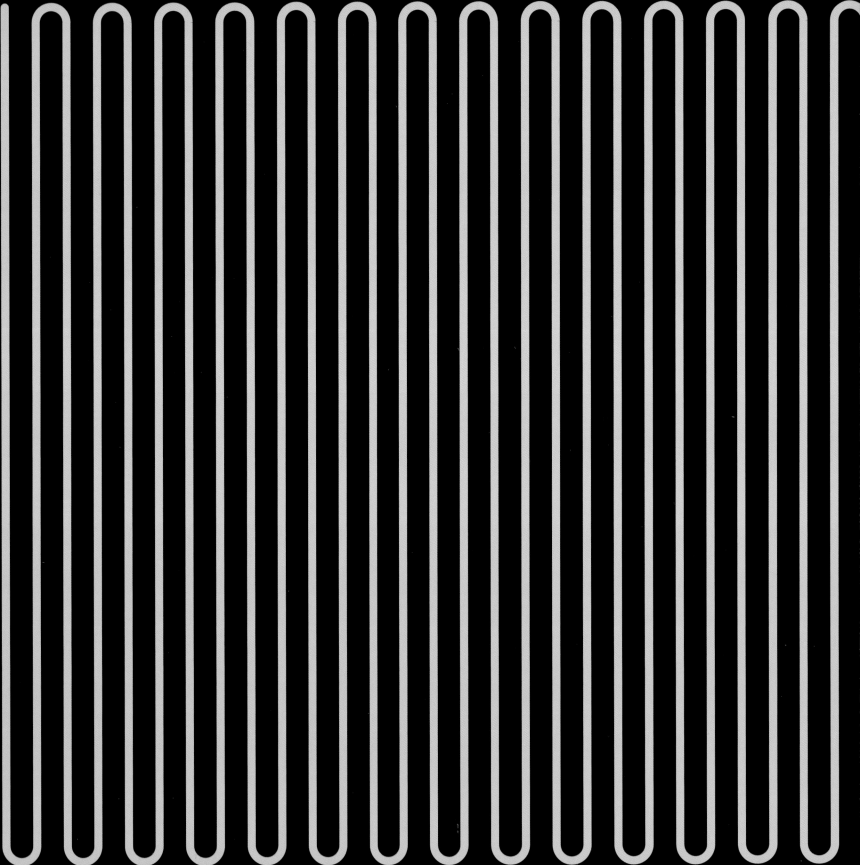

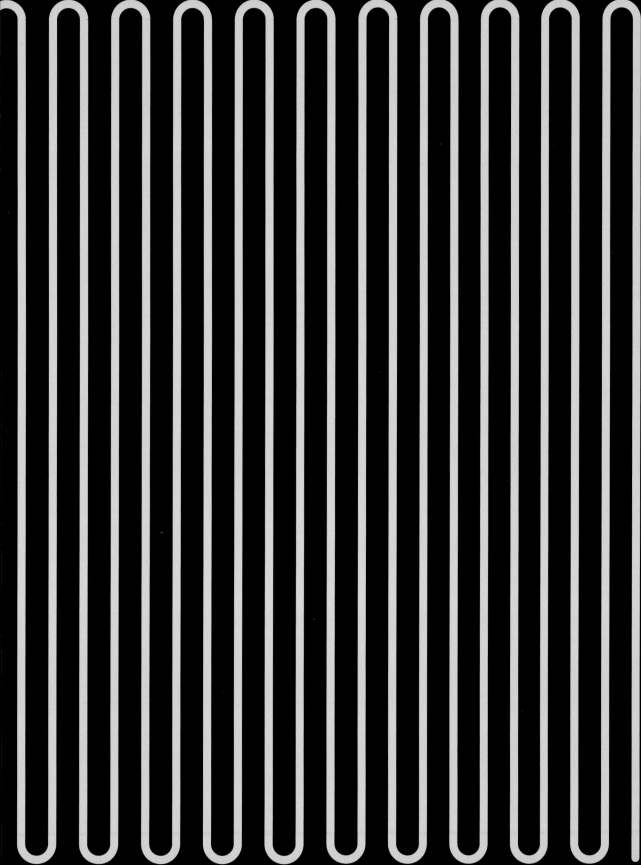

VIETNAMESE VODKA
ESPRESSO

I DREAM OF
LYCHEE

CUCUMBER AND
LEMONGRASS MARTINI

I DREAM OF LYCHEE

MAKES 1 STEMLESS WINE GLASS

2 lychees, cut in half, peeled and deseeded
30 ml lime juice
45 ml Ketel One vodka
15 ml St-Germain elderflower liqueur
20 ml lemongrass-infused sugar syrup*
½ egg white
ice
a dash of soda water
1 sliver of lemongrass

METHOD

Muddle the lychees in a Boston mixing glass, add the lime juice, vodka, elderflower liqueur, sugar syrup, egg white and ice, and shake hard. (Note: the egg white is used to give a frothy appearance.) Double strain (using a hawthorn strainer followed by a tea strainer) into a chilled stemless wine glass, add the soda water and garnish with the lemongrass.

To make the lemongrass-infused sugar syrup, put 500 g sugar into a saucepan, add 1½ cups water and heat to a simmer. Add 2 lemongrass stalks (each stalk broken into 3 pieces) and simmer on medium temperature for 10 minutes. Cool.

One for a night in with the girls, but not one the boys should overlook.

VIETNAMESE VODKA ESPRESSO

MAKES 1 MARTINI GLASS

30 ml sweetened condensed milk
30 ml Ketel One vodka
45 ml freshly made espresso coffee, chilled
15 ml Kahlua
ice

METHOD

Shake condensed milk, vodka and ice in a Boston mixing glass, then pour into the bottom of a martini glass. Rinse out the Boston mixing glass then pour in espresso coffee and Kahlua and shake over ice. Gently pour over the condensed milk layer, giving a two-tier effect.

Filter coffee sweetened with condensed milk is a popular drink in Vietnam, so I thought it would be great to put a twist on this and another popular drink, the espresso martini. I, personally, would drink this anytime of the day but it's probably best suited for after dinner.

CUCUMBER AND LEMONGRASS MARTINI

MAKES 1 MARTINI GLASS

2 thick slices of cucumber
2 teaspoons finely chopped lemongrass, white part only
1 lime wedge
30 ml apple juice
60 ml Ketel One vodka
1 tablespoon cucumber sorbet*
ice
twist of a telegraph cucumber, to garnish

METHOD

Muddle the cucumber, lemongrass and lime wedge in a Boston mixing glass, add the apple juice, vodka, sorbet and ice, and shake. Double strain (using a hawthorn strainer, then a tea strainer) into a chilled martini glass, and garnish with a cucumber twist.

To make the cucumber sorbet, deseed and chop one large cucumber, add 250 ml (1 cup) water and 250 ml (1 cup) sugar syrup (see page 242). Place in the bowl of a food processor, blend and strain through a fine sieve. Churn in an ice-cream machine according to the manufacturer's instructions.

A subtle twist on a classic.

GINGER GIRL

MAKES 1 ROCKS GLASS

6 coriander leaves, picked and washed, plus 1 extra leaf, to garnish
1 teaspoon finely chopped fresh ginger
2 lime wedges
45 ml pineapple juice
30 ml Ketel One vodka
30 ml Massanez crème de gingembre (ginger liqueur)
4 mint leaves, roughly chopped
ice
1 piece of candied ginger, to garnish

METHOD

Muddle the coriander, chopped ginger and the lime wedges in a Boston mixing glass, add the pineapple juice, vodka, ginger liqueur, mint leaves and ice, and shake. Pour straight into a chilled rocks glass, and garnish with the candied ginger and the remaining coriander leaf.

Taken from gingerboy's very first cocktail list, this has been a popular drink since the day we opened.

GIN NO NAME

MAKES 1 MARTINI GLASS

1 kaffir lime leaf, torn, plus 1 extra leaf, to garnish
1 teaspoon finely chopped lemongrass, white part only
45 ml Tanqueray gin
15 ml Massanez lychee liqueur
15 ml sugar syrup (see page 242)
ice

METHOD

Muddle the torn lime leaf and the lemongrass in a Boston mixing glass, add the gin, lychee liqueur, sugar syrup and ice, and shake. Double strain (using a hawthorn strainer, then a tea strainer) into a chilled martini glass and garnish with the extra lime leaf.

One of, if not the most, popular cocktails ever to grace the pages of the gingerboy cocktail menu.

THAI MOON

MAKES 1 TALL GLASS

6 coriander leaves
2 coriander roots, washed and roughly chopped
1 teaspoon finely chopped fresh ginger
½ small red chilli (e.g. bird's eye chilli), split lengthways and roughly chopped
½ lime
15 ml gula melaka (see page 238)
45 ml chilli-infused vodka*
15 ml Licor 43
2 lychees, cut in half, peeled and deseeded
ice
soda water
1 lemongrass stem, white part only, cut in half lengthways
1 Thai basil leaf, to garnish
½ small red chilli, split lengthways and deseeded, to garnish

METHOD

Muddle the coriander leaves and roots, ginger, chilli and lime in a Boston mixing glass. Add the gula melaka, vodka, Licor 43, lychees and ice, and shake. Pour straight into a chilled highball glass and top with the soda water. Pound the lemongrass with a muddling stick, or a rolling pin on a chopping board, to release the aroma. Clap the basil leaf between your hands to release the natural oils and flavour. Garnish with the lemongrass, basil and split chilli.

To make the chilli-infused vodka, cut 2 red bird's eye chillies in half, place in a bottle of vodka and leave until the desired heat is achieved.

The quintessential flavours of gingerboy in a glass.

GIN NO NAME

GINGER GIRL

THAI MOON

MR MIYAGI'S DRAGON FIST PUNCH

SERVE IN A 1-LITRE JUG WITH 4 GLASSES AND ICE

1 handful of Thai basil leaves
240 ml dark rum
120 ml DOM Benedictine
30 ml Pama pomegranate liqueur*
120 ml lime juice
180 ml ruby grapefruit juice
1 dash of Angostura bitters
ice
ruby red grapefruit slices
8 mint leaves, thinly sliced
5 Thai basil leaves, thinly sliced

METHOD

Clap the basil between your hands to release the aroma and place in a 1-litre jug. Add the rum, Benedictine, pomegranate liqueur, lime and grapefruit juices and bitters, fill with the ice and stir for 30 seconds with a bar spoon to mix the ingredients together. Pour the punch into rocks glasses filled with ice, and garnish with slices of grapefruit, mint and basil.

* Pama pomegranate liqueur can be hard to find in most liquor stores; however, you can find it on the internet. Otherwise, pomegranate syrup is just as good and can be found in most supermarkets.

This drink was originally a single-serve punch, but it's too good for one person to drink by themselves. Great for dinner parties and hot summer afternoons.

AN EAST SIDE STORY

MAKES 1 COCKTAIL GLASS

2 slices of cucumber, plus an extra slice
  to garnish
30 ml lime juice
45 ml Matusalem Platino white rum
15 ml St-Germain elderflower liqueur*
15 ml sugar syrup (see page 242)
ice

METHOD

Muddle the cucumber in a Boston mixing glass, add the remaining ingredients and shake hard. Double strain (using a hawthorn strainer, then a tea strainer) into a chilled cocktail glass. Garnish with the remaining cucumber slice.

* St-Germain can be hard to find in liquor stores but can be found on the internet; however, elderflower cordial can be used in its place and is available from specialist food stores and some supermarkets. When using elderflower cordial, I find it best to use 60 ml of rum and 20 ml of cordial to replace the sugar syrup; this keeps the cocktail balanced and tasting close to the original recipe.

For every cocktail menu at gingerboy, we like to put a twist on the classic – here's our version of a Cuban daiquiri. The lighter style white rum marries well with the perfume elderflower and the soft tones of cucumber.

BANGKOK MULE

APEROL, POMEGRANATE
AND GINGER SOUR

CORIANDER COBBLER

APEROL, POMEGRANATE AND GINGER SOUR

MAKES 1 MARTINI GLASS

1 tablespoon peeled and finely chopped
    fresh ginger
50 ml Aperol
20 ml Pama pomegranate liqueur*
30 ml lemon juice
½ egg white
15 ml sugar syrup (see page 242)
ice
1 mint leaf

METHOD

Muddle the ginger in a Boston mixing glass, add the Aperol, pomegranate liqueur, lemon juice, egg white and sugar syrup and give it a dry shake first. (Note: dry shaking the egg white will give your drink a great foamy effect.) Add ice and shake again. Double strain (using a Hawthorn strainer, then a tea strainer) into a martini glass and garnish with the mint leaf.

Pama pomegranate liqueur can be hard to find in most liquor stores; however, you can find it on the internet. Otherwise, pomegranate syrup is just as good and can be found in most supermarkets.

A new member to the gingerboy cocktail list that is sure to stir up a fuss. It's always nice to have something fruity and sour for those hot summer days.

BANGKOK MULE

MAKES 1 HIGHBALL GLASS

3 slices of spiced pear*
½ lime
15 ml poaching syrup*
45 ml vodka
15 ml Poire William liqueur
ice
ginger beer, to finish
3 slices of pear, to garnish

METHOD

Muddle the spiced pear and lime in a Boston mixing glass, add the poaching syrup, vodka, Poire William and ice, and shake. Strain into a chilled highball glass full of ice, top with the ginger beer and garnish with the slices of pear in a fan-like shape.

To make the spiced pears, peel 2 pears, place in a saucepan with 2 cardamom pods, 2 whole cloves, 2 cinnamon sticks and 2 whole star anise. Add a syrup of 4 parts water to 1 part sugar, bring to a light simmer and cook till the pears are soft and the syrup has reduced. Cool the pears in the syrup to let the flavours infuse. Thinly slice the pears and keep the poaching syrup, as it is used in the cocktail.

Bartenders at gingerboy have always liked putting our unique twist on classic drinks and this take on a Moscow mule is no different.

CORIANDER COBBLER

MAKES 1 ROCKS GLASS

5 coriander leaves, plus 1 extra to garnish
30 ml ruby grapefruit juice
30 ml lime juice
30 ml DOM Benedictine
20 ml sweet Italian vermouth
10 ml Campari
ice
crushed ice*
1 ruby grapefruit wedge, to garnish

METHOD

Lightly press the coriander leaves into a Boston mixing glass, add the grapefruit and lime juices, Benedictine, vermouth, Campari and ice, and shake hard. Strain into a rocks glass filled with crushed ice, and garnish with the extra coriander leaf and the grapefruit wedge.

To make crushed ice, put half a glass of ice into a metal Boston tumbler and, using a muddling stick, pound the ice into small crushed pieces.

The bartenders at gingerboy wanted to create a drink using a combination of bitter and herbal flavours. This drink is incredibly refreshing and is great as an aperitif.

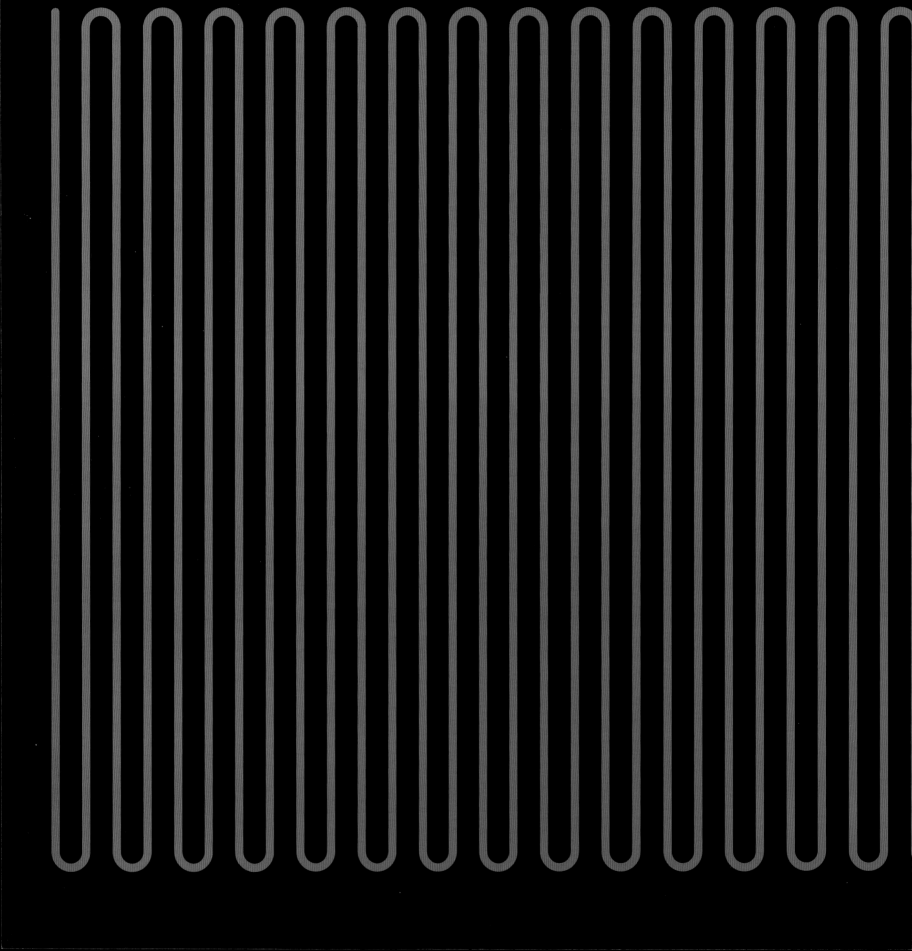

SHARED PLATES

Duck san choi bao, a very easy eating dish, is a favourite at most Asian restaurants. To get the best duck san choi bao, you need to use top quality minced duck and pork. If you can't find this, you can ask your butcher to make it for you.

DUCK SAN CHOI BAO
WITH WATER CHESTNUTS AND LAP CHEONG

DUCK SAN CHOI BAO

300 g minced duck leg meat
100 g minced pork shoulder
100 ml oyster sauce
3½ tablespoons light soy sauce
2 tablespoons sesame oil
3 tablespoons gula melaka
  (see page 238)
sesame oil, extra, for stir-frying
4 tablespoons shaoxing rice wine
5 garlic cloves, finely chopped
4 red shallots, finely chopped
25 g (approx 5 cm) fresh ginger,
  peeled and finely chopped
50 g lap cheong sausage,
  cut in half lengthways and
  thinly sliced
70 g water chestnuts, cut into
  quarters
1 teaspoon prickly ash
  (see page 240)
80 ml lime juice
12 iceberg lettuce cups
  (see page 238)
1 tablespoon white sesame seeds,
  lightly toasted
1 handful of coriander leaves
4 spring onions, white part only,
  thinly sliced on an angle

METHOD

Duck san choi bao Combine the minced duck and pork in a bowl and set aside for 15 minutes to come to room temperature.

In another bowl, combine the oyster and soy sauces, sesame oil and gula melaka and set aside.

Heat the extra sesame oil in a wok over high heat, add the minced duck and pork and fry for 2–3 minutes, stirring, to colour the mince well. Pour in the shaoxing rice wine and stir to break up the mince. Add the garlic, shallots and ginger, cook for 2 minutes, then stir in the lap cheong and water chestnuts. Cook for 1 minute, pour in the oyster sauce mix and cook for 3–4 minutes until caramelised and golden brown. Season with the prickly ash and lime juice.

TO SERVE

Place three lettuce cups on each serving plate and spoon 1–2 tablespoons of the san choi bao mixture into each one. Garnish with a sprinkle of sesame seeds, a couple of coriander leaves and a pinch of spring onion.

This dish is great when you can get fresh sashimi-grade kingfish. The tamarind helps to balance this dressing and the flavours and textures of the fish are not hidden away. You'll need to start this recipe a day ahead.

COCONUT-MARINATED KINGFISH
WITH PEANUT AND TAMARIND DRESSING AND CRISPY NOODLES

Serves four to share

PEANUT AND TAMARIND DRESSING

250 ml (1 cup) coconut cream
1 lemongrass stem, white part
   only, thinly sliced
2 green bird's eye chillies,
   thinly sliced
3 garlic cloves, finely chopped
30 g (approx 6 cm) fresh ginger,
   peeled and finely chopped
30 g light palm sugar, grated
3 red shallots, thinly sliced
4 tablespoons fried chilli peanuts
   (see page 236), crushed in a
   mortar and pestle
2 kaffir lime leaves, thinly sliced
4 tablespoons tamarind paste
   (see page 242)
80 ml lime juice
3 tablespoons fish sauce
600 g kingfish fillets,
   skin removed, pin-boned

CRISPY NOODLES

300 ml vegetable oil
100 g rice vermicelli noodles
sea salt

GARNISH

1 tablespoon fried chilli peanuts
   (see page 236), extra, crushed
   in a mortar and pestle
1 red bird's eye chilli, finely sliced
1 handful of coriander leaves
2 kaffir lime leaves, finely sliced

METHOD

Peanut and tamarind dressing Combine the coconut cream, lemongrass, chilli, garlic, ginger, palm sugar and shallots in a saucepan over medium heat and bring to a gentle simmer. Take off the heat and set aside for 15 minutes. Add the chilli peanuts, lime leaves, tamarind pulp, lime juice, fish sauce and taste for a balance of sweet, sour, salty and hot. Adjust if required. Set aside to cool completely.

Cut the fish in half lengthways, then cut out the centre part, removing the bones and blood line. Place the two fillets of fish in a container and pour on half of the peanut and tamarind dressing. Gently massage the marinade into the fish with your fingertips. Cover the container and transfer to the refrigerator to marinate the kingfish overnight. Pour the remaining dressing into an airtight container and place in the refrigerator.

Crispy noodles Heat the oil in a wok to 180°C (you can test if the oil is the right temperature by dropping in a cube of bread; if the bread browns in 30 seconds, the oil is ready), gently add the noodles and fry for a few seconds until puffed. Flip over with a slotted spoon and fry for a further ten seconds to make sure they are evenly cooked. Drain on paper towel and season with the salt.

TO SERVE

With a thin, sharp knife, thinly slice the kingfish across the grain. Arrange the slices of kingfish on a serving plate and pour on 2 tablespoons of the dressing. Garnish with the extra chilli peanuts. Mix the crispy rice noodles, chilli, coriander and kaffir lime leaf in a small bowl and place a neat pile alongside the fish.

The success of this dish relies heavily on a hot chargrill pan for the moreton bay bugs. If you don't have a chargrill pan, other options would be a very hot barbecue or grill.

CHARGRILLED MORETON BAY BUGS
WITH TURMERIC AND COCONUT DRESSING AND CUCUMBER AND LIME SALAD

TURMERIC AND COCONUT DRESSING

10 g (approx 2 cm) fresh turmeric, peeled and finely chopped
3 garlic cloves, finely chopped
4 red shallots, finely chopped
20 g (approx 4 cm) fresh ginger, peeled and finely chopped
250 ml (1 cup) coconut cream
2 tablespoons fish sauce
80 ml lime juice
2 green bird's eye chillies, thinly sliced
3 tablespoons gula melaka (see page 238)
6 raw moreton bay bugs, cut in half lengthways and cleaned

CUCUMBER AND LIME SALAD

1 telegraph (long) cucumber, peeled and thinly sliced
2 large red chillies, deseeded and thinly sliced
4 spring onions, white part only, thinly sliced
2 limes, segmented
1 handful of Thai basil leaves
1 handful of coriander leaves
50 ml hot and sour dressing (see page 238)

METHOD

Turmeric and coconut dressing Combine the turmeric, garlic, shallots, ginger and coconut cream in a saucepan over medium heat and bring to a gentle simmer. Remove from the heat and set aside to cool for 10 minutes. Add the fish sauce, lime juice, chilli and gula melaka and refrigerate for 10 minutes.

Place the bugs in a large container, pour on half of the coconut dressing, reserving the rest, and transfer to the refrigerator for 2 hours for the flavours and colour to infuse.

Cucumber and lime salad Mix the cucumber, chilli, spring onion, lime segments, basil and coriander in a bowl and reserve until needed.

TO SERVE

Remove the bugs from the refrigerator 20 minutes before cooking, to allow them to return to room temperature. Heat a chargrill pan or barbecue to really hot. Cook the bug halves for 2 minutes. Flip over and cook for another 3 minutes until a nice golden colour with a few really charred spots.

Dress the salad with the hot and sour dressing and divide among serving plates. Criss cross three bug halves on top and pour 3 tablespoons of the reserved turmeric and coconut dressing over the top.

Serves four to share

Serves four to share

This is our version of a classic Vietnamese dish. Banana blossom can be found at a local Asian markets and is best eaten in summer, when it is in abundance.

BANANA BLOSSOM AND CRISPY DUCK SALAD
WITH GINGER NUOC CHAM

CRISPY DUCK

4 duck marylands
1.5 litres (6 cups) Asian chicken
  stock (see page 232)
300 g yellow rock sugar
250 ml (1 cup) shaoxing rice wine
300 ml light soy sauce
750 ml (3 cups) vegetable oil
1 teaspoon prickly ash
  (see page 240)

GINGER NUOC CHAM

30 g (approx 6 cm) fresh ginger,
  peeled and finely chopped
250 ml (1 cup) nuoc cham
  (see page 239)

BANANA BLOSSOM SALAD

1 banana blossom
40 ml lemon juice
1 red onion, thinly sliced
6 spring onions, white part only,
  thinly sliced on an angle
20 g (approx 4 cm) fresh ginger,
  peeled and thinly sliced
2 bird's eye chillies, thinly sliced
1 large handful of Vietnamese
  mint leaves
1 large handful of coriander leaves
1 large handful of Thai basil leaves
120 ml lime juice
2 tablespoons fish sauce

METHOD

Crispy duck Preheat the oven to 180°C.

Heat a large frying pan over medium heat, add the duck legs, and gently seal on each side for 4 minutes until golden brown and the fat is rendered.

Meanwhile, combine the stock, sugar, shaoxing rice wine and soy sauce in a large pot and bring to the boil.

Transfer the duck legs to a 3-litre (12 cup) casserole dish, pour on the stock and cover with a lid. Place in the oven for 2½ hours, or until the meat falls off the bone when you pick up a leg. Remove the duck legs with a slotted spoon and place on a wire rack over a tray until cool. When cool enough to handle, remove the meat from each leg in five or six pieces and reserve until needed.

Ginger nuoc cham Mix the ginger into the nuoc cham and set aside for at least 25 minutes to allow the flavours to infuse.

Banana blossom salad Cut the banana blossom in half, peel off and discard the top four layers, then cut crossways into 1 mm thick slices. Place in a bucket of water with the lemon juice to prevent oxidising. Combine the rest of the salad ingredients in a large bowl.

TO SERVE

Heat the oil in a wok to 170°C (you can test if the oil is the right temperature by dropping in a cube of bread; if the bread browns in 40 seconds, the oil is ready), add the reserved duck meat and deep-fry for 2–3 minutes until crisp. Drain on paper towel and lightly season with the prickly ash.

Remove the banana blossom from the acidulated water and squeeze to remove any excess liquid. Add to the remaining salad ingredients and toss well.

Spoon the ginger nuoc cham into four shallow serving bowls, arrange the duck neatly on top and finish with a handful of the banana blossom salad.

The sweet, sour, salty, hot and fresh relish that we serve with these dumplings is great with all seafood.

PORK, SHIITAKE AND GARLIC CHIVE DUMPLINGS
WITH CORIANDER AND MINT RELISH

CORIANDER AND MINT RELISH

3 garlic cloves, roughly chopped
3 red shallots, roughly chopped
20 g (approx 4 cm) fresh ginger, peeled and roughly chopped
2 green bird's eye chillies, roughly chopped
80 g light palm sugar, grated
1 handful of coriander leaves, roughly chopped
1 handful of mint leaves, roughly chopped
3½ tablespoons fish sauce
80 ml lime juice

PORK, SHIITAKE AND GARLIC CHIVE DUMPLINGS

1 tablespoon vegetable oil
200 g shiitake mushrooms, stalks removed, cut into 5 mm dice
400 g minced pork
½ cup finely chopped garlic chives
20 g (approx 4 cm) fresh ginger, peeled and finely chopped
3 garlic cloves, finely chopped
2 red bird's eye chillies, deseeded and finely chopped
4 coriander roots, washed and finely chopped
4 spring onions, white part only, thinly sliced
2 tablespoons light soy sauce
2 tablespoons fish sauce
½ teaspoon freshly ground white peppercorns
12 round gyoza skins
1 handful of coriander leaves

METHOD

Coriander and mint relish Pound the garlic, shallots, ginger and chilli in a mortar and pestle to make a fine paste. Transfer the paste to a small saucepan and cook over medium–high heat for 3–4 minutes until coloured. Add the palm sugar and cook for 4 minutes until aromatic and pale golden. Set aside to cool.

Place the herbs in the bowl of a food processor, add the paste and blitz until smooth and combined. Transfer to a bowl and add the fish sauce and lime juice.

Pork, shiitake and garlic chive dumplings Heat a wok over high heat, add the oil and mushrooms and stir-fry for 1 minute until the mushrooms are golden. Transfer the mushrooms to a tray to cool.

Combine the mushrooms, pork, chives, ginger, garlic, chilli, coriander root, spring onion, soy and fish sauces and pepper in a large bowl and mix thoroughly with your hands to work the proteins in the meat. Working the proteins in the meat helps infuse flavour through the pork and retain moisture when cooking.

Taking one gyoza skin at a time, place 1 tablespoon of the pork mixture in the middle, lightly brush around the edge with water and fold in half to form a semicircle. Press around the edge to seal, then tap the dumpling on the bench to create a flat base. Using your fingers, mould the rim of the dumpling to create a wavy appearance.

TO SERVE

Place a perforated stainless steel disc insert in a bamboo steamer, spray with cooking spray and add the dumplings in a single layer, leaving a 5 mm space around each one so they don't stick together. Cover and steam over a wok of simmering water for 4–5 minutes, or until cooked through.

Spoon 2 tablespoons of the coriander and mint relish into a ramekin. Arrange the dumplings on a platter, garnish with the coriander leaves and place the relish to one side.

Here is our version of an old Chinese classic from the Sichuan province.

MA-PO TOFU
WITH CHERRY TOMATOES AND HOLY BASIL

MA-PO TOFU

1 tablespoon sesame oil
500 g minced pork
5 red shallots, finely chopped
5 garlic cloves, finely chopped
25 g (approx 5 cm) fresh ginger,
   peeled and finely chopped
8 cherry tomatoes, cut in half
2 tablespoon gula melaka
   (see page 238)
3 red bird's eye chillies,
   thinly sliced
150 ml shaoxing rice wine
250 ml (1 cup) Asian chicken
   stock (see page 232)
150 g firm tofu, cut into 1 cm dice
3 tablespoons light soy sauce
1 tablespoon prickly ash
   (see page 240)
40 ml lemon juice
1 handful of Thai basil leaves

METHOD

Ma-po tofu Heat a wok over high heat, add the oil and pork and stir-fry for 4 minutes until golden brown. Add the shallots, garlic, ginger and cherry tomatoes and stir-fry for 3 minutes, then add the gula melaka and chilli and cook for 1 minute until caramelised. Pour in the shaoxing rice wine and reduce by half, then add the stock and again reduce by half. Add the tofu, soy sauce, prickly ash and lemon juice and stir gently.

TO SERVE

Transfer the tofu mixture to a serving bowl, garnish with the basil and place in the middle of the table.

If you can't get minced wagyu beef get your butcher to mince beef topside with shoulder and add a small amount of pork fat. Betel leaves, also known as la-lot leaves, originate from south and Southeast Asia and can be purchased from most large fruit and vegetable markets, especially Asian markets. We love betel leaves at gingerboy and this dish really releases their flavour.

GRILLED WAGYU BEEF IN BETEL LEAVES
WITH SOUR CHILLI VINEGAR

WAGYU BEEF IN BETEL LEAVES

400 g minced wagyu beef
5 spring onions, white part only, thinly sliced
1 lemongrass stem, white part only, finely chopped
2 kaffir lime leaves, thinly sliced
3 red bird's eye chillies, finely chopped
3 garlic cloves, finely chopped
50 g fresh bamboo shoots, cut into 5 mm slices (see page 235)
3 coriander roots, washed and finely chopped
1 handful of coriander leaves
2 tablespoons fish sauce
3 tablespoons soy sauce
1 pinch of salt
12 large betel leaves, wiped with damp paper towel

SOUR CHILLI VINEGAR

5 garlic cloves, roughly chopped
3 red shallots, roughly chopped
25 g (approx 5 cm) fresh ginger, peeled and roughly chopped
4 large green chillies, roughly chopped
1 handful of coriander root, washed and roughly chopped
100 g light palm sugar, grated
150 ml coconut vinegar
4 tablespoons fish sauce

GARNISH

½ telegraph (long) cucumber, peeled and sliced into thin ribbons on a mandolin

METHOD

Wagyu beef in betel leaves Combine the wagyu beef, spring onion, lemongrass, kaffir lime leaves, chilli, garlic, bamboo shoots, coriander root and leaves, fish and soy sauces and salt in a large chilled bowl. Knead the mixture with the back of your hand for about 4 minutes (this will help retain flavour when cooking). Cover the bowl with plastic wrap and place in the refrigerator for 20 minutes for the flavours to infuse, then knead again for a further 3 minutes.

Spread the betel leaves, shiny side up, in a single layer on a tray lined with damp paper towel.

Roll a golf ball-sized amount of the wagyu beef mixture into a cigar shape that is as long as your betel leaves are wide. Place the cigar across the bottom of a betel leaf, and roll tightly up towards the tip of the leaf. Betel leaves are very strong and will help to keep the moisture in while cooking. Repeat with the remaining wagyu beef mixture and betel leaves. Cover the tray with plastic wrap and transfer to the refrigerator until needed.

Sour chilli vinegar Pound the garlic, shallots, ginger, chilli and coriander root to a fine paste using a mortar and pestle.

Heat a saucepan over medium heat, add the paste and sweat for 5 minutes until coloured. Add the palm sugar and cook for a further 4 minutes until pale golden and aromatic. Take out of the pan and cool in a mixing bowl. Once the paste is cool, add the vinegar and fish sauce and mix well.

TO SERVE

Heat a chargrill pan or barbecue to hot, then cook the wagyu beef in betel leaves for 1 minute on each side (including both sides of the cigar, as well as top and bottom) or until aromatic. They take about 4 minutes to cook altogether. Rest in a warm place for 1 minute.

Spoon the sour chilli vinegar into a ramekin and place at one end of a rectangular platter. Spread the cucumber ribbons lengthways on the platter, then place wagyu in betel leaves on top.

CRISPY YELLOW CURRY-MARINATED GARFISH
WITH CUCUMBER AND CHERRY TOMATO SALAD

Serves four to share

CRISPY YELLOW CURRY-MARINATED GARFISH

1 cup yellow curry paste
  (see page 243)
90 g light palm sugar, grated
5½ tablespoons fish sauce
130 ml lime juice
8 x 80–100 g garfish fillets,
  pin-boned and cut in half
12 thick bamboo skewers, soaked
  in water for 20 minutes
500 ml (2 cups) rice flour batter
  (see page 240)
750 ml (3 cups) vegetable oil
1 tablespoon salt and pepper mix
  (see page 241)

CUCUMBER AND CHERRY TOMATO SALAD

1 cup bean shoot pickle dressing
  (see page 232)
100 g bean shoots, trimmed
1 telegraph (long) cucumber,
  cut in half, deseeded and
  thickly sliced
6 cherry tomatoes, cut in half

GARNISH

8 lemon cheeks
1 handful of coriander leaves

METHOD

Crispy yellow curry-marinated garfish Place the curry paste, sugar, fish sauce and lime juice in a bowl and mix until well combined. Add the fish, cover the bowl with plastic wrap and leave in the refrigerator for 30 minutes to marinate.

Cucumber and cherry tomato salad Mix the bean shoot pickle and the bean shoots in a small bowl and set aside to pickle for 2 minutes. Remove the bean shoots, discarding the pickling liquid, and place in a bowl with the cucumber, shallots and tomato. Reserve until needed.

TO SERVE

Remove the garfish from the refrigerator and take out of the marinade. Thread each piece of garfish onto a skewer.

Heat the oil in a wok to 180°C (you can test if the oil is the right temperature by dropping in a cube of bread; if the bread browns in 30 seconds, the oil is ready). Dip the garfish in the batter, shake off the excess, and deep-fry in the hot oil for 2–3 minutes until crisp. Drain on paper towel, then lightly season with the salt and pepper mix.

Toss the salad gently, then evenly divide between four serving plates. Place three garfish skewers on each plate and garnish with two lemon cheeks and the coriander.

Wagyu beef rib meat, also known as intercostals, is ideal for braising.
It has great marbling and once cooked is nice and gelatinous and extremely
tasty. We like to roll it in the roasted rice and then deep-fry for texture.

TWICE-COOKED CRUSTED WAGYU BEEF RIBS
WITH YELLOW BEAN CHILLI SOY SAUCE AND CITRUS SALAD

TWICE-COOKED CRUSTED WAGYU BEEF RIBS

1.5 litres (6 cups) master stock
  (see page 239)
600 g wagyu beef ribs, on
  the bone
750 ml (3 cups) vegetable oil
6 egg whites
1 cup roasted rice (see page 240)
2 tablespoons prickly ash
  (see page 240)
500 ml (2 cups) water

YELLOW BEAN CHILLI SOY SAUCE

100 ml kecap manis
100 ml rice wine vinegar
1 tablespoon Chinese black
  vinegar
3 tablespoons yellow bean paste
2 tablespoons light soy sauce
70 g caster sugar
2 red bird's eye chillies,
  roughly chopped
20 g (approx 4 cm) fresh ginger,
  peeled and roughly chopped
3 garlic cloves, roughly chopped
80 ml lime juice
3 tablespoons water

CITRUS SALAD

1 cup bean shoots
1 orange, segmented
1 ruby grapefruit, segmented
2 limes, segmented
1 large handful of mint leaves
1 small handful of coriander cress

METHOD

Twice-cooked crusted wagyu beef ribs Preheat the oven to 170°C.

Bring the master stock to a gentle simmer in a saucepan over medium heat. Place the wagyu beef in a casserole dish and pour on the stock. Cover with a cartouche*, then with a lid and place in the oven for 2½ hours until the meat is gelatinous and falls apart when you pick it up. Remove the wagyu beef and place on a tray to cool. Then transfer to the refrigerator for 45 minutes. Cut the chilled wagyu beef into 5 cm lengths.

Heat the oil in a wok to 180°C (you can test if the oil is the right temperature by dropping in a cube of bread; if the bread browns in 30 seconds, the oil is ready). Lightly whisk the egg whites in a bowl until frothy. Place the roasted rice in a large shallow bowl. Dip the wagyu beef into the egg white, let the excess drip off then dust in the roasted rice, making sure that all sides are coated. Deep-fry for 2 minutes until crispy and lightly golden. Drain on paper towel.

Yellow bean chilli soy sauce Combine all of the ingredients in a saucepan, place over medium heat and bring to the boil. Reduce the heat to low and simmer for 5 minutes to allow the flavours to infuse. Set aside for 30 minutes, then strain through a fine sieve into a small saucepan and reheat.

Citrus salad Place the bean shoots, citrus segments, mint and coriander cress in a large shallow serving bowl. Toss gently to combine.

TO SERVE

Pour 2–3 tablespoons of yellow bean chilli soy into a small bowl. Cut the wagyu beef pieces in half on a slight angle and place on top of the salad.

* *To make a cartouche*, cut out a circle of greaseproof paper slightly larger than your casserole dish.

Silver whiting is a small eating fish that barbecues really well. Ask your fishmonger to scale the fish for you. Throughout Southeast Asia you find small fish on skewers at street vendors.

BARBECUED SILVER WHITING
WITH CHINESE VINEGAR AND CHILLI DRESSING

SILVER WHITING

3 red shallots, finely chopped

3 garlic cloves, finely chopped

1 large green chilli, finely chopped

4 coriander roots, washed and finely chopped

3 tablespoons light soy sauce

12 x 70 g whole silver whiting, scaled, cleaned, and scored both sides to the bone

12 thick bamboo skewers, soaked in water for 20 minutes

2 tablespoons vegetable oil

2 tablespoons salt and pepper mix (see page 241)

CHINESE VINEGAR AND CHILLI DRESSING

4 tablespoons pat chun (sweetened Chinese vinegar)

120 ml Chinese black vinegar

3 tablespoons coconut vinegar

40 g butter

40 ml lime juice

1 teaspoon spiced chilli salt (see page 241)

200 g light palm sugar, grated

2 tablespoons water

GARNISH

700 ml vegetable oil

250 g rice vermicelli noodles

1 large handful of coriander cress

6 spring onions, white part only, thinly sliced on an angle

METHOD

Silver whiting Combine the shallots, garlic, chilli, coriander root and soy sauce in a large shallow bowl.

Transfer the fish to the bowl and gently rub the marinade into the skin. Cover with plastic wrap and place in the refrigerator to marinate for 1 hour.

Remove the fish from the marinade, then thread each fish onto a skewer, starting at the mouth and working down to the tail.

Chinese vinegar and chilli dressing Combine the pat chun, vinegars, butter, lime juice and chilli salt in a jug and mix well.

Place the palm sugar and water in a saucepan over medium heat. Stir to completely dissolve the sugar, then bring to the boil and cook for about 6 minutes or until you have a golden brown caramel. Carefully pour the pat chun mixture into the caramel, standing back a little bit in case it splashes up, and bring to the boil over medium heat. Set aside to cool.

Garnish Heat the oil in a wok to 180°C (you can test if the oil is the right temperature by dropping in a cube of bread; if the bread browns in 30 seconds, the oil is ready). Add the noodles and fry for 10 seconds or until puffed. Flip over using a slotted spoon and fry for a further 5–10 seconds. Drain on paper towel.

TO SERVE

Heat a barbecue to hot. Drizzle the oil over the fish and season with the salt and pepper mix. Barbecue on each side for 1–2 minutes or until the skin is golden and the flesh is white.

Pile the noodles onto a platter and place the skewered silver whiting on top. Pour on the Chinese vinegar and chilli dressing and garnish with the coriander and spring onion.

Fresh finger limes are available over the summer months and are natively grown in Australia. You can purchase finger limes from specialty food markets. Inside the finger limes are small caviar-like lime pearls.

BANANA PRAWNS
WITH BANDIT SAUCE

FINGER LIME SALAD

2 large red chillies, deseeded and thinly sliced

½ pomelo, segmented

1 red onion, thinly sliced

1 cup sliced baby coconut (see page 232)

1 large handful of Thai basil leaves

3 large (approx 6 cm) finger limes, cut in half lengthways, flesh scraped out

25 ml lime juice

½ tablespoon fish sauce

BANDIT SAUCE

150 g light palm sugar, grated

½ long green chilli, deseeded and roughly chopped

½ long red chilli, deseeded and roughly chopped

3 coriander roots, washed and roughly chopped

3 garlic clove, thinly sliced

5 tablespoons fish sauce

130 ml lime juice

2 kaffir lime leaves, thinly sliced

2 red shallots, peeled and thinly sliced

2 tablespoons fried chilli peanuts (see page 236)

BANANA PRAWNS

8 very large raw banana prawns, head removed, peeled and deveined

1 tablespoon fish sauce

60 ml lime juice

METHOD

Finger lime salad Place the chilli, pomelo, onion, coconut, basil and finger lime flesh in a bowl and set aside.

Bandit sauce Pound the palm sugar, chillies, coriander root and garlic to a fine paste in a mortar and pestle. Add the fish sauce, lime juice, lime leaves, shallots and peanuts and taste for seasoning. The sauce should be sweet, salty, hot and sour; adjust if necessary.

Banana prawns Heat a barbecue until extremely hot. Season the prawns with the fish sauce and lime juice and place on the barbecue for 2–5 minutes each side, or until they are golden.

TO SERVE

Place two prawns, flesh side up, on each serving plate. Spoon the bandit sauce over the prawns, then dress the salad with the lime juice and fish sauce. Gently toss the salad and place a small handful on each plate.

Cooking quails in master stock gets the flavour right through the flesh but does not cook them completely. When you fry them and cut them in half, they should be pink and moist. Popcorn shoots are sweet and have a great texture and add a different flavour to the dish. They can be ordered in by some fruit and vegetable shops if they are given a bit of notice. You'll need to start this recipe a day ahead.

CRISPY QUAIL
WITH PICKLED BEAN SHOOT SALAD

CRISPY QUAIL

2 litres (8 cups) master stock
  (see page 239)
6 large whole quails
750 ml (3 cups) vegetable oil
2 tablespoons prickly ash
  (see page 240)

PICKLED BEAN SHOOT SALAD

1 cup bean shoot pickle dressing
  (see page 232)
100 g bean shoots, trimmed
1 handful of coriander cress
30 g popcorn shoots
1 red bird's eye chilli, thinly sliced
1 red onion, thinly sliced
4 spring onions, white part only
  thinly sliced

GARNISH

250 ml (1 cup) green chilli soy
  (see page 237)

METHOD

Crispy quail Pour the master stock into a large saucepan and bring to a simmer over high heat. Immediately remove from the heat and set aside. Add the quails, pressing down so they are completely covered. Cover with a lid and leave for 10 minutes, then move the quails around and leave for 20–30 minutes until the stock has cooled. Take the quails out of the stock and transfer to a wire rack over a tray and place, uncovered, in the refrigerator overnight. (This is done to dry out the skin, which will give the quails a really nice crispy texture when fried.) Strain the stock, let it cool, then store in an airtight container in the freezer, for future use.

Pickled bean shoot salad Place the bean shoot pickle and bean shoots in a bowl and set aside to pickle for 2 minutes. Remove the bean shoots, discarding the pickling liquid, and transfer to a serving bowl. When ready to serve, add the coriander, popcorn shoots, chilli, onion and spring onion and toss gently.

TO SERVE

Take the quails out of the refrigerator. Heat the oil in a wok to 180°C (you can test if the oil is the right temperature by dropping in a cube of bread; if the bread browns in 30 seconds, the oil is ready) and deep-fry the quails, in batches of two or three at a time, for 2 minutes or until golden brown. Drain on paper towel for 2 more minutes, then season with the prickly ash. Cut the quails in half through the breast bone, and arrange on a serving plate. Pour the green chilli soy into a small jug, and serve on the side with the salad.

This dish has become a bit of a gingerboy signature; the soy cures the trout nicely overnight. The dressing uses fresh turmeric, which adds great colour and flavour. You'll need to start this recipe a day ahead to allow time for the trout to cure.

SOY-CURED OCEAN TROUT
WITH TURMERIC AND COCONUT CARAMEL AND PICKLED DAIKON

SOY-CURED OCEAN TROUT

400 ml light soy sauce

4 whole star anise, lightly toasted

zest and juice of 2 lemons

4 spring onions, white part only, roughly chopped

3 garlic cloves, roughly chopped

30 g (approx 6 cm) fresh ginger, peeled and roughly chopped

1 tablespoon caster sugar

600 g ocean trout fillets, skin removed, pin-boned

TURMERIC AND COCONUT CARAMEL

150 g light palm sugar, grated

4 tablespoons water

10 g (approx 2 cm) fresh turmeric, peeled and finely chopped

1–2 large green chillies, finely sliced

150 ml coconut cream

3 tablespoons shiso vinegar

80 ml lime juice

2 pinches of sea salt

3 spring onions, white part only, thinly sliced

PICKLED DAIKON

1 small daikon, peeled and thinly sliced into ribbons

250 ml (1 cup) sichuan pepper pickling liquid (see page 241)

METHOD

Soy-cured ocean trout Combine the soy sauce, star anise, lemon zest and juice, spring onion, garlic, ginger and sugar in a large shallow bowl. Set aside for 10 minutes so the flavours can infuse. Add the ocean trout, cover with plastic wrap and place in the refrigerator for 20–24 hours to cure. Pull out after 10 hours, flip the trout over and return to the refrigerator.

Turmeric and coconut caramel Place the palm sugar and water in a saucepan over medium heat and bring to the boil, stirring until the sugar dissolves. Continue to simmer for 6–8 minutes until the syrup is golden. Add the turmeric and chilli (reserving a few slices of the chilli for garnish), cook for 30 seconds then pour in the coconut cream and vinegar. Bring back to a gentle simmer then remove from the heat. Set aside for 20 minutes to cool, then stir in the lime juice, salt and spring onion.

Pickled daikon Combine the daikon and pickling liquid in a bowl and set aside for 20 minutes. Drain and discard the pickling liquid.

TO SERVE

Cut the trout into 1–2 mm thick slices and arrange on the serving plates in a neat line. Spoon the turmeric and coconut caramel into a small serving bowl. Place a small pile of the pickled daikon on top of the trout and garnish with remaining chilli.

CHAR SIU PORK
AND SPRING ONION RICE PAPER ROLLS

CHAR SIU PORK

600 g pork fillet
500 ml (2 cups) char siu
    marinade (see page 233)
1 teaspoon sea salt

RICE PAPER ROLLS

100 g rice vermicelli noodles
12 small round rice paper
    wrappers
1 telegraph (long) cucumber,
    deseeded and cut into 5 cm
    julienne
1 handful of coriander leaves
1 handful of mint leaves
1 red onion, peeled and
    thinly sliced
4 spring onions, white part only,
    thinly sliced on an angle
1 large handful of garlic chives,
    cut into 2.5 cm batons
1 tablespoon prickly ash
    (see page 240)
250 ml (1 cup) char siu marinade
    (see page 233), for dipping

METHOD

Char siu pork Place the pork in a shallow bowl. Pour half of the char siu marinade over the pork and gently massage into the flesh and skin. Cover with plastic wrap and leave in the refrigerator for one hour. Reserve the remaining char siu marinade for serving.

Preheat the oven to 180°C and also heat a barbecue until really hot. Remove the pork from the marinade, then place the pork on the barbecue and char for 4–5 minutes until some nice grill lines appear on the meat. Transfer to a wire rack over a baking tray and place in the oven for 15 minutes. Remove from oven, cover with foil and set aside to rest for 10 minutes. Once rested, cut the pork against the grain into 2 mm thick slices, place on a plate and set aside until needed.

Rice paper rolls Cook the noodles in boiling water for 4 minutes. Drain and run under cold water for 30 seconds, then drain again.

Using one rice paper wrapper at a time, soak the wrapper in a bowl of cold water for 30 seconds or until it starts to soften. Remove and gently pat dry with paper towel. Place a cucumber baton in the centre, add a couple of pieces of the pork, a couple of coriander and mint leaves, spread on a small amount of the noodles and scatter some red onion, spring onion and chives over the top. Lightly season with some prickly ash and fold over one end to form a base. Roll over the right side and then pull tightly and roll over the left side, being careful not to tear as the rice paper is fragile, to enclose the filling.

TO SERVE

Place three rice paper rolls on each serving plate and serve accompanied by ramekins of the reserved char siu marinade.

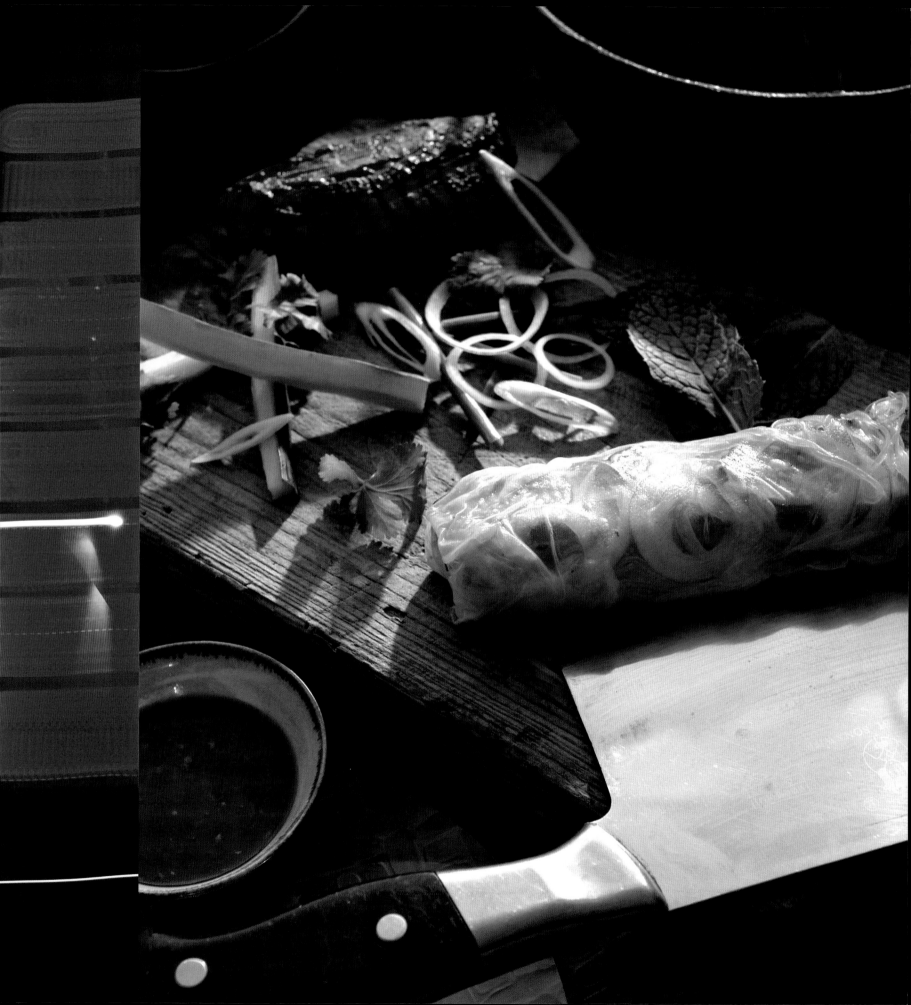

Bun dough flour is available from your local Asian grocer. It is a great product, as you can cook the dough and use it to accompany soups or curries.

GINGERBOY'S STEAMED BARBECUE PORK BUNS

BARBECUE PORK

600 g pork belly, cut into 3 pieces
350 ml char siu marinade
  (see page 233)
6 spring onions, white part only,
  thinly sliced
½ teaspoon prickly ash
  (see page 240)
1 red bird's eye chilli, thinly sliced
3 red shallots, thinly sliced
40 ml lime juice
1 tablespoon gula melaka
  (see page 238)

BUNS

300 g bun dough flour
120 ml milk
60 g caster sugar
1 teaspoon vegetable oil

GARNISH

4 spring onions, white part only,
  thinly sliced on an angle
250 ml (1 cup) green chilli soy
  (see page 237)

METHOD

Barbecue pork Place the pork in a shallow bowl, pour 170 ml ($^2/_3$ cup) of the char siu marinade over the top and gently massage it into the flesh and skin. Cover with plastic wrap and refrigerate for 1 hour to marinate.

Preheat the oven to 180°C. Place a wire rack on a baking tray.

Remove the pork belly from the marinade, place it on the wire rack and roast for 30 minutes until golden brown and caramelised. Set aside to cool. Cut the pork belly into small dice and transfer to a bowl. Add the remaining char siu marinade, the spring onion, prickly ash, chilli, shallots, lime juice and gula melaka and mix well. Cover with plastic wrap and leave in the refrigerator until needed.

Buns Place 270 g of the bun dough flour, the milk and sugar in the bowl of an electric mixer (the dough can also be made in a food processor or by hand in a large mixing bowl). Using a paddle attachment on a medium speed, work until the dough comes together. Once it comes together turn it onto a low speed for a further 3 minutes and gently work it. Transfer the dough to a lightly floured surface and knead for a couple of minutes until smooth, soft and shiny. Cover with plastic wrap and rest in the refrigerator for 10 minutes.

Lightly dust the bench with the remaining bun flour and roll the dough into a sausage shape. Cut into 12 evenly sized pieces. Roll out each piece of dough to form a round 12 cm in diameter. Place 1 large tablespoon of the barbecue pork in the centre, then pinch the dough in towards the middle to enclose the filling. Press firmly to seal the edges and expel the air, then turn over so that the seam side is underneath.

TO SERVE

Place a perforated stainless steel disc insert in a bamboo steamer, spray with cooking spray and add the buns, seam side down, in a single layer, leaving a 2 cm space around each one so they don't stick together. Cover and steam over a wok of simmering water for 6 minutes, or until cooked through. To check if they are cooked, gently squeeze the base of bun; it should be nice and firm.

Place three buns on each plate and scatter on the spring onion. Pour the green chilli soy into a small dish, and serve alongside the buns.

This is a very simple dish but the texture of the silken tofu when crispy on the outside and silky smooth on the inside is sublime. This is a great vegetarian option for a dinner party.

SALT AND PEPPER SILKEN TOFU

SALT AND PEPPER SILKEN TOFU

200 g (1⅓ cups) plain flour
600 g silken tofu, cut into
  2 cm dice
750 ml (3 cups) vegetable oil
1 tablespoon salt and pepper mix
  (see page 241)
lemon cheeks, to serve

METHOD

Salt and pepper silken tofu Place half of the flour in a large bowl, gently add the tofu, sprinkle the remaining flour over the top and gently move the tofu around to completely coat each piece.

Heat the oil in a wok to 180°C (you can test if the oil is the right temperature by dropping in a cube of bread; if the bread browns in 30 seconds, the oil is ready). Deep-fry the tofu for 2–3 minutes until golden. Remove with a slotted spoon and drain on paper towel. Season evenly with the salt and pepper mix.

TO SERVE

Divide the tofu evenly between four serving bowls and serve with lemon cheeks.

BLUE SWIMMER CRAB AND POMELO SALAD
WITH SWEET AND SOUR CHILLI DRESSING

Serves four to share

SWEET AND SOUR CHILLI DRESSING

5 garlic cloves, roughly chopped

5 red shallots, roughly chopped

30 g (approx 6 cm) fresh ginger, peeled and roughly chopped

6 coriander roots, washed and roughly chopped

4 large green chillies, roughly chopped

150 g light palm sugar, grated

5 tablespoons fish sauce

200 ml coconut vinegar

BLUE SWIMMER CRAB AND POMELO SALAD

1 pomelo, peeled and segmented

100 g desiccated coconut

1 baby coconut (see page 232), flesh thinly sliced

1 red onion, thinly sliced

1 telegraph (long) cucumber, deseeded and thinly sliced into ribbons using a vegetable peeler

20 g (approx 4 cm) fresh ginger, peeled and thinly sliced

2 tablespoons dried shrimp

1 mango, diced

1 avocado, diced

1 cup blue swimmer crabmeat (see page 233)

1 large handful of Thai basil leaves

1 large handful of sawtooth coriander leaves

1 cup fried onion (see page 236)

METHOD

Sweet and sour chilli dressing Pound the garlic, shallots, ginger, coriander root and chilli to a fine paste in a mortar and pestle.

Place a saucepan over medium heat, add the garlic paste and sweat for 5 minutes until lightly coloured. Add the palm sugar and cook for a further 5 minutes until caramelised, aromatic and a light golden colour. Add the fish sauce and vinegar and bring to the boil, stirring to dissolve the sugar. Set aside to cool.

Blue swimmer crab and pomelo salad Preheat the oven to 170°C.

Spread the desiccated coconut on a baking tray and toast in the oven for 5 minutes. Take the tray out of the oven and move the coconut around. Return the tray to the oven for a further 3 minutes until lightly golden brown all over. Set aside to cool.

Combine the pomelo, toasted coconut, baby coconut, onion, cucumber, ginger, dried shrimp, mango, avocado, crabmeat, basil and coriander in a large bowl and gently mix.

TO SERVE

Arrange the crab and pomelo salad in the middle of each serving plate and scatter the fried onion on top. To keep the salad fresh and crisp, place the dressing on the side and pour on at the table.

These quick, tasty and crispy sweet crab won tons are a fantastic small course to serve as a canapé for a function.

BLUE SWIMMER CRAB WON TONS
WITH BEAN SHOOT SALAD

BEAN SHOOT SALAD

150 g bean shoots, trimmed
1 cup bean shoot pickle dressing (see page 232)
½ iceberg lettuce, finely shredded
3 red shallots thinly sliced
½ cup coriander leaves
1 large red chilli, deseeded and thinly sliced

BLUE SWIMMER CRAB WON TONS

150 g bream fillet, skin removed, pin-boned
1 cup blue swimmer crabmeat (see page 233)
4 spring onions, white part only, thinly sliced
2 red bird's eye chillies, thinly sliced
3 garlic cloves, finely chopped
20 g (approx 4 cm) fresh ginger, peeled and finely chopped
4 coriander roots, washed and finely chopped
2 tablespoons fish sauce
12 square yellow won ton wrappers
750 ml (3 cups) vegetable oil
1 cup nuoc cham (see page 239), to serve as a dipping sauce
coriander leaves, to garnish

METHOD

Bean shoot salad Mix the bean shoots and the bean shoot pickle in a bowl and leave for 2 minutes. Drain the bean shoots and set aside. Combine the lettuce, shallots, coriander and chilli in a bowl, then stir through the bean shoots.

Blue swimmer crab won tons Place the bream in the bowl of a food processor and blitz to form a smooth ball.

Combine the crabmeat and fish in a large bowl, add the spring onion, chillies, garlic, ginger, coriander root and, using your hands, mix well. Stir in the fish sauce.

Cut each won ton wrapper into a disc with an 8 cm round cutter. Using one won ton wrapper at a time, place 1 tablespoon of the crab mixture in the centre, brush a little water round the edge and close over into a semicircle, pressing the edges firmly to seal. Stand the won tons up so that the folded edge is facing up.

Heat the oil in a wok to 180°C (you can test if the oil is the right temperature by dropping in a cube of bread; if the bread browns in 30 seconds, the oil is ready). Add the won tons, about six at a time, and deep-fry for 2–3 minutes or until golden. Drain on paper towel.

TO SERVE

Divide the salad evenly among four large plates. Place three dumplings on each plate, garnish with coriander leaves and serve accompanied by small dishes of the nuoc cham.

Smoked trout and avocado salad
with betel leaves and coconut dressing

Freshly shucked oysters with chilli lime dressing

This great summer salad has texture, and the flavour is a balance of creamy and smoky. Betel leaves originated in Asia but are readily available in most countries these days. They can be found in fresh vegetable markets and are available most of the year.

SMOKED TROUT AND AVOCADO SALAD
WITH BETEL LEAVES AND COCONUT DRESSING

Serves four to share

COCONUT DRESSING

120 g light palm sugar, grated
110 ml coconut vinegar
110 ml rice wine vinegar
4 tablespoons peanut oil
80 ml lime juice
2 limes, zested and segmented
6 red shallots, thinly sliced
2 red bird's eye chillies,
   thinly sliced
2 tablespoons fish sauce

SMOKED TROUT AND
AVOCADO SALAD

100 g rice vermicelli noodles
500 ml (2 cups) boiling water
2 avocados, cut into 1 cm dice
400 g smoked trout, skin and
   bones removed, cut into
   1 mm thick slices
1 large handful of chives, cut
   into 5 cm batons
100 g water chestnuts,
   finely diced
5 spring onions, white part only,
   sliced on an angle
2 large red chillies, thinly sliced
10 large betel leaves, wiped
   with damp paper towel, finely
   shredded
½ telegraph (long) cucumber,
   peeled, deseeded and cut into
   5 cm batons
1 red onion, thinly sliced
40 g salmon roe

METHOD

Coconut dressing Combine the palm sugar and vinegars in a small saucepan and cook, stirring over low heat until the sugar has dissolved. Remove from the heat and set aside to cool. Whisk in the oil and lime juice, then add the lime zest and segments, shallots, chilli and fish sauce.

Smoked trout and avocado salad Soak the noodles in the boiling water for 10 minutes, drain well and roughly chop into 5 cm lengths. Transfer to a large bowl, add the avocado, trout, chives, water chestnuts, spring onion, chilli, betel leaves, cucumber and onion, pour over half of the coconut dressing and gently toss.

TO SERVE

Place a neat pile of the salad in four shallow serving bowls, spoon 1 tablespoon of salmon roe over the top and drizzle on 1 extra tablespoonful of the dressing.

This is a great dressing for oysters as it is not overpowering and complements the flavour. There is no garnish as it doesn't need anything else.

FRESHLY SHUCKED OYSTERS
WITH CHILLI LIME DRESSING

CHILLI LIME DRESSING

90 g grated light palm sugar
1 tablespoon water
60 ml lime juice
2 tablespoons fish sauce
2 red bird's eye chillies,
   finely chopped
1 garlic clove, finely chopped
12 large oysters, freshly shucked

METHOD

Chilli lime dressing Combine the palm sugar and water in a saucepan over low heat and cook, stirring, until the sugar has dissolved. Take off the heat and stir in the lime juice, fish sauce, chilli and garlic. Set aside until needed.

TO SERVE

Place two oysters on each serving plate, then spoon 1 tablespoon of the chilli lime dressing on top.

We get our beautiful, sweet school prawns from Lakes Entrance in Victoria. When they are rolled in flour and fried, they have an amazing texture.

SALT AND PEPPER SCHOOL PRAWNS
WITH RED CHILLI DRESSING

RED CHILLI DRESSING

4 roma tomatoes, cored and cut in half
100 ml pat chun (sweetened Chinese vinegar)
4 large red chillies, roughly chopped
3 red shallots, roughly chopped
2 garlic cloves, roughly chopped
5 coriander roots, washed and roughly chopped
50 g light palm sugar, grated
150 ml lime juice
4 tablespoons fish sauce

SALT AND PEPPER PRAWNS

750 ml (3 cups) vegetable oil
150 g (1 cup) plain flour
2 tablespoons prickly ash (see page 240)
500 g raw school prawns, cleaned and spikes removed

GARNISH

3 cups crispy fried sweet potato (see page 235)
6 spring onions, white part only, thinly sliced on an angle
1 large handful of coriander leaves

METHOD

Red chilli dressing Combine the tomatoes and pat chun in a small saucepan over low heat and cook, covered, for 20 minutes. Strain the tomato in a colander and set aside to cool for 10 minutes. When cool enough to handle, peel, discarding the skin.

Place the chilli, shallots, garlic and coriander root in a mortar and pestle and pound to a fine paste. Add the tomato and pound to form a chunky sauce. Stir in the palm sugar and lime juice, a little at a time, and continue to pound until incorporated. Slowly mix in the fish sauce and taste. You want a good balance of sweet, sour and salty. Reserve until ready to use.

Salt and pepper prawns Heat the oil in the wok to 180°C (you can test if the oil is the right temperature by dropping in a cube of bread; if the bread browns in 30 seconds, the oil is ready). In a large bowl, mix together the flour and prickly ash, then add the prawns and toss until well coated. Remove the prawns from the bowl, shaking off any excess flour. Fry the prawns, in two batches, for 2 minutes, or until pale golden. Drain on paper towel.

TO SERVE

Evenly divide the red chilli dressing between four shallow serving bowls. Place the prawns on top and garnish with the crispy sweet potato, spring onion and coriander.

The red duck leg curry, a signature dish at gingerboy that has been on the menu since we opened, is a great recipe with a lot of depth and flavour.

RED DUCK LEG CURRY
WITH CONFIT OF SHALLOTS AND FRESH LYCHEES

BRAISED DUCK LEGS

8 duck legs
2.5 litres (10 cups) Asian chicken
   stock (see page 232)
200 g yellow rock sugar
200 ml shaoxing rice wine
200 ml light soy sauce

RED CURRY PASTE

1 tablespoon coriander seeds,
   lightly toasted
3 whole star anise, lightly toasted
½ cinnamon stick, lightly toasted
1 tablespoon cumin seeds,
   lightly toasted
1 teaspoon white peppercorns
6 red shallots, roughly chopped
4 garlic cloves, roughly chopped
30 g (approx 6 cm) fresh ginger,
   peeled and roughly chopped
25 g (approx 5 cm) galangal,
   roughly chopped
1 lemongrass stem, white part
   only, thinly sliced
3 kaffir lime leaves, thinly sliced
5 dried large red chillies,
   deseeded and soaked in water
   for 30 minutes, drained and
   roughly chopped
4 coriander roots, washed and
   roughly chopped
1 tablespoon roasted belacan
   shrimp paste
200 ml coconut milk
200 g light palm sugar, grated
4 tablespoons fish sauce
700 ml coconut cream
120 ml lime juice

CONFIT OF SHALLOTS

750 ml (3 cups) vegetable oil
300 g red shallots, peeled

GARNISH

coconut cream, extra, to serve
12 whole lychees, peeled and
   deseeded
1 large handful of Thai basil leaves
2 red bird's eye chillies, thinly
   sliced (if you like it hot)

METHOD

Braised duck legs Preheat the oven to 180°C.

Heat a large frying pan over medium heat, add the duck legs, and cook for 8 minutes or until golden brown. (This also renders the fat on the legs.) Transfer the duck legs to a 5 litre casserole dish.

Place the stock, sugar, shaoxing rice wine and soy sauce in a saucepan and bring to the boil. Pour the hot stock over the duck in the casserole dish, cover with a lid and place in the oven for 2½ hours until the meat is falling off the bone. Using a slotted spoon, transfer the braised duck legs to a wire rack over a tray and allow to cool completely.

Red curry paste Individually pound the spices in a mortar and pestle until fine. Place in a bowl and add the shallots, garlic, ginger, galangal, lemongrass, lime leaves, chilli, coriander root and shrimp paste and mix to form a paste.

Heat the coconut milk, stirring with a wooden spoon and scraping the base of the pan to stop if from sticking and burning, in a saucepan over medium heat for 6–8 minutes until light golden brown and the coconut milk has split. Be careful as it tends to spit. Add the curry paste and cook, constantly stirring, over low heat for 25 minutes until the star anise and lemongrass are fragrant. Add the palm sugar and cook for another 20 minutes to caramelise the sugar. The paste is ready when you see orange oil oozing out. Pour in 3 tablespoons of the fish sauce, stir, then whisk in the coconut cream and bring to a gentle simmer. Take the saucepan off the heat and set aside.

Confit of shallots Place the oil and shallots in a wok over low–medium heat and cook for 40 minutes. Remove the shallots with a slotted spoon, drain on paper towel, leaving the oil in the wok for the duck legs.

TO SERVE

Place the wok over medium heat and heat the oil to 170˚C (you can test if the oil is the right temperature by dropping in a cube of bread; if the bread browns in 40 seconds, the oil is ready). Add the duck legs and fry for 2–3 minutes until crisp and golden brown. Drain on paper towel.

While the duck is frying, return the curry paste to the stove top over a low heat. Add the lime juice, the remaining fish sauce and the shallots to the curry paste and stir until well combined and the sauce is heated through.

Divide the duck legs and shallots between four serving plates and cover with the red curry sauce. Dot with the extra coconut cream and top with the lychees, basil leaves and extra chilli, if desired.

This dish is gingerboy's interpretation of the famous sweet and sour pork. We serve it as a small-course salad. You'll need to start this recipe a day ahead.

SWEET AND SOUR PORK BELLY
WITH CHERRY TOMATO, CORIANDER AND PEANUT SALAD

PORK BELLY

2 litres master stock
  (see page 239)
600 g pork belly
750 ml (3 cups) vegetable oil
1 tablespoon prickly ash
  (see page 240)

CHERRY TOMATO, CORIANDER AND PEANUT SALAD

8 cherry tomatoes, cut into
  quarters
1 telegraph (long) cucumber,
  peeled and sliced into noodles
  on a mandolin
1 red onion, thinly sliced
2 long red chillies, deseeded and
  thinly sliced
1 cup fried chilli peanuts
  (see page 236)
½ iceberg lettuce, finely shredded
15 g (approx 3 cm) fresh ginger,
  peeled and thinly sliced
1 large handful of coriander leaves
1 large handful of Thai basil leaves
200 ml green chilli pickle dressing
  (see page 237)

SWEET AND SOUR CARAMEL

200 g light palm sugar, grated
100 ml water
2 tablespoons tomato paste
220 ml coconut vinegar
5 garlic cloves, finely chopped
20 g (approx 4 cm) fresh ginger,
  peeled and finely chopped
6 red bird's eye chillies,
  finely chopped
2 large red chillies, thinly sliced
3 tablespoons lime juice
2 tablespoons fish sauce

METHOD

Pork belly Preheat the oven to 180°C.

Bring the stock to the boil in a saucepan and remove from the heat.

Place the pork belly in a 4-litre casserole dish and pour on the hot stock, place a cartouche* on top and cover with the lid. Braise in the oven for 2–2½ hours until the pork is tender and falling apart. Transfer the pork to a wire rack with a tray underneath to catch any juices and cool for 30 minutes, then cover with plastic wrap and leave in the refrigerator overnight to cool completely. The next day, cut the pork into 3 cm pieces.

Cherry tomato, coriander and peanut salad Place the tomatoes, cucumber, onion, chilli, chilli peanuts, lettuce, ginger, coriander and basil in a large bowl, mix well and reserve.

Sweet and sour caramel Combine the palm sugar and water in a saucepan and bring to the boil, stirring to dissolve the sugar. Reduce to a simmer and cook for 6–7 minutes until golden brown in colour. Add the tomato paste, vinegar, garlic, ginger and chillies and cook for 30 seconds, then remove from the heat and set aside to cool. Once cool, stir in the lime juice and fish sauce.

TO SERVE

Heat the vegetable oil in a wok over high heat, add the pork and deep-fry for 2 minutes until crispy and golden brown. Drain on paper towel. Season with the prickly ash, then mix into the salad and dress with the green chilli pickle.

Divide the pork belly and cherry tomato salad between serving bowls and drizzle the sweet and sour caramel over the top.

* *To make a cartouche*, cut out a circle of greaseproof paper slightly larger than your casserole dish.

YELLOW CURRY-CURED KINGFISH AND OCEAN TROUT
ON BETEL LEAVES WITH FRIED ONION

Serves four to share

YELLOW CURRY DRESSING

2 tablespoons yellow curry paste
   (see page 243)
30 ml lime juice
5 teaspoons fish sauce
5 teaspoons gula melaka
   (see page 238)

KINGFISH AND TROUT

300 g kingfish fillet, skin
   removed, pin-boned and
   cut into 5 mm dice
300 g ocean trout fillet, skin
   removed, pin-boned and
   cut into 5 mm dice
1 avocado, cut into 1 cm dice

GARNISH

12 large betel leaves, wiped with
   damp paper towel
seeds of ½ pomegranate
1 small handful of coriander cress
1 cup fried onion (see page 236)

METHOD

Yellow curry dressing Combine the yellow curry paste, lime juice, fish sauce and gula melaka in a bowl and mix well.

Kingfish and trout Place the fish in a bowl, pour on the yellow curry dressing and mix well. Set aside to cure for 3 minutes. Gently mix in the avocado.

TO SERVE

Place three betel leaves on each serving plate and spoon 1 heaped tablespoon of cured fish onto each leaf. Garnish with the pomegranate seeds, coriander cress and fried onion.

Eel is great to cook with if you know how to prepare it. The meat has a distinctive flavour and texture and is known as a delicacy in China and Japan. If you can't get it to smoke yourself, you can buy it already smoked from specialist seafood stores. If not, you can get soy-glazed eel from an Asian grocer and smoke it yourself.

SALT AND PEPPER SMOKED EEL
WITH SWEET AND SOUR APPLE SALAD

SOY REDUCTION

1 apple, cut into quarters
200 ml light soy sauce
100 ml kecap manis
300 ml apple juice
2 tablespoons caster sugar

SALT AND PEPPER SMOKED EEL

140 g woodchips (manuka is the
    best but any from your local
    barbecue store will work),
    soaked in water for 30 minutes
    then drained
700 g freshwater eel, filleted
750 ml (3 cups) vegetable oil
350 ml tempura batter
    (see page 242)
1 tablespoon salt and pepper mix
    (see page 241)
250 ml (1 cup) mustard soy sauce
    (see page 239)

SWEET AND SOUR APPLE SALAD

2 green apples, cut into 2 mm
    thick slices
3 red shallots, thinly sliced
1 large handful of sawtooth
    coriander leaves
5 spring onions, white part only,
    thinly sliced on an angle
125 ml (½ cup) green ginger wine
    dressing (see page 238)

METHOD

Soy reduction Place the apple, soy sauce, kecap manis, apple juice and sugar in a small saucepan over medium heat and simmer until reduced by two-thirds. Set aside to cool for 20 minutes.

Salt and pepper smoked eel Bring a large saucepan of water to the boil. Plunge the eel into the water for 15 seconds, then transfer to a bowl of iced water to cool completely. Once cool, place the eel, flesh side down, on a chopping board and scrape all of the goo from the skin with the back of a knife.

Heat the grill to high. Place the eel, skin side up, on a baking tray and grill for 3–4 minutes, or until light golden brown. Flip the eel over, brush with the soy reduction and place under the grill for 2 minutes. Pull out, brush again with the soy reduction and grill for a further 2 minutes. Repeat this process about three times, making sure you keep an eye on the eel as you don't want it to burn. The eel takes about 6 minutes to caramelise. Place a perforated stainless steel disc insert in a steamer basket, then transfer the eel to the steamer. Place a foil-lined wok over medium heat, and sprinkle in a handful of the soaked woodchips. Move the woodchips around until they start to smoke, then add the bamboo steamer and cover with a lid. Smoke over the heat for 30 seconds, then turn off the heat and leave the eel to smoke for 4 minutes. Remove the lid, move the woodchips around and repeat this process. Remove the steamer and woodchips from the wok.

Cut the eel into 10 cm lengths. Heat the oil in the wok to 180°C. To check if the oil is hot enough, drip a teaspoonful of the batter into the oil; if it floats to the surface after 2–3 seconds, it's ready. Coat the eel in the batter, letting the excess drip off. Deep-fry the eel for 1–2 minutes until golden brown. Drain on paper towel and season with the salt and pepper mix.

Sweet and sour apple salad Combine the apple, shallots, coriander and spring onion and green ginger wine dressing in a bowl and toss well.

TO SERVE

Arrange a neat pile of the salad in the centre of each serving plate and lean two pieces of salt and pepper eel up against it. Pour 2 tablespoons of mustard soy sauce into ramekins and place to one side.

Son-in-law eggs is one of our signature dishes. The salty sourness of the prik nam pla balances out the hot sweetness of the chilli jam, and the explosion of the runny egg in your mouth is fantastic. Always cook an extra couple of eggs just to be safe, as they are fragile and you might break some when peeling them.

SON-IN-LAW EGGS
WITH PRIK NAM PLA, CHILLI JAM AND ASIAN HERBS

Serves four to share

SON-IN-LAW EGGS

6–8 large eggs, at room
   temperature
700 ml vegetable oil

GARNISH

1 cup chilli jam (see page 234)
½ cup prik nam pla
   (see page 240)
1 handful of coriander leaves
1 handful of mint leaves
1 handful of Thai basil leaves
½ cup fried shallots
   (see page 237)

METHOD

Son-in-law eggs Bring a large saucepan of water to the boil, add the eggs and simmer for 5 minutes. Remove the eggs with a slotted spoon and gently lower into a bowl of iced water to cool for 10 minutes before carefully peeling.

Heat the oil in a wok to 180°C (you can test if the oil is the right temperature by dropping in a cube of bread; if the bread browns in 30 seconds, the oil is ready), add the eggs and deep-fry for 1–2 minutes until golden brown and crispy on the outside but runny in the middle.

TO SERVE

Cut each egg in half. Spoon 3 tablespoons of the chilli jam into each serving bowl, drizzle on 1 teaspoon of prik nam pla and top with two egg halves, cut side up. Garnish with the coriander, mint, basil and fried shallots.

Jellyfish is great in salads; it has a wonderful texture and adds another dimension. You can get jellyfish from most Asian grocers, more commonly Japanese grocers. The colour, texture and flavour of yellow pickled daikon, from the Japanese section of Asian supermarkets, works great with this dish.

BROKEN CHICKEN
AND JELLYFISH SALAD

Serves four to share

BROKEN CHICKEN

2.5 litres (10 cups) Asian chicken stock (see page 232)
350 g yellow rock sugar
400 ml shaoxing rice wine
10 garlic cloves, roughly chopped
50 g (approx 10 cm) fresh ginger, peeled and roughly chopped
3 whole star anise, lightly toasted
3 cinnamon sticks, lightly toasted
1 brown onion, roughly chopped
1.5 kg whole chicken

YELLOW PICKLED DAIKON

250 ml green chilli pickle dressing (see page 237)
1 drop orange food dye
1 small white radish, peeled, cut in half and sliced into 2 mm thick pieces

JELLYFISH SALAD

200 ml rice wine vinegar
80 g caster sugar
2 tablespoons light soy sauce
250 g dried jellyfish sheets
1 telegraph (long) cucumber, deseeded and cut into 5cm batons
1 handful of coriander leaves
1 handful of mint leaves
4 spring onions, white part only thinly sliced on an angle
4 large red chillies, deseeded and thinly sliced
150 ml lime juice
½ cup fried garlic (see page 236)

TOASTED SESAME DRESSING

1 tablespoon peanut oil
2 tablespoons sesame oil
3 red bird's eye chillies, thinly sliced
20 g (approx 4 cm) fresh ginger, peeled and finely chopped
2 garlic cloves, finely chopped
2 tablespoons rice wine vinegar
2 tablespoons kecap manis
4 tablespoons light soy sauce
2 tablespoons mirin
80 ml lemon juice
3 tablespoons toasted sesame seeds

METHOD

Broken chicken Bring the stock, sugar, shaoxing rice wine, garlic, ginger, star anise, cinnamon and onion to the boil in a large saucepan over high heat. Add the chicken, bring to the boil, then reduce the heat to low and simmer gently for 40 minutes. Take the chicken out of the stock and set aside to cool for 20 minutes. When cool enough to handle, remove and finely chop the skin, then remove and gently shred the meat with your fingers. Reserve until needed.

Yellow pickled daikon Pour the green chilli pickle into a saucepan over medium heat and bring to a simmer. Add the food dye by dipping the end of a wooden skewer into the dye and then stirring the skewer in the green chilli pickle. Add the radish and simmer for 1 minute. Remove from the heat and set aside for 15 minutes. Transfer the mix to an air-tight container and set aside to cool completely. Refrigerate until needed.

Jellyfish salad Combine the vinegar, sugar and soy sauce in a small saucepan and bring to a gentle simmer. Set aside to cool.

Soak the dried jellyfish sheets in cold water for 15 minutes, changing the water and rinsing the jellyfish once every 5 minutes. Drain and finely slice. Place the sliced jellyfish in the pan with the vinegar mixture, stir well, and set aside for 20 minutes.

Toasted sesame dressing Heat the peanut oil and sesame oil in a frying pan and gently sauté the chilli, ginger and garlic for 2–3 minutes until fragrant. Set aside to cool. Stir in the vinegar, kecap manis, soy sauce, mirin, lemon juice and sesame seeds.

TO SERVE

Remove the jellyfish from the vinegar mixture and combine with the chicken, daikon, cucumber, coriander, mint, spring onion, chilli and lime juice in a large bowl, add the dressing and gently toss. Taste for seasoning and chilli – you want a nice amount of heat in this salad. Place a neat pile of salad on each serving plate and sprinkle with fried garlic to serve.

PORK AND PRAWN SIU MAI
WITH BLACK VINEGAR CARAMEL

PORK AND PRAWN SIU MAI

250 g finely minced pork shoulder

150 g small–medium sized raw
prawns, peeled, deveined and
finely chopped

5 garlic cloves, finely chopped

4 red shallots, finely chopped

15 g (approx 3 cm) fresh ginger,
peeled and finely chopped

2 red bird's eye chillies,
finely chopped

6 spring onions, white part only,
thinly sliced

2 tablespoons pat chun
(sweetened Chinese vinegar)

2 tablespoons soy sauce

1 teaspoon prickly ash
(see page 240)

12 square yellow won ton skins,
cut into rounds with a 9 cm
cutter

½ cup black vinegar caramel
(see page 233)

METHOD

Pork and prawn siu mai Combine the pork and chopped prawns in a large bowl and knead well for 3 minutes with the back of your hands. Add the garlic, shallots, ginger, chilli, spring onion, pat chun, soy sauce and prickly ash and incorporate with your hands. Cover with plastic wrap and leave in the refrigerator for 20 minutes to chill, making it easier to work with.

Place a won ton wrapper in the palm of your hand, spoon 1 heaped tablespoon of the siu mai mixture into the centre and use a crimping motion to fold the edges of the wrapper up around the sides of the meat, leaving the top open. Tap the base on the bench to flatten it slightly so the dumpling can sit upright. Repeat with the remaining wrappers and siu mai mixture.

TO SERVE

Place a perforated stainless steel disc insert in a bamboo steamer, spray with cooking spray and add the dumplings in a single layer, leaving a 2 cm space around each one so they don't stick together. Cover and steam over a wok of simmering water for 4–5 minutes, or until the bases of the dumplings are firm and they are cooked through.

Arrange the siu mai dumplings on a plate and serve with a small dish of the black vinegar caramel.

COCONUT-BATTERED PRAWNS
WITH YELLOW CURRY SAUCE

Serves four to share

COCONUT-BATTERED PRAWNS

45 g desiccated coconut
3 tablespoons coconut cream
1 teaspoon prickly ash
  (see page 240)
2 cups tempura batter
  (see page 242)
12 x very large green tiger prawns,
  peeled and deveined, leaving
  the tail intact
750 ml (3 cups) vegetable oil
1 pinch of sea salt

YELLOW CURRY SAUCE

1 tablespoon vegetable oil
130 g (½ cup) yellow curry paste
  (see page 243)
60 g light palm sugar, grated
200 ml coconut cream
80 ml lime juice
3 tablespoons fish sauce

METHOD

Coconut-battered prawns Combine the coconut, coconut cream, prickly ash and tempura batter in a bowl and whisk well. Place in the refrigerator to chill completely.

Yellow curry sauce Heat the oil in a saucepan over medium heat and fry the yellow curry paste for 6 minutes until fragrant. Add the sugar and fry the paste for a further 5 minutes until a nice golden brown. Stir in the coconut cream and bring to a gentle simmer. Remove from the heat and set aside to cool for 10 minutes. Mix in the lime juice and fish sauce and reserve until needed.

TO SERVE

Remove the prawns from the refrigerator and allow to come to room temperature for 10 minutes. Heat the oil in a wok over high heat to 170°C (you can test if the oil is the right temperature by dropping in a cube of bread; if the bread browns in 40 seconds, the oil is ready). Holding a prawn by the tail, dip into the batter and let the excess drip off. The prawn should be well coated, not smothered. Carefully lower the prawn into the oil and cook for 1–2 minutes, or until golden brown. Remove from the oil with a slotted spoon and drain on paper towel. Cook the prawns in batches until all of the prawns are cooked.

Lightly season the prawns with the salt, place three on each serving plate and serve with a small bowl of the yellow curry sauce.

Fresh water red claw crayfish are from North Queensland. You might be able to order them through your fishmonger, otherwise you can use yabbies or large king prawns.

RED CLAW CRAYFISH,
MUSSEL AND GLASS NOODLE SALAD WITH CHILLI LIME DRESSING

Serves four to share

CHILLI LIME DRESSING

170 g light palm sugar, grated
1 tablespoon water
200 ml lime juice
4 tablespoons fish sauce
2 red bird's eye chillies, finely
   chopped
½ teaspoon chilli powder
3 garlic cloves, finely chopped

RED CLAW CRAYFISH, MUSSEL AND GLASS NOODLE SALAD

1 kg mussels, scrubbed and
   de-bearded
300 ml white wine
12 live red claw crayfish (each
   weighing approx 100–110 g)
1 garlic head, cut in half
2 carrots, roughly chopped
1 tablespoon sea salt, extra
100 ml vegetable oil
1 teaspoon sea salt
200 g glass noodles
1 litre boiling water
150 g green beans, topped
   and tailed and cut into
   2.5 cm lengths
80 g water chestnuts, cut into
   3 pieces
1 avocado, cut into 1 cm dice
1 bunch asparagus, trimmed and
   cut into 2.5 cm lengths
1 zucchini, cut into 1 cm thick
   slices
1 large handful of holy basil leaves

METHOD

Chilli lime dressing Combine the palm sugar and water in a saucepan over low heat and bring to the boil, stirring until the sugar dissolves. Remove from the heat, stir in the lime juice and fish sauce, then add the chilli and garlic. Set aside until needed.

Red claw crayfish, mussel and glass noodle salad Heat a large saucepan over high heat, add the mussels and wine, cover with a tight-fitting lid and steam until the mussels open. Strain the mussels through a fine sieve, discarding the cooking liquid, and set aside until cool enough to handle. Take the mussels out of the shells, and discard the shells.

Place the crayfish in the freezer for 20 minutes so they go to sleep. Fill a large bucket with iced water. Fill a large saucepan with water, add the garlic, carrot and salt and bring to the boil. Plunge the crayfish into the boiling water and cook for 6 minutes, then transfer to the iced water to cool for 6 minutes. Pull the tails off the crayfish and remove the meat. Crack open the claws and extract the meat. Place the crayfish meat in a bowl and drizzle 1 tablespoon of the oil over the top and season with a little salt.

Place the glass noodles in a large heatproof bowl and pour on the boiling water. Cover with plastic wrap and set aside to soak for 5 minutes. Drain the noodles through a fine sieve and run under cold water for 2 minutes to cool. Drain again and transfer to a large bowl.

Blanch the beans in a saucepan of boiling water for 1–2 minutes. Drain and refresh in iced water for 2 minutes. Drain again. Divide the mussels, noodles, beans, water chestnuts and avocado between four shallow serving bowls.

Heat a barbecue to hot. Drizzle the remaining oil over the asparagus and zucchini and season with salt. Place the asparagus and zucchini on the barbecue and cook, turning, until golden and charred all over. Remove from the barbecue and place in the bowls with the other salad ingredients. Place the crayfish meat on the barbecue for 1 minute, then turn and cook for 1 minute or until lightly golden.

TO SERVE

Divide the crayfish meat between the bowls. Drizzle 2 tablespoons of the chilli lime dressing over the top and gently toss. Tear up the basil and sprinkle over each salad.

Wagyu beef short ribs on the bone are deliciously gelatinous and extremely tasty when done well. So here is a favourite of ours.

BLACK PEPPERED WAGYU BEEF SHORT RIBS
WITH PAT CHUN DRESSING

Serves four to share

BLACK PEPPERED WAGYU BEEF SHORT RIBS

600 g wagyu beef short ribs, on the bone
300 ml kecap manis
1 tablespoon freshly ground black pepper
700 ml vegetable oil

BRAISING STOCK

1.5 litres (6 cups) Asian chicken stock (see page 232)
150 g yellow rock sugar
4 cinnamon sticks, lightly toasted
4 whole star anise, lightly toasted
6 garlic cloves, roughly chopped
30 g (approx 6 cm) fresh ginger, roughly chopped
1 teaspoon sichuan peppercorns
1 tablespoon black peppercorns

PAT CHUN DRESSING

200 ml pat chun (sweetened Chinese vinegar)
1 teaspoon freshly ground black pepper
3 tablespoons light soy sauce
1 red onion, finely chopped
3 large green chillies, thinly sliced
2 garlic cloves, finely chopped
6 coriander roots, washed and finely chopped
1 tablespoon grated light palm sugar
80 ml lime juice

METHOD

Black peppered wagyu beef short ribs Place the ribs in a deep container, pour on the kecap manis and massage the pepper into the meat. Cover with plastic wrap and leave in the refrigerator for one hour.

Heat the oil in a wok to 180°C (you can test if the oil is the right temperature by dropping in a cube of bread; if the bread browns in 30 seconds, the oil is ready). Remove the ribs from the refrigerator and cook, in batches, for 2 minutes to caramelise. Remove with a slotted spoon and transfer to a flameproof casserole dish and set aside while the braising stock is made.

Braising stock Preheat the oven to 170°C. Combine the stock, rock sugar, spices, garlic, ginger and peppercorns in a large saucepan over low heat and bring to a gentle simmer. Pour the braising stock over the wagyu beef, cover with a cartouche* and a lid. Place in the oven for 2½ hours, or until the meat is gelatinous and falling apart when you pick it up. Remove the wagyu beef with a slotted spoon and place on a tray to cool. Once the wagyu beef has cooled to room temperature, cover the tray with plastic wrap and transfer to the refrigerator to cool completely.

Place the casserole dish on the stovetop over medium heat and simmer the stock until reduced to 200 ml. Cool and reserve for the pat chun dressing.

Pat chun dressing Combine the pat chun, pepper, soy sauce, onion, chilli, garlic, coriander, sugar, lime juice and the reduced braising stock in a bowl and whisk well.

TO SERVE

Pour the pat chun dressing into a large saucepan, add the wagyu beef and bring to a gentle simmer over medium heat.

Evenly divide the wagyu beef between four shallow serving bowls and spoon on the pat chun dressing.

* *To make a cartouche*, cut out a circle of greaseproof paper slightly larger than your saucepan.

GRILLED PORK SKEWERS
WITH PICKLED MUSTARD GREENS

Serves four to share

PORK SKEWERS

500 g pork belly, skin off, cut
   into 3 cm pieces
12 thick bamboo skewers, soaked
   in water for 20 minutes
3 tablespoons kecap manis
3 tablespoons light soy sauce
1 tablespoon freshly ground
   black pepper
3 tablespoons Chinese black
   vinegar
3 tablespoons peanut oil
250 ml (1 cup) mustard soy sauce
   (see page 239)

PICKLED MUSTARD GREENS

200 g table salt
1 litre (4 cups) water
300 g mustard greens, trimmed
   (mustard greens are available
   from Asian grocers)
300 ml rice wine vinegar
145 g caster sugar
1 red bird's eye chilli, thinly sliced

METHOD

Pork skewers Push two pieces of pork belly on to each skewer. Transfer the pork skewers to a small shallow tray.

Combine the kecap manis, soy sauce, pepper and vinegar in a bowl and pour over the pork skewers. Cover with plastic wrap and refrigerate for 1 hour.

Pickled mustard greens Combine the salt and water in a large bowl, add the mustard greens and set aside for 3–4 hours. Drain, then rinse off the salt and drain again. Transfer to a large container.

Place the vinegar, sugar and chilli in a small saucepan and bring to a gentle simmer. Take off the heat and set aside to cool. Pour over the mustard greens, cover with plastic wrap and place in the refrigerator overnight.

TO SERVE

Take the pork out of the refrigerator and leave for 15 minutes to come to room temperature.

Heat a chargrill pan or barbecue until nice and hot. Remove the pork skewers from the tray, reserving the marinade, and drizzle the skewered meat with the oil. Cook the pork skewers for 2 minutes on each side, remove from the heat and rest for 5 minutes. Pour the reserved marinade over the skewers and cook for a further 10 seconds on each side.

Place a small pile of mustard greens on each serving plate, then place three skewers alongside. Serve with the mustard soy sauce on the side.

CRISPY PRAWN WON TONS
WITH SWEET FISH SAUCE

SWEET FISH SAUCE

100 g light palm sugar
1 red bird's eye chilli, thinly sliced
½ long green chilli, deseeded and
  finely chopped
½ long red chilli, deseeded
  and finely chopped
3 coriander roots, washed
  and finely chopped
2 garlic cloves, thinly sliced
7½ tablespoons fish sauce
100 ml lime juice
2 red shallots, thinly sliced

CRISPY PRAWN WON TONS

12 very large raw king prawns,
  peeled and deveined, leaving
  the tail intact
12 square yellow won ton
  wrappers
750 ml (3 cups) vegetable oil
sea salt

GARNISH

12 iceberg lettuce cups
  (see page 238)
1 handful of Vietnamese mint
  leaves
1 handful of coriander leaves
1 spring onion, white part only,
  thinly sliced on an angle

METHOD

Sweet fish sauce Pound the sugar, chillies, coriander root and garlic in a mortar and pestle to form a fine paste. Add the fish sauce, lime juice and shallots and taste for seasoning. The dressing should be hot, sour, a little bit sweet and mostly salty. Pour into a serving bowl and set aside.

Crispy prawn won tons Wrap each prawn in a won ton wrapper, using a little water to seal the edges.

Heat the oil in a wok to 180˚C (you can test if the oil is the right temperature by dropping in a cube of bread; if the bread browns in 30 seconds, the oil is ready). Deep-fry the won tons in two batches, moving them around so they cook evenly, for 2–3 minutes until golden brown all over. Drain on paper towel. Season with the salt.

TO SERVE

Place a won ton in each lettuce cup, garnish with mint, coriander and a few slices of spring onion and serve with the sweet fish sauce on the side.

If you can't get lobster medallions from your fishmonger, buy about 500 grams of large lobster tails and cut them into four even pieces. Cook and serve with the shell on. Coriander cress is available at fruit and vegetable shops.

SAKE AND SOY POACHED LOBSTER MEDALLIONS
WITH RED VINEGAR CARAMEL AND FRIED STICKY RICE BALLS

Serves four to share

SAKE AND SOY POACHED LOBSTER MEDALLIONS

200 ml sake
200 ml light soy sauce
100 ml mirin
60 g unsalted butter
2 tablespoons rice wine vinegar
4 x 130 g lobster medallions
2 tablespoons sesame oil

SALAD

½ telegraph (long) cucumber,
    halved lengthways and cut into
    1 mm thick slices
½ cup green chilli pickle dressing
    (see page 237)
4 spring onions, white part only,
    thinly sliced on an angle
6 cherry tomatoes, cut into
    quarters
4 tablespoons red vinegar
    caramel (see page 131)
1 handful of coriander cress
1 cup fried sticky rice balls
    (see page 237)

METHOD

Sake and soy poached lobster medallions Combine the sake, soy sauce, mirin, butter and vinegar in a large saucepan over low heat and bring up to 75°C (the mix should be almost simmering). Add the lobster and poach for 10 minutes, flipping the medallions over halfway through cooking. Remove the lobster and set aside to cool.

Heat a barbecue to hot. Rub the oil into the lobster medallions and place them on the barbecue for 2 minutes on each side. Rest for 1 minute.

Salad Meanwhile, place the cucumber and green chilli pickle dressing in a small mixing bowl and set aside for 15 minutes. Drain and discard half of the pickling liquid from the cucumber mix, then add the spring onion and cherry tomatoes and mix well.

TO SERVE

Evenly divide the salad between two serving plates. Place two lobster medallions on each plate and drizzle the red vinegar caramel over and around the lobster. Scatter the coriander cress and fried sticky rice balls around the plate.

Wok-fried eggs with Thai salad of crab,
corn and green chilli

Sichuan fried taro prawns with chilli jam

WOK-FRIED EGGS
WITH THAI SALAD OF CRAB, CORN AND GREEN CHILLI

WOK-FRIED EGGS

2 tablespoons vegetable oil
8 large eggs

THAI SALAD

1 tablespoon vegetable oil
5 red shallots, thinly sliced
kernels cut from 2 corn cobs
2 large green chillies, thinly sliced
300 g blue swimmer crabmeat
  (see page 233)
6 cherry tomatoes, quartered
3 tablespoons oyster sauce
2 tablespoons fish sauce
120 ml lime juice
4 tablespoons caster sugar

GARNISH

1 handful of holy basil leaves, torn
2 limes, peeled and segmented
1 cup fried shallots (see page 237)

METHOD

Wok-fried eggs Heat the oil in a wok over high heat. Crack the eggs into a bowl and whisk for 10 seconds. Tip the egg into the hot oil, tilting the wok to spread the egg over the base, and cook until the egg starts to set. Drag one side of the cooked egg into the centre and tilt the wok to allow any remaining uncooked egg to flow to the edge and set. Roll up the omelette to form a cigar shape and slide out onto a chopping board. Cut into 1 cm thick slices.

Thai salad Wipe out the wok, add the oil, shallots, corn and chilli and stir-fry over high heat for 2 minutes. Stir in the crabmeat, tomatoes, oyster sauce, fish sauce, lime juice and sugar, turn off the heat and transfer the mixture to a large bowl.

TO SERVE

Arrange the omelette slices on two large serving plates. Top with the Thai salad and garnish with the basil, lime segments and fried shallots.

SICHUAN FRIED TARO PRAWNS
WITH CHILLI JAM

SICHUAN FRIED TARO PRAWNS

12 short thick wooden skewers

12 raw tiger prawns, peeled and deveined, leaving the tail intact

1 taro (about 500 g), peeled and thinly sliced on a mandolin

750 ml (3 cups) peanut oil

2 tablespoons sichuan peppercorns

1 tablespoon black peppercorns

4 dried large red chillies, deseeded

1 teaspoon prickly ash (see page 240)

½ cup chilli jam (see page 234)

4 lime cheeks

METHOD

Sichuan fried taro prawns Skewer the prawns then wrap each one in a slice of taro, leaving the tails exposed.

Pour the oil into a wok. Add the sichuan and black peppercorns, place over medium heat and bring the oil to 160°C (you can test if the oil is the right temperature by dropping in a cube of bread; if the bread browns in 50 seconds, the oil is ready). Strain the pepper oil through a fine sieve, discard the peppercorns and return the oil to the wok. Heat the wok over medium heat, add the chillies and fry for 15 seconds. Remove the chillies with a slotted spoon and discard. Fry the prawns in the oil for 1–2 minutes, then drain on paper towel. Season the prawns with the prickly ash.

TO SERVE

Divide the prawns between serving plates and serve with a small bowl of the chilli jam and the lime cheeks.

These salt and pepper oysters are awesome. We get great feedback about
this dish; even customers who don't like oysters love eating these!

SALT AND PEPPER OYSTERS
WITH PRIK NAM PLA

SALT AND PEPPER OYSTERS

12 large oysters, freshly shucked
750 ml (3 cups) vegetable oil
500 ml (2 cups) tempura batter
    (see page 242)
2 teaspoons salt and pepper mix
    (see page 241)
1 egg white
50 g table salt
½ small iceberg lettuce, finely
    shredded
lime cheeks, to serve
½ cup prik nam pla
    (see page 240)

METHOD

Salt and pepper oysters Take the oysters out of the shells and place in
a small bowl. Put the shells in a saucepan, just cover with water and
bring to the boil. Drain and run the shells under cold water to clean
thoroughly.

Heat the oil in a wok to 180˚C. To test if the oil is hot enough, dip a
teaspoon in the tempura batter, then hold it about 2.5 cm above the oil
and let a little bit drip in. If the batter sinks and then comes back to the
top, the oil is ready; if the batter stays at the bottom, you need to let the
oil heat up for longer. Use chopsticks to dip the oysters, one at a time,
in the batter, shake off excess and fry in the hot oil for 2 minutes until
crispy. Drain on paper towel and season with the salt and pepper mix.

Whisk the egg white and table salt in a bowl until light and fluffy.

TO SERVE

To hold each oyster shell in place, spoon 3 tablespoons of the egg white
and salt mixture on each serving plate or board and place an oyster
shell on top of each. Arrange a small amount of shredded lettuce in
each shell and top with an oyster. Place 1 teaspoon of prik nam pla on
top of each oyster and serve with lime cheeks.

SEARED SCALLOPS
WITH SWEET POTATO, BLACK VINEGAR CARAMEL AND KING BROWN MUSHROOMS

Serves four to share

KING BROWN MUSHROOMS

2 king brown mushrooms,
    quartered lengthways
3½ tablespoons light soy sauce
3 tablespoons rice wine vinegar
2 tablespoons cooking sake
20 g unsalted butter

SWEET POTATO

200 g sweet potato, peeled and
    cut into 2 cm dice
2 garlic cloves, roughly chopped
10 g (approx 2 cm) fresh ginger,
    peeled and finely chopped
2 tablespoons thickened cream
10 g unsalted butter
1 pinch of sea salt

SCALLOPS

12 large scallops, on the half shell
1 teaspoon sea salt
2 tablespoons vegetable oil

GARNISH

½ cup black vinegar caramel
    (see page 233)
1 small handful of coriander cress
4 spring onions, white part only,
    finely sliced on an angle

METHOD

King brown mushrooms Preheat the oven to 180°C.

Line a baking tray with foil. Place the mushrooms on the foil and gather up the sides to create a bowl shape. Pour in the soy sauce, vinegar and sake and dot the butter over the top. Bring the foil edges together and fold over to seal the parcel. Roast for 30 minutes. Set aside to cool.

Sweet potato Combine the sweet potato, garlic and ginger in a saucepan, cover with water and bring to the boil over high heat. Reduce the heat to low and simmer for 25 minutes until the sweet potato is tender. Drain and set aside in the sieve for 2 minutes to allow the excess water to drain.

Place the cream and butter in a saucepan over medium heat and bring to the boil. Remove from the heat.

Transfer the sweet potato to the bowl of a food processor and blitz to form a puree. Slowly pour in the cream and butter and process until well combined. Pour the puree into a small saucepan and gently reheat.

Scallops To clean the scallop shells, place the shells in a small saucepan, cover with water and bring to the boil. Strain and reserve.

Season the scallops with salt. Heat a frying pan over high heat. Add the oil and scallops, in two batches, and fry for 1 minute, then flip them over and cook for a further 10 seconds. Remove from the heat.

TO SERVE

Arrange the scallop shells on serving plates. Place 1 tablespoon of the sweet potato puree in each shell, then place a scallop and a slice of mushroom on top. Lightly drizzle on the black vinegar caramel and garnish with the coriander cress and spring onion.

HOT AND SOUR TROUT
AND BANANA BLOSSOM SALAD WITH ROASTED SHRIMP DRESSING

HOT AND SOUR TROUT AND BANANA BLOSSOM SALAD

500 g ocean trout fillet, chopped into large pieces
250 g banana blossom
lemon juice
½ red onion, thinly sliced
5 spring onions, white part only, thinly sliced on an angle
3 kaffir lime leaves, thinly sliced
1 handful of Vietnamese mint leaves
1 handful of coriander leaves
1 handful of Thai basil leaves
½ teaspoon dried chilli flakes
1 telegraph (long) cucumber, peeled, thinly sliced on a mandolin then cut into long thin strips
1 cup fried sticky rice balls (see page 237)

ROASTED SHRIMP DRESSING

30 g belacan shrimp paste
3 garlic cloves, roughly chopped
3 red bird's eye chillies, roughly chopped
3 roma cherry tomatoes, cut in half
3 tablespoons pat chun (sweetened Chinese vinegar)
80 ml tamarind paste (see page 242)
3 tablespoons fish sauce
100 ml lime juice

METHOD

Hot and sour trout and banana blossom salad Preheat the oven to 180˚C. Place the ocean trout on a baking tray and roast for 50 minutes until golden brown. Once cooked take out and set aside.

Cut the banana blossom in half, peel off and discard the four outer layers, then cut crossways into 1 mm thick slices. Place in a bucket of water with some lemon juice to prevent oxidising. Combine the red onion, spring onion, kaffir lime leaves, mint, coriander, basil, chilli flakes and cucumber in a large bowl.

Roasted shrimp dressing Preheat the oven to 180˚C.

Wrap the shrimp paste in a large piece of foil and roast for 20 minutes. The paste will have dried out a bit while roasting. Set aside to cool for 15 minutes.

Pound the garlic and chilli to a paste in a mortar and pestle, then add the shrimp paste and cherry tomatoes and pound again to combine. Slowly incorporate the pat chun, tamarind paste, fish sauce and lime juice. Set aside for 15 minutes to allow the flavours to infuse.

TO SERVE

Drain the banana blossom and add it to the onion, herb and cucumber mix. Use your hands to roughly break up the trout and add it to the banana blossom salad mix.

Spoon 3 tablespoons of the dressing onto the centre of each serving plate. Pile the trout and banana blossom salad over the dressing and then use your hands to crumble the fried glutinous rice balls over the salads.

CHARGRILLED JUMBO PRAWNS
WRAPPED IN GRAPE VINE LEAVES WITH PEANUT, CHILLI AND PINEAPPLE RELISH

Serves four to share

**PEANUT, CHILLI AND
PINEAPPLE RELISH**

1 tablespoon vegetable oil
½ red onion, finely chopped
2 garlic cloves, finely chopped
1 long red chilli, deseeded and
   finely chopped
1 red bird's eye chilli, thinly sliced
15 g (approx 3 cm) fresh ginger,
   peeled and finely chopped
200 g ripe pineapple, peeled,
   cored and cut into 1 cm pieces
½ teaspoon freshly ground black
   peppercorns
60 g fried chilli peanuts
   (see page 236)
80 ml lime juice
1 teaspoon sea salt

**CHARGRILLED JUMBO PRAWNS
WRAPPED IN GRAPE VINE LEAVES**

2 litres (8 cups) cold water
12 large grape vine leaves
12 very large raw tiger prawns,
   peeled and deveined
750 ml (3 cups) vegetable oil
1 pinch of salt

METHOD

Peanut, chilli and pineapple relish Heat the oil in a saucepan over medium heat, add the onion, garlic, chillies and ginger and cook for 1 minute. Add half of the pineapple and cook for 5 minutes until soft, then add the remaining pineapple, season with the pepper, and cook for a further 1 minute. Set aside to cool. Crush the peanuts to a paste in a mortar and pestle. Add the lime juice, salt and crushed peanuts to the pineapple mixture and mix to combine. Transfer to an airtight container and place in the refrigerator until needed.

Chargrilled jumbo prawns wrapped in vine leaves Pour the water into a large bowl, add the vine leaves and soak for 15 minutes. Take the vine leaves out of the water, pat them dry with paper towel, transfer to a chopping board and trim the leaves so that they will wrap around the prawns twice. Tightly wrap the prawns in the vine leaves, place on a tray and set aside.

Heat a chargrill pan or barbecue until really hot, then cook the vine leaf-wrapped prawns on each side for 1 minute. Leave in a warm place to rest for 2 minutes.

TO SERVE

Place three prawns on each serving plate and spoon 1 tablespoon of the peanut, chilli and pineapple relish over the top.

GARLIC AND CHILLI-SALTED BLUE SWIMMER
SOFT SHELL CRABS WITH THREE SAUCES

GARLIC AND CHILLI-SALTED SOFT SHELL CRABS

6 blue swimmer soft shell crabs, halved and deveined

2 tablespoons fried garlic (see page 236), crushed in a mortar and pestle

1 tablespoon spiced chilli salt (see page 241)

2 cups (500 ml) tempura batter (see page 242)

750 ml (3 cups) vegetable oil

THREE SAUCES

BONITO MAYONNAISE

½ cup dried bonito flakes

2 garlic cloves, roughly chopped

1 tablespoon dijon mustard

4 tablespoons coconut vinegar

1 egg yolk

300 ml vegetable oil

½ teaspoon sea salt

STICKY SOY SAUCE

200 ml kecap manis

3½ tablespoons apple juice

3½ tablespoons light soy sauce

1 apple, peeled and roughly chopped

2 tablespoons rice wine vinegar

1 tablespoon honey

CHILLI SAUCE

4 large red chillies, deseeded and roughly chopped

1 red bird's eye chilli, deseeded and roughly chopped

4 red shallots, roughly chopped

2 garlic cloves, roughly chopped

5 coriander roots, washed and roughly chopped

80 g grated light palm sugar

2½ tablespoons water

120 ml lime juice

4 tablespoons fish sauce

METHOD

Garlic and chilli-salted soft shell crabs Place the crabs on a tray lined with paper towel, cover with plastic wrap and leave in the refrigerator until needed. Mix the fried garlic and the chilli salt in a bowl and combine with your hands.

Bonito mayonnaise Place the bonito flakes, garlic, mustard, vinegar and egg yolks in the chilled bowl of a food processor and pulse until combined. With the motor running, slowly pour in the oil in a thin steady stream until thick and creamy and emulsified. Add the salt and pulse to combine. Transfer to a bowl and leave in the refrigerator for at least an hour to chill.

Sticky soy sauce Place the kecap manis, apple juice, soy sauce, apple, vinegar and honey in a small saucepan over medium heat, bring to a gentle simmer and cook for 15 minutes until reduced by two-thirds. Transfer to a small container and place in the refrigerator to chill for 30 minutes.

Chilli sauce Place the chillies, shallots, garlic and coriander root in a mortar and pestle and pound to a fine paste.

Combine the palm sugar and water in a small saucepan over medium heat and simmer for 6 minutes until a golden brown caramel. Add the chilli paste and cook for 5 minutes, then pour in the lime juice and fish sauce. Cool for 15 minutes, then taste. You want to have a good balance of hot, sweet, sour and salty. Reserve until ready to use.

TO SERVE

Heat the oil in a wok over high heat to 180°C (you can test if the oil is the right temperature by dropping in a cube of bread; if the bread browns in 30 seconds, the oil is ready). Use chopsticks to dip the crab in the tempura batter, shake off excess batter and deep-fry in batches of three for 2–3 minutes, or until golden and crispy. Drain on paper towel. Lightly season with the fried garlic and chilli salt and serve with the three sauces.

DUCK SPRING ROLLS
WITH CHILLI, PLUM AND HOISIN DRESSING

Serves four to share

CHILLI, PLUM AND HOISIN DRESSING

150 g light palm sugar, grated

150 ml water

300 g blood plums, roughly chopped

2 green bird's eye chillies, finely chopped

30 g (approx 6 cm) fresh ginger, peeled and finely chopped

4 garlic cloves, finely chopped

3 tablespoons hoisin sauce

80 ml lime juice

2 tablespoons fish sauce

6 spring onions, white part only, thinly sliced

BRAISED DUCK

3 duck marylands

1 litre Asian chicken stock (see page 232)

200 ml light soy sauce

250 g yellow rock sugar

200 ml shaoxing rice wine

DUCK SPRING ROLLS

80 g rice vermicelli noodles

500 ml (2 cups) boiling water

½ handful of coriander leaves, roughly chopped

6 spring onions, white part only, thinly sliced

4 garlic cloves, finely chopped

1 red bird's eye chilli, finely chopped

15 g (approx 3 cm) fresh ginger, peeled and finely chopped

1 teaspoon prickly ash (see page 240)

2 tablespoons hoisin sauce

2 tablespoons plain flour

3 tablespoons water

12 spring roll wrappers

750 ml (3 cups) vegetable oil

METHOD

Chilli, plum and hoisin dressing Combine the sugar and water in a large saucepan over medium heat. Simmer until the sugar has dissolved and the syrup is pale golden. Add the plums, chilli, ginger, garlic and hoisin and cook, stirring continuously to stop the mixture from sticking to the base of the pan, for 45 minutes until a thin jam forms. Take off the heat and set aside to cool. Transfer to the bowl of a food processor and blitz to form a smooth paste. Add the lime juice, fish sauce and spring onion and blitz again.

Braised duck Preheat the oven to 180°C.

Heat a large frying pan over medium heat, add the duck and cook for 8 minutes until golden brown. (This also renders the fat on the duck.) Transfer the duck legs to a casserole dish.

Place the stock, soy sauce, sugar and shaoxing rice wine in a saucepan and bring to the boil. Pour the hot stock over the duck in the casserole dish, cover with a lid and place in the oven for 2½ hours until the meat is falling off the bone. Using a slotted spoon, transfer the braised duck to a wire rack over a tray and allow to cool completely.

Duck spring rolls Place the rice noodles in a separate bowl and pour on the boiling water. Cover with plastic wrap and set aside for 10 minutes for the noodles to cook through. While the noodles are soaking, shred the cooled duck meat into a large bowl. Drain the noodles, roughly chop into 2.5 cm lengths and mix in with the duck. Add the coriander, spring onion, garlic, chilli, ginger, half of the prickly ash and the hoisin sauce and mix with your hands until well combined. Cover with plastic wrap and leave in the refrigerator for 25 minutes to chill completely.

Combine the flour and water in a bowl and mix well. Divide the duck mixture into 12 equal portions, then place a couple of spring roll wrappers on the bench at a time. Place 2 tablespoons of the duck mixture evenly across the bottom third of each spring roll wrapper. Brush the edges with the flour and water paste and roll up tightly, folding in the sides to completely enclose the filling.

Heat the oil in a wok to 180°C (you can test if the oil is the right temperature by dropping in a cube of bread; if the bread browns in 30 seconds, the oil is ready). Fry the spring rolls in two batches for 2 minutes, or until golden. Drain on paper towel.

TO SERVE

Cut some of the spring rolls in half on the diagonal, lightly season with the remaining prickly ash, pile on a plate, and serve with a small dish of the chilli, plum and hoisin dressing.

Jinhua ham is a Chinese-style salted pork. If you cannot find it, you can substitute prosciutto.

CHARGRILLED BABY SQUID
STUFFED WITH JINHUA HAM AND SCALLOPS AND BLACK VINEGAR CARAMEL

Serves four to share

JINHUA HAM AND SCALLOP FILLING

200 g blue eye or sea bream fillets, skin removed, pin-boned and roughly chopped

100 g jinhua ham, diced

200 g scallop meat, thinly sliced

4 red shallots, finely chopped

3 garlic cloves, finely chopped

2 tablespoons kecap manis

1 handful of garlic chives, thinly sliced

1 tablespoon sea salt

2 tablespoons sesame oil

SQUID

4 x 15 cm fresh baby squid tubes, cleaned

8 toothpicks

4 lime cheeks

½ cup black vinegar caramel (see page 233)

METHOD

Jinhua ham and scallop filling Place the fish in the chilled bowl of a food processor and blitz to a smooth ball. Transfer to a large bowl and add the jinhua ham, scallop meat, shallots, garlic, kecap manis, chives and half of the salt and mix until well combined. Cover with plastic wrap and place in the refrigerator for 30 minutes to chill.

Squid Using a tablespoon, fill the squid tubes with the jinhua ham mixture until almost full, making sure you don't overfill the squid tubes as they will burst when you cook them. Thread the toothpicks through each opening to close. Place the squid tubes on a plate, cover with plastic wrap and place in the refrigerator until needed.

TO SERVE

Remove the squid from the refrigerator 10 minutes before cooking, to allow it to return to room temperature. Preheat the oven to 160°C and heat a chargrill pan or barbecue until very hot.

Season the squid with the remaining salt and the sesame oil. Cook for 20 seconds on the chargrill pan or barbecue until sealed on all sides. Transfer the squid to a baking tray and roast in the oven for 8 minutes until cooked through. Slice each squid tube into five pieces, place on serving plates and serve with lime cheeks and the black vinegar caramel.

These dumplings are a favourite of ours; the cashew chilli soy cuts through the fat in the wagyu beef dumplings and the bamboo adds great texture.

STEAMED WAGYU BEEF AND BAMBOO DUMPLINGS
WITH CASHEW CHILLI SOY

Serves four to share

CASHEW CHILLI SOY

75 g unsalted roasted cashews
1 tablespoon mirin
2 tablespoons rice wine vinegar
2 tablespoons kecap manis
2 tablespoons light soy sauce
3 green bird's eye chillies,
    thinly sliced
1 teaspoon caster sugar
1 pinch of sea salt

WAGYU BEEF AND BAMBOO DUMPLINGS

100 g fresh bamboo shoots
    (see page 235)
350 g minced wagyu beef (or ask
    your butcher to mince beef
    topside with shoulder and a
    small amount of pork fat)
3 coriander roots, washed and
    finely chopped
½ handful of coriander leaves,
    finely chopped
6 spring onions, white part only,
    thinly sliced
4 red bird's eye chillies,
    finely chopped
4 garlic cloves, finely chopped
2 tablespoons fish sauce
3 tablespoons light soy sauce
1 pinch of sea salt
12 gyoza skins

METHOD

Cashew chilli soy Pound the cashews to a coarse paste in a mortar and pestle then transfer to a bowl. Add the mirin, vinegar, kecap manis, soy sauce, chilli, sugar and salt and mix well. Taste for seasoning and adjust if required.

Wagyu beef and bamboo dumplings Preheat the oven to 180°C.

Place the bamboo on a baking tray and roast for 45 minutes until tender. Cut off the outside layer of the bamboo and discard. Cut the bamboo into small dice.

Combine the wagyu beef, bamboo, coriander roots and leaves, spring onion, chilli, garlic, fish sauce, soy sauce and salt in a large chilled bowl and knead, working the proteins in the meat, for 5 minutes.

Using one gyoza skin at a time, place 1 tablespoon of the wagyu beef mixture in the middle, brush around the edge of the skin with water and fold the skin over the filling to form a half moon shape. Press firmly to seal the edges and expel the air.

TO SERVE

Place a perforated stainless steel disc insert in a steamer basket, spray with cooking spray and add the wagyu beef dumplings in a single layer, leaving a 2 cm space around each one so they don't stick together. Cover and steam over a wok of simmering water for 4–5 minutes, or until cooked through.

Put 2 tablespoons of cashew chilli soy in a ramekin and arrange the dumplings on a serving plate.

These dumplings were inspired by our travels in Hong Kong. Our version uses sharp pickled cucumber to complement the spicy dumplings.

CHICKEN SATAY DUMPLINGS
WITH CUCUMBER PICKLE

CHICKEN SATAY DUMPLINGS

500 ml (2 cups) coconut cream
50 g (approx 6 cm) fresh
   turmeric, peeled and
   finely chopped
30 g light palm sugar, grated
4 green bird's eye chillies,
   finely chopped
4 red shallots, finely chopped
5 garlic cloves, finely chopped
3½ tablespoons fish sauce
80 ml lime juice
3 teaspoons coriander seeds,
   toasted and freshly ground
5 teaspoons cumin seeds,
   toasted and freshly ground
500 g boneless and skinless
   chicken thighs
1 cup fried chilli peanuts
   (see page 236)
24 square yellow won ton
   wrappers

CUCUMBER PICKLE

125 ml (½ cup) coconut vinegar
2 tablespoons rice wine vinegar
2 tablespoons caster sugar
1 teaspoon sea salt
1 red bird's eye chilli, thinly sliced
4 red shallots, thinly sliced
2 coriander roots, washed and
   thinly sliced
1 telegraph (long) cucumber,
   peeled and thinly sliced into
   ribbons

METHOD

Chicken satay dumplings Preheat the oven to 180°C.

Combine the coconut cream, turmeric, sugar, chilli, shallots, garlic, fish sauce, lime juice and ground coriander and cumin in a saucepan over low–medium heat and bring to a gentle simmer.

Place the chicken in a roasting tin, pour on half of the coconut cream mixture. Transfer to the oven to roast for 25 minutes, or until the chicken is golden brown and cooked through. Set aside to cool.

Remove the chicken, reserving the roasting juices, cut into fine dice and place in a large bowl. Add half the chilli peanuts, the reserved roasting juices and 2 tablespoons of the remaining coconut mixture.

Using one won ton wrapper at a time, place a heaped tablespoonful of the chicken mixture in the centre, brush around the edges with a little water and place another won ton wrapper on top. Press firmly around the filling to seal the edges and expel the air. Using the blunt side of a 4 cm round cutter, push down around the dumpling filling firmly. Then using the sharp side of a 6 cm round cutter, cut off the excess wrapper.

Cucumber pickle Combine the vinegars, sugar and salt in a small bowl and whisk well. Stir in the chilli, shallots and coriander root, then add the cucumber. Set aside for 15 minutes to pickle.

TO SERVE

Place a perforated stainless steel disc insert in a bamboo steamer, spray with cooking spray and add the dumplings in a single layer, leaving a 2 cm space around each one so they don't stick together. Cover and steam over a wok of simmering water for 4–5 minutes, or until cooked through. The underside of the dumpling skin will be translucent when cooked. Reheat the remaining coconut cream mixture, stirring through the remaining chilli peanuts to make a satay sauce.

Place the dumplings on a serving plate, spoon 2 tablespoons of the satay sauce over the top, then add a small pile of cucumber pickle in the centre.

Jumbo mussels are best for this recipe, but large oysters could also be used.

PANKO-CRUMBED MUSSELS
WITH ROASTED CHILLI DRESSING AND COCONUT SALAD

ROASTED CHILLI DRESSING

750 ml (3 cups) vegetable oil
10 large dried red chillies, deseeded
6 red shallots, thinly sliced
½ teaspoon sea salt
1 teaspoon icing sugar
8 garlic cloves, thinly sliced
150 ml milk
150 g light palm sugar, grated
50 ml water
150 ml lime juice
5 tablespoons fish sauce

COCONUT SALAD

1 cup sliced baby coconut (see page 232)
½ red onion, thinly sliced whole
6 spring onions, white part only, thinly sliced on an angle
2 large red chillies, deseeded and thinly sliced
2 avocadoes, cut into small dice
½ pomelo, segmented
1 large handful of Thai basil leaves
1 large handful of coriander leaves

PANKO-CRUMBED MUSSELS

16 fresh jumbo mussels, scrubbed and de-bearded
200 ml white wine
6 eggs
100 ml milk
150 g (1 cup) plain flour
100 g panko breadcrumbs
750 ml vegetable oil, for deep-frying
2 tablespoons sea salt

METHOD

Roasted chilli dressing Heat 500 ml (2 cups) of the oil in a wok to 160°C (you can test if the oil is the right temperature by dropping in a cube of bread; if the bread browns in 50 seconds, the oil is ready). Deep-fry the chillies for 20 seconds until nutty and aromatic and a deep red colour, being careful not to let them burn. Drain on paper towel. Add the shallots to the wok and deep-fry, moving the slices around and flipping them over, for 30–40 seconds until pale golden brown. Drain on paper towel and separate with a fork. Season with salt and dust with the icing sugar to enhance and balance the flavour.

Place the garlic in a small saucepan and pour in the milk. Bring to the boil, then remove from the heat. Strain and run under cold water to rinse away any excess milk. Return the garlic to the cleaned pan, add the remaining oil and cook over high heat for 1 minute until lightly golden. Strain the hot oil through a fine sieve into a small saucepan and reserve. Drain the garlic on paper towel.

Combine the palm sugar and water in a saucepan and bring to the boil, stirring to dissolve the sugar. Remove from the heat and set aside to cool.

Place the fried chilli, shallots and garlic in the bowl of a food processor and blitz to form a fine paste. With the motor running, slowly pour in the palm sugar syrup and process until a smooth paste forms. Pour in the lime juice and fish sauce and process until combined. Taste for seasoning; you want the dressing to be sweet, salty, sour and hot.

Coconut salad Gently toss together the coconut, onion, spring onion, chilli, avocado, pomelo, basil and coriander.

Panko-crumbed mussels Place a large saucepan over high heat, add the mussels and wine, cover with a lid and cook for 1 minute until mussels open. Discard any mussels that don't open. Strain the mussels through a colander, discarding the cooking liquid, and set the mussels aside until cool enough to handle. Take the mussels out of the shells, then refrigerate until needed.

Crack the eggs into a shallow bowl, add the milk and lightly whisk, place the flour in another bowl and the panko crumbs in a third bowl. Dip the mussels, one by one, into the flour, then in the egg wash and finally in the panko crumbs. Place on a tray.

Heat the oil in the wok to 180°C (you can test if the oil is the right temperature by dropping in a cube of bread; if the bread browns in 30 seconds, the oil is ready). Deep-fry the mussels, in batches, for 1–2 minutes in the oil until golden brown. Drain on paper towel and lightly season with salt.

TO SERVE

Spoon 3 tablespoons of the roasted chilli dressing onto each serving plate and scatter on four mussels. Place a neat pile of the salad on top of the mussels.

Minced chicken thighs have a lot more flavour and texture than breasts.
Ask your butcher in advance for straight minced chicken thighs.

CHICKEN AND CHINESE CABBAGE DUMPLINGS
WITH BLACK VINEGAR DRESSING

BLACK VINEGAR DRESSING

3 red shallots, thinly sliced

15 g (approx 3 cm) fresh ginger, peeled and finely chopped

4 coriander stems and roots, washed and finely chopped

3 tablespoons kecap manis

3 tablespoons light soy sauce

3 tablespoons black vinegar

1 tablespoon sesame oil

2 tablespoons gula melaka (see page 238)

40 ml lime juice

CHICKEN AND CHINESE CABBAGE DUMPLINGS

1 teaspoon vegetable oil

1 cup shredded Chinese cabbage (wong bok)

350 g minced chicken thighs

15 g (approx 3 cm) fresh ginger, peeled and finely chopped

5 garlic cloves, finely chopped

6 spring onions, white part only, thinly sliced

3 red shallots, finely chopped

2 tablespoons light soy sauce

1 tablespoon fish sauce

1 pinch of sea salt

12 square yellow won ton wrappers, cut into 9 cm rounds

METHOD

Black vinegar dressing Combine the ingredients in a bowl, mix well and set aside.

Chicken and Chinese cabbage dumplings Heat the oil in a wok over high heat and add the Chinese cabbage and fry for 2 minutes. Transfer the cabbage to a large bowl and set aside to cool.

Add the chicken, ginger, garlic, spring onions and shallots to the cabbage and mix thoroughly. Season with the soy and fish sauces and salt. Refrigerate the dumpling mix for 1 hour.

Using one won ton wrapper at a time, place 1 tablespoon of the chicken mixture in the centre, brush around the edge with a little water and fold to form a half moon shape. Press firmly to seal the edges and expel the air. To give each dumpling a nice flat base, hold the pinched edge in your fingers and press down on the bench.

TO SERVE

Place a perforated stainless steel disc insert in a bamboo steamer, then spray with cooking spray and add the dumplings in a single layer, leaving a 2 cm space around each one so they don't stick together. Cover and steam over a wok of simmering water for 4–6 minutes, or until cooked through. To check if they are cooked, gently squeeze the base of dumpling; it should be nice and firm.

Pour the black vinegar dressing into a ramekin and place the dumplings on a serving plate.

Atari goma is a white sesame paste which can be bought from most Asian supermarkets. Tahini is the same product. Kangkong is Chinese water spinach and can be found at any fresh Asian produce market.

LOBSTER, KANGKONG
AND WATER CHESTNUT DUMPLINGS WITH SESAME PONZU SAUCE

Serves four to share

SESAME PONZU SAUCE

20 g silken tofu
3 tablespoons atari goma
1 tablespoon caster sugar
3½ tablespoons hot water
3 tablespoons Chinese
   black vinegar
2 tablespoons ponzu sauce
1 teaspoon spiced chilli salt
   (see page 241)

LOBSTER, KANGKONG AND
WATER CHESTNUT DUMPLINGS

150 g blue eye fillet, skin removed,
   cut into chunks
250 g raw lobster meat, chopped
   into a small dice
10 kangkong leaves, thinly sliced
40 g water chestnuts, cut into
   1 mm thick slices
6 spring onions, white part only,
   thinly sliced
4 garlic cloves, finely chopped
2 red bird's eye chillies,
   finely chopped
1 tablespoon kecap manis
2 tablespoons fish sauce
1 teaspoon sea salt
12 gyoza skins

METHOD

Sesame ponzu sauce Place the tofu in the bowl of a food processor and blitz for 30 seconds, then pour in the atari goma and sugar and, with the motor running, add the hot water and process until combined. Pour in the vinegars and blitz until combined. Now add the chilli salt and blitz again. Transfer to a small bowl and place in the refrigerator until needed.

Lobster, kangkong and water chestnut dumplings Place the fish in the chilled bowl of a food processer and blitz to form a smooth ball.

Combine all of the ingredients for the dumplings in a large chilled bowl and mix well for 3 minutes, to work the proteins in the fish and infuse the flavours. Cover with plastic wrap and refrigerate to chill.

Using one gyoza skin at a time, place 1 tablespoon of the lobster mixture in the centre, brush around the edge with a little water, then fold in half to form a semicircle. Press firmly to seal the edges and expel the air.

TO SERVE

Place a perforated stainless steel disc insert in a bamboo steamer, spray with cooking spray and add the dumplings in a single layer, leaving a 2 cm space around each one so they don't stick together. Cover and steam over a wok of simmering water for 4–5 minutes, or until cooked through.

Divide the dumplings between four serving plates, then pour 2 tablespoons of the sesame ponzu over the top.

CRISPY SINGAPORE NOODLES
WITH SPICED VEGETABLES

SPICED VEGETABLES

700 ml vegetable stock
  (see page 242)
4 red shallots, thinly sliced
3 garlic cloves, finely chopped
15 g (approx 3 cm) fresh ginger,
  peeled and thinly sliced
200 g lotus root, peeled and
  thickly sliced
2 tablespoons vegetable or
  peanut oil
1 large eggplant, peeled, cut in
  half lengthways, then cut into
  quarters
1 teaspoon sea salt
12 cherry tomatoes, cut in half
100 ml pat chun (sweetened
  Chinese vinegar)
200 g silk melon, peeled, cut in
  half lengthways, then into thirds
100 g garlic shoots, cut into
  5 cm batons
120 g snake beans, cut into
  5 cm batons

SOY AND SESAME DRESSING

300 ml vegetable stock
  (see page 242)
100 ml light soy sauce
2½ tablespoons sesame oil
125 ml (½ cup) kecap manis
2 green bird's eye chillies,
  thinly sliced

CRISPY SINGAPORE NOODLES

750 ml (3 cups) vegetable oil
500 g thin yellow egg noodles
  (Singapore noodles)
100 g Chinese broccoli (gai larn),
  leafy part only, thinly sliced
1 teaspoon sea salt

METHOD

Spiced vegetables Pour the stock into a large saucepan, add the shallots, garlic, ginger and lotus root and bring to the boil. Reduce the heat to low and simmer for 1 hour until the lotus root is still firm but easy to bite through.

Heat a chargrill or barbecue over very high heat. Drizzle the oil over the eggplant and season lightly with the salt. Chargrill for 30–40 seconds on each side, or until charred.

Meanwhile, preheat the oven to 140°C. Spread the tomatoes on a baking tray and pour the pat chun over the top and lightly season with salt. Add the charred eggplant to the tray, cover with foil and bake for 30 minutes. Set aside to cool, then pour the roasting juices from the tomatoes into a large bowl and reserve for the dressing.

Soy and sesame dressing Mix the vegetable stock, soy sauce, sesame oil, kecap manis, chilli and the reserved roasting juices from the tomatoes and set aside.

Crispy Singapore noodles Heat the oil in a wok to 180°C (you can test if the oil is the right temperature by dropping in a cube of bread; if the bread browns in 30 seconds, the oil is ready). Add the noodles, in batches, and deep-fry for 1 minute until puffed. Drain on paper towel. Scoop any residue from the noodles out of the oil. Deep-fry the Chinese broccoli in the hot oil for 15 seconds. Drain on paper towel, transfer to a large serving bowl and season with the salt.

TO SERVE

Stir-fry the silk melon, garlic shoots and snake beans in a wok for 2 minutes until cooked and shiny. Add the eggplant and lotus root and stir-fry for a further minute. Toss in the tomatoes and pour in half of the dressing and stir-fry for 2 minutes.

Divide the spiced vegetables and remaining dressing between serving bowls and serve with the crispy Singapore noodles.

This is a great dish any time of the year. The lime and lemongrass barbecued cuttlefish has lots of flavour and works well for a dinner party or on a hot summer's day with a nice cold apple cider. If you can't get cuttlefish, you can substitute it with calamari. Ask your fishmonger to clean it for you. Banana blossom is available from your local Asian market. If you can't get banana blossom, you can leave it out.

LIME AND LEMONGRASS CUTTLEFISH
WITH GREEN CHILLI MAYONNAISE

Serves four to share

LIME AND LEMONGRASS CUTTLEFISH

600 g cuttlefish, cleaned and scored
2 lemongrass stems, white part only, finely chopped
3 kaffir lime leaves, thinly sliced
3 garlic cloves, finely chopped
2 limes, zested and segmented
6 red shallots, finely chopped
3 tablespoons vegetable oil
1 banana blossom
1 tablespoon sea salt

GREEN CHILLI MAYONNAISE

1 garlic clove, roughly chopped
10 g (approx 2 cm) fresh ginger, peeled and finely chopped
2 large green chillies, roughly chopped
4 coriander roots, washed and roughly chopped
1 tablespoon dijon mustard
1 egg yolk
70 ml coconut vinegar
½ handful of coriander leaves, picked and washed
350 ml vegetable oil
2 pinches of sea salt
lime cheeks, to serve

METHOD

Lime and lemongrass cuttlefish Cut the cuttlefish in half, then slice into six pieces and place in a bowl. Add the lemongrass, kaffir lime leaves, garlic, lime zest, shallots and oil and mix well. Cover with plastic wrap and leave in the refrigerator for 2 hours to marinate.

Cut the banana blossom in half, peel off and discard the four outer layers. Gently peel off the next four layers and trim the base. Place in the refrigerator until needed.

Green chilli mayonnaise Combine the garlic, ginger, chilli, coriander root, mustard and egg yolk in the chilled bowl of a food processor and blitz to form a paste. Add the vinegar and coriander leaves and, with the motor running, slowly pour in the oil in a thin steady stream until the sauce is thick and creamy. Season with the lime juice and salt and leave in the refrigerator for at least an hour to chill.

TO SERVE

Remove the cuttlefish from the refrigerator and leave to come to room temperature for 15 minutes.

Heat the barbecue to medium–high heat. Season the cuttlefish with the salt and barbecue for 3 minutes. Transfer to a bowl, add the lime segments and mix well.

Place a banana leaf in the centre of each serving plate, evenly divide the cuttlefish between the plates and garnish with the fried chilli peanuts. Serve with a small dish of the green chilli mayonnaise and lime cheeks.

This dish is a great salad for the warmer months of the year; it is spicy, aromatic, sour, salty and full of flavour. Very similar flavours to tom kha.

COCONUT CHICKEN SALAD
WITH CHILLI, BEANS, PEANUTS AND MANGO

Serves four to share

POACHED CHICKEN

2 litres (8 cups) Asian chicken stock (see page 232)
100 g fresh ginger, roughly chopped
6 garlic cloves, roughly chopped
2 cinnamon sticks, lightly toasted
250 ml (1 cup) shaoxing rice wine
100 g yellow rock sugar
2 green bird's eye chillies, roughly chopped
1.6 kg whole chicken

COCONUT DRESSING

300 ml coconut cream
20 g (approx 4 cm) fresh ginger, peeled and finely chopped
3 garlic cloves, finely chopped
3 green bird's eye chillies, thinly sliced
3 red shallots, thinly sliced
2 kaffir lime leaves, thinly sliced
80 ml lime juice
3½ tablespoons fish sauce
3 tablespoons gula melaka (see page 238)

SALAD

½ cup fried chilli peanuts (see page 236)
100 g green beans, quartered lengthways and blanched
2 large red chillies, deseeded and thinly sliced
1 large ripe mango, diced
1 handful of coriander leaves
1 handful of mint leaves

METHOD

Poached chicken Pour the stock into a stockpot or large saucepan, add the ginger, garlic, cinnamon, shaoxing rice wine, sugar and chilli and bring to the boil over high heat. Add the chicken, bring back to the boil and reduce the heat to low. Cover and gently simmer for 45 minutes until the chicken is cooked through.

Take the chicken out of the stock, place on a tray and let cool. When cool enough to handle, remove the skin and meat and place in separate bowls. Use your fingers to shred the poached chicken meat. Finely chop the skin and mix it into the shredded chicken.

Coconut dressing Combine the coconut cream, the ginger, garlic, chilli, shallots, lime leaves, lime juice, fish sauce and gula melaka in a large bowl and mix well. Set aside for 20 minutes to allow the flavours to infuse. It should be perfectly balanced: hot, salty, sour and sweet.

Salad Place the chilli peanuts, green beans, half the chilli and half the mango in a large bowl, spoon over half of the dressing and mix thoroughly. Add the herbs and taste for seasoning.

Serve Combine the shredded chicken meat and skin with the salad and divide it between serving bowls. Spoon 2 tablespoons of the remaining dressing over the top of each. In a separate bowl, combine the remaining chilli and mango, then top each salad with 2 tablespoons of the chilli mango mixture.

KINGFISH TARTARE
WITH BETEL LEAVES AND MUSTARD MAYONNAISE

KINGFISH TARTARE

350 g kingfish fillets, skin
   removed, pin-boned and
   finely chopped
4 spring onions, white part only,
   thinly sliced
½ white onion, finely chopped
1 green bird's eye chilli,
   thinly sliced
20 g (approx 4 cm) fresh ginger,
   peeled and finely chopped
1 teaspoon sea salt
1 tablespoon light soy sauce
1 tablespoon pat chun
   (sweetened Chinese vinegar)
12 medium–large betel leaves,
   wiped with damp paper towel

MUSTARD MAYONNAISE

1 egg yolk
2½ tablespoons rice wine vinegar
½ teaspoon mustard powder
4 tablespoons dijon mustard
40 ml lime juice
300 ml vegetable oil
1 pinch of salt
1 pinch of freshly ground
   white pepper

GARNISH

1 tablespoon yellow mustard
   seeds, soaked for 10 minutes,
   then drained
1 lime, segmented

METHOD

Kingfish tartare Combine the kingfish, spring onion, onion, chilli, ginger, salt, soy sauce and pat chun in a chilled bowl and mix well. Cover with plastic wrap and leave in the refrigerator until needed.

Mustard mayonnaise Place the egg yolk, vinegar, mustard powder and lime juice in the bowl of a food processor and blitz until combined. With the motor running, slowly pour in the oil in a thin steady stream until the sauce is thick and creamy. Season with the salt and pepper.

TO SERVE

Divide the betel leaves, shiny side up, between four serving plates, spoon 1 heaped tablespoon of kingfish tartare into the centre of each leaf and top with 1 teaspoon of the mustard mayonnaise. Garnish with a sprinkle on the yellow mustard seeds and a lime segment.

Serves four to share

CUMIN-SPICED BROWN RICE
WITH SOY-GLAZED CHICKEN

CUMIN-SPICED BROWN RICE

185 g (1 cup) brown rice
750 ml (3 cups) water
1 tablespoon cumin seeds,
   lightly toasted
3 red shallots, finely chopped
3 garlic cloves, finely chopped
20 g (approx 4 cm) fresh ginger,
   peeled and finely chopped
1 tablespoon white sesame seeds,
   lightly toasted
2 tablespoons vegetable oil

SOY-GLAZED CHICKEN

2 tablespoons shaoxing rice wine
3 tablespoons kecap manis
3 tablespoons light soy sauce
1 tablespoon honey
2 boneless chicken breasts,
   skin on
1 tablespoon sesame oil
1 pinch of sea salt
6 cherry tomatoes, cut in half
1 large red chilli, thinly sliced
125 g double smoked bacon, diced

METHOD

Cumin-spiced brown rice Place the rice in a strainer and rinse under cold water for 5 minutes, moving the rice around with your hand to wash it really well. Transfer the rice to a saucepan, add the water and cumin seeds and place over high heat. Bring to the boil, reduce the heat to low, cover with a lid on it and cook for 16 minutes until tender. Mix in the shallots, garlic, ginger and sesame seeds and spread the rice on a tray to cool.

Soy-glazed chicken Combine the shaoxing rice wine, kecap manis, soy sauce and honey in a bowl, then pour half into a small roasting tin, reserving the other half for the rice. Add the chicken and massage the marinade into the flesh, then cover with plastic wrap and leave in the refrigerator for 1 hour.

Preheat the oven to 180°C.

Remove the chicken from the marinade and pat dry with paper towel. Season the chicken breast with the salt.

Heat an ovenproof frying pan over medium heat, add the sesame oil and chicken and fry the chicken on one side for 2 minutes, then flip over and cook for a further 2 minutes. Transfer the pan to the oven and roast for 8–10 minutes or until cooked through. You want the chicken to caramelise but not burn. Set aside to rest for 5 minutes, then cut across the grain into 2 mm thick slices.

TO SERVE

Heat a wok over high heat, add the oil and the cumin-spiced brown rice and stir-fry for 1 minute. Add the tomato, chilli and bacon and stir-fry for 3 minutes. Pour in the reserved marinade and cook for 1 minute. Pile the rice onto a platter and place the chicken alongside.

Sichuan cuisine is very distinct; it is often spicy, incorporating sichuan peppercorns, chilli, star anise, garlic and ginger. They often use a bean chilli paste made from broad beans to season.

SICHUAN-STYLE PORK, PRAWN AND SCALLOPS
IN LETTUCE CUPS

SICHUAN-STYLE PORK, PRAWN AND SCALLOPS

300 ml vegetable oil
4 dried large red chillies, deseeded
4 red shallots, thinly sliced
4 garlic cloves, finely chopped
20 g (approx 4 cm) fresh ginger, peeled and finely chopped
100 g minced pork
250 g raw tiger prawns, peeled, deveined and roughly chopped
4 tablespoons shaoxing rice wine
2 tablespoons oyster sauce
2 tablespoons grated light palm sugar
12 large scallops, cut into quarters
2 tablespoons light soy sauce
1 red bird's eye chilli, thinly sliced
80 ml lime juice
1 teaspoon prickly ash
12 iceberg lettuce cups (see page 238)
3 spring onions, white part only, thinly sliced on an angle
1 tablespoon white sesame seeds, toasted

METHOD

Sichuan-style pork, prawn and scallops Heat the oil in a wok to 140°C (you can test if the oil is the right temperature by dropping in a cube of bread; if the bread browns in 1 minute and 30 seconds, the oil is ready). Add the dried chillies and fry for 1–2 minutes. Strain the oil into a heatproof bowl and reserve. Drain the chillies on paper towel and, when cool enough to handle, crumble into a few pieces.

Place the wok over high heat. Add 1 tablespoon of the reserved chilli oil, the shallots, garlic and ginger and stir-fry for 1 minute. Add the pork and prawns and cook, stirring, for 1 minute, then pour in the shaoxing rice wine and cook for 1 minute. Stir in the oyster sauce and sugar and caramelise for 1 minute. Add the scallops, soy sauce, crumbled dried chilli, fresh chilli and lime juice and stir-fry for 1 minute. Season with the prickly ash and mix well.

TO SERVE

Place three lettuce cups on each serving plate. Spoon 1–2 tablespoons of the sichuan pork, prawn and scallop mixture into each cup and garnish with the spring onion and sesame seeds.

This is gingerboy's version of a deconstructed satay-style tataki dish.
Smoke salt can be bought from most fine foods stores.

SATAY-SPICED SWORDFISH TATAKI
WITH PICKLED CUCUMBER

Serves four to share

TURMERIC AND COCONUT DRESSING

15 g (approx 3 cm) fresh turmeric, peeled and roughly chopped
3 garlic cloves, roughly chopped
3 red shallots, roughly chopped
20 g (approx 4 cm) fresh ginger, peeled and roughly chopped
150 ml coconut cream
3 green bird's eye chillies, thinly sliced
2 tablespoons fish sauce
80 ml lime juice
2 tablespoons gula melaka (see page 238)

PICKLED CUCUMBER

½ telegraph (long) cucumber, peeled and thinly sliced into thin ribbons using a mandolin
150 ml green chilli pickle dressing (see page 237)
1 handful of coriander leaves
2 large red chillies, deseeded and thinly sliced
5 spring onions, white part only, thinly sliced on an angle
3 kaffir lime leaves, thinly sliced

SATAY-SPICED SWORDFISH TATAKI

½ teaspoon ground turmeric
1 teaspoon white sesame seeds
1 teaspoon sea salt
½ teaspoon smoke salt
1 teaspoon freshly ground black pepper
½ teaspoon freshly ground toasted cumin seeds
500 g mid-loin swordfish fillet, skin removed, cut in half
1 teaspoon vegetable oil

GARNISH

4 tablespoons fried chilli peanuts (see page 236), pounded in a mortar and pestle

METHOD

Turmeric and coconut dressing Place the turmeric, garlic, shallots and ginger in the bowl of a food processor and blitz to form a fine paste. You might need to add 3–4 tablespoons of water to help the paste come together. Transfer the paste to a large bowl and add the coconut cream, chilli, fish sauce, lime juice and gula melaka. Reserve until needed.

Pickled cucumber Put the cucumber and chilli pickle in a bowl and let it sit for 5 minutes. Drain and discard the pickling liquid, place the cucumber in a bowl and add the coriander, chilli, spring onion and kaffir lime leaf and combine well.

Satay-spiced swordfish tataki Combine the turmeric, sesame seeds, sea salt, smoke salt, pepper and cumin seeds in a large bowl. Season the swordfish with the spice mixture.

Heat a frying pan over high heat, add the oil and swordfish and cook on each side for 10 seconds. Take the swordfish out of the pan and set aside to cool.

Cut the swordfish into 2 mm thick slices.

TO SERVE

Layer the swordfish in a straight line on each plate, and sprinkle the fried chilli peanuts over and around the fish. Place a neat pile of salad next to the fish and serve with a small dish of the turmeric and coconut dressing.

Wing beans, in season during winter, have a great texture and are very
visually appealing. If you can't get wing beans you can use green beans or
snow peas. Pomelo is a large citrus fruit that is native to Southeast Asia; if you
can't find it, use ruby grapefruit. You'll need to start this recipe a day ahead.

SMOKED DUCK, POMELO AND WING BEAN SALAD
WITH TAMARIND DRESSING

Serves four to share

SMOKED DUCK

2 tablespoons kecap manis
2 tablespoons shaoxing rice wine
2 garlic cloves, roughly chopped
40 g (approx 8 cm) fresh ginger,
　roughly chopped
1 tablespoon honey
2 boneless duck breasts, skin on
100 g woodchips (manuka is the
　best but any from your local
　barbecue store will work),
　soaked in 100 ml water for 20
　minutes, then drained

POMELO AND WING BEAN SALAD

200 g wing beans, cut into
　2.5 cm pieces
½ red onion, thinly sliced
2 kaffir lime leaves, very
　thinly sliced
½ pomelo, segmented
8 spring onions, white part only,
　thinly sliced on an angle
1 handful of Vietnamese mint
　leaves
1 large handful of sawtooth
　coriander leaves, cut into
　2.5 cm lengths
4 tablespoons roasted rice
　(see page 240)

TAMARIND DRESSING

20 g belacan shrimp paste
3 garlic cloves, roughly chopped
3 red bird's eye chillies,
　roughly chopped
5 cherry tomatoes, cut in half
3 tablespoons pat chun
　(sweetened Chinese vinegar)
4 tablespoons tamarind paste
　(see page 242)
3 tablespoons fish sauce
90 ml lime juice

METHOD

Smoked duck Combine the kecap manis, shaoxing rice wine, garlic,
ginger and honey in a large shallow bowl. Score the skin on the duck
breasts using a sharp knife. Place the duck, skin side up, in the marinade,
cover with plastic wrap and place in the refrigerator overnight.

Preheat the oven to 180°C. Remove the duck from the refrigerator and
leave for 10 minutes to come to room temperature. Remove the duck
from the marinade and pat dry with paper towel. Place a perforated
stainless steel disc insert in a steamer basket, add the duck and cover
with the lid. Line the base of a wok with foil, sprinkle in a half of the
soaked woodchips and place over medium heat. Stir the woodchips
around until they start to smoke, then place the steamer on top. Cover
and smoke for 30 seconds, then turn off the heat and leave for 4 minutes.
Remove the steamer from the wok, move the woodchips around, replace
the steamer and repeat the smoking process. Remove the foil from the
wok and replace with a fresh sheet. Repeat the smoking process with the
remaining woodchips. Remove the duck from the steamer.

Place a large ovenproof frying pan over medium heat, add the smoked
duck breast, skin side down, and fry for 4–5 minutes, then flip over and
seal for 2 minutes. Transfer to the oven for 5 minutes until golden brown.
Allow the duck to rest in a warm place for 15 minutes, then cut into
1–2 mm thick slices.

Pomelo and wing bean salad Blanch the wing beans in boiling water
for 10 seconds. Drain, refresh in iced water and drain again. Place in a
large bowl and add the duck, onion, kaffir lime leaves, pomelo, spring
onion, mint and coriander and toss well.

Tamarind dressing Preheat the oven to 180°C. Wrap the shrimp paste
in foil and roast for 20 minutes. Set aside to cool. Pound the garlic and
chilli to a paste in a mortar and pestle, mix in the shrimp paste and
cherry tomatoes, then slowly incorporate the pat chun, tamarind paste,
fish sauce and lime juice.

TO SERVE

Pour 3 tablespoons of the dressing over the salad and mix gently. Pour
2 tablespoons of the dressing into each serving dish, add a handful of
the salad and scatter on 1 tablespoon of the roasted rice.

PORK, PRAWN AND GINGER DUCK NECK SAUSAGE
WITH RED VINEGAR CARAMEL

RED VINEGAR CARAMEL

100 g light palm sugar, grated
3 tablespoons water
1 garlic clove, finely chopped
1 red bird's eye chilli,
  finely chopped
3½ tablespoons red vinegar
2 tablespoons rice wine vinegar
2 tablespoons light soy sauce

PORK, PRAWN AND GINGER
DUCK NECK SAUSAGE

150 g raw tiger prawns, peeled,
  deveined and roughly chopped
250 g minced pork
2 spring onions, white part only,
  thinly sliced
2 red bird's eye chillies, finely
  chopped
20 g (approx 4 cm) fresh ginger,
  peeled and finely chopped
3 garlic cloves, finely chopped
1 small handful of coriander
  leaves, roughly chopped
1 teaspoon prickly ash
  (see page 240)
2½ tablespoons light soy sauce
2½ tablespoons gula melaka
  (see page 238)
2 medium-large duck necks,
  deboned and trimmed
2 m kitchen twine, cut into
  25 cm lengths
2 litres (8 cups) master stock
  (see page 239)
700 ml vegetable oil
1 teaspoon sea salt

METHOD

Red vinegar caramel Place the palm sugar and water in a small saucepan over medium heat and stir until the sugar is dissolved. Simmer for 8 minutes until the syrup thickens and turns golden brown. Stir through the garlic and chilli. Carefully add the remaining liquids, standing back a step as the caramel tends to spit and bubble over. Bring the caramel back to the boil and simmer for 3 minutes. Set aside to cool.

Pork, prawn and ginger duck neck sausage Place the prawns and pork in a large mixing bowl, add the spring onion, chilli, ginger, garlic and coriander and mix well, kneading with the back of your hands for 3 minutes to ensure a nice smooth stuffing for the duck neck. Mix in the prickly ash, soy sauce and gula melaka, cover with plastic wrap and leave in the refrigerator for up to 2 hours to help the proteins relax and make the mixture easier to work with.

Tightly tie one end of the duck neck with twine to ensure no stuffing can escape. Using a piping bag, fill the duck neck with the prawn mixture, packing it in tightly and making sure you have enough neck skin left to tie up the open end. Seal the open end with twine. Repeat this process with the remaining duck neck.

Heat the master stock in a saucepan until it just comes to the boil, add the sausages and cook for 25–30 minutes. Place on a wire rack to cool for 25 minutes.

Heat the oil in a wok over high heat, add the sausages and fry for 2–3 minutes until golden. Drain on paper towel.

TO SERVE

Cut the sausages into 1 cm thick slices, arrange on a platter and drizzle 4 tablespoons of red vinegar caramel over the top.

Make sure you get two 500 g chickens as that will be the perfect amount to share between four people.

SMOKED BABY CHICKEN
WITH TOMATO AND EGGPLANT SAMBAL

Serves four to share

SMOKED BABY CHICKEN

85 ml light soy sauce

15 g (approx 3 cm) fresh ginger, peeled and finely chopped

3 tablespoons green ginger wine

2 tablespoons shaoxing rice wine

2 x 500 g baby chickens, butterflied (ask your butcher to do this)

100 g woodchips (manuka is the best but any from your local barbecue store will work), soaked in water for 20 minutes, then drained

2 tablespoons jasmine tea leaves

1 tablespoon vegetable oil

TOMATO AND EGGPLANT SAMBAL

2 eggplants, peeled and sliced lengthways into 12 wedges

1 tablespoon vegetable oil

1 tablespoon sea salt

4 roma tomatoes, cut in half lengthways

250 ml (1 cup) pat chun (Chinese sweetened vinegar)

2 red shallots, thinly sliced

2 garlic cloves, finely chopped

1 red bird's eye chilli, thinly sliced

2 tablespoons shaoxing rice wine

2 tablespoons kecap manis

1 large handful of coriander leaves

1 cup crispy fried sambal (see page 234)

METHOD

Smoked baby chicken Combine the soy sauce, ginger, green ginger wine and shaoxing rice wine in a large container, add the chickens, skin side down, and rub the marinade into the flesh. Cover and place in the refrigerator for 2 hours to marinate. Remove the chickens from the refrigerator and leave for 10 minutes to come to room temperature.

Place a perforated stainless steel disc insert in a steamer basket, then add the chicken and cover with the lid. Line the base of a wok with foil, sprinkle in half of the soaked woodchips and place over medium heat. Stir the woodchips around until they start to smoke, then place the steamer on top. Cover and smoke for 30 seconds, then turn off the heat and leave for 4 minutes. Remove the steamer from the wok, turn the heat back on, stir the woodchips around, replace the steamer and repeat the smoking process. Remove the steamer from the wok and then remove the foil and the woodchips. Replace with a fresh sheet of foil and the remaining woodchips and repeat the smoking process. The last time you move the woodchips around, place the wok over medium heat and, once the woodchips start to smoke, sprinkle on the tea leaves. Place the steamer on top, cover and leave to smoke for 3 minutes. Turn off the heat and leave for 5 minutes.

Tomato and eggplant sambal Preheat the oven to 180°C.

Spread the eggplant in a single layer on a baking tray, drizzle on the oil and season with 1 teaspoon of the salt. Roast for 25 minutes until golden brown and soft. Set aside to cool.

Arrange the tomatoes, cut side up, in a single layer on a baking tray. Pour the pat chun over the top, season lightly with the remaining salt and cover with foil. Roast for 30 minutes until the tomatoes are cooked but still hold their shape. Leave the tomatoes to cool in the liquid. Once cool, the skin can be easily removed. Strain, reserving 80 ml (1/3 cup) of the pat chun liquid.

Heat a wok over medium heat, add the eggplant and stir-fry for 1 minute, then add the shallots, garlic, chilli and tomatoes and stir-fry for 1 minute. Pour in the shaoxing rice wine, cook for 20 seconds, then add the kecap manis and caramelise for a further 30 seconds. Stir in the reserved pat chun liquid, cook for 2 minutes, then remove from the heat.

TO SERVE

Preheat the oven to 180°C.

Season the chicken lightly on the skin side. Place a non-stick frying pan over high heat, add the oil and chicken, skin side down, and cook for 1–2 minutes, then flip over, cover and cook for a further 4 minutes or until the chicken is cooked through. Cut each chicken into quarters.

Spoon some sambal into the centre of two serving plates, top with the chicken and garnish with the coriander and crispy fried sambal.

RED CURRY-SPICED WAGYU BEEF TARTARE
ON BETEL LEAVES WITH LIME MAYONNAISE

LIME MAYONNAISE

2 tablespoons dijon mustard
2 tablespoons Chinese black
   vinegar
2 egg yolks
200 ml vegetable oil
½ teaspoon sea salt
80 ml lime juice
zest of 1 lime
3 kaffir lime leaves, thinly sliced

RED CURRY-SPICED WAGYU
BEEF TARTARE

10 g (approx 2 cm) fresh ginger,
   peeled and finely chopped
10 g (approx 2 cm) galangal,
   finely chopped
½ lemongrass stem, white part
   only, finely chopped
2 large red chillies, finely chopped
2 red shallots, finely chopped
2 garlic cloves, finely chopped
2 coriander roots, washed and
   finely chopped
½ cinnamon stick, lightly toasted
   and ground to a powder
1 teaspoon cumin seeds, lightly
   toasted and ground to a powder
1 teaspoon coriander seeds,
   lightly toasted and ground to a
   powder
1 whole star anise, lightly toasted
   and ground to a powder
40 ml lime juice
2 tablespoons fish sauce
2 tablespoons gula melaka
   (see page 238)
400 g minced wagyu beef
5 g belacan shrimp paste, roasted
12 betel leaves, wiped with damp
   paper towel
½ cup sliced baby coconut
   (see page 232)
½ telegraph (long) cucumber,
   halved lengthways, seeds
   scraped and cut into 2 mm
   thick slices

METHOD

Lime mayonnaise Combine the mustard, vinegar and egg yolk in the chilled bowl of a food processor and blitz to incorporate. With the motor running, slowly pour in the oil in a thin steady stream until smooth and creamy. Add the salt, lime juice and lime zest and blitz to combine. Transfer the mayonnaise to a small bowl and fold in the kaffir lime leaves. Cover with plastic wrap and refrigerate until needed.

Red curry-spiced wagyu beef tartare Place the ginger, galangal and lemongrass in the chilled bowl of a food processor and blitz until incorporated. Add the chilli, shallots, garlic and coriander root and process to a paste. With the motor running, add the ground spices, the lime juice, fish sauce and gula melaka and combine well. Transfer the red curry paste to a bowl, add the wagyu beef, mix well and leave to stand for 5 minutes.

TO SERVE

Place three betel leaves, shiny side up, on each serving plate, then, using 2 tablespoons, spoon a quenelle of the tartare onto each leaf and garnish with a slice each of baby coconut and cucumber. Spoon the lime mayonnaise into a small bowl and serve alongside.

OVEN-DRIED BEEF
AND SMASHED GREEN MANGO SALAD

Serves four to share

OVEN-DRIED BEEF

600 g grass-fed beef sirloin, thinly
    sliced into 10 cm strips
2 tablespoons spiced chilli salt
    (see page 241)
1 tablespoon light soy sauce
2 tablespoons sesame oil

SMASHED GREEN MANGO SALAD

100 g snake beans, cut into 1 cm
    lengths
3 garlic cloves, peeled
1 tablespoon dried shrimp
2 green mangoes, cut into 2 mm
    thick batons on a mandolin
2 red bird's eye chillies, thinly
    sliced
6 roma cherry tomatoes,
    cut in half
½ cup fried chilli peanuts
    (see page 236)
120 ml lime juice
5 tablespoons fish sauce
80 ml tamarind paste
    (see page 242)
1 handful of coriander leaves
1 handful of Thai basil leaves
3 kaffir lime leaves, thinly sliced

METHOD

Oven-dried beef Preheat the oven to 120°C. Line a baking tray with baking paper.

Place the beef, chilli salt, soy sauce and sesame oil in a bowl and massage the marinade into the meat. Cover the bowl with plastic wrap and leave in the refrigerator for 1 hour.

Spread the beef in a single layer on the prepared tray, so the strips aren't touching each other. Place in the oven for 4 hours until the beef has dried out. Set aside to cool.

Smashed green mango salad Blanch the snake beans in a saucepan of boiling water for 1 minute. Drain and plunge into iced water for 2 minutes to stop the cooking process. Drain again and set aside.

Pound the garlic and dried shrimp to a paste in a mortar and pestle. Add the mango and lightly pound until bruised. Add the snake beans, chilli and cherry tomatoes and lightly pound until bruised. Transfer to a large bowl, add the chilli peanuts, lime juice, fish sauce and tamarind paste and mix well. Scatter on the coriander and basil, then mix in the dried beef.

TO SERVE

Evenly divide the salad between four shallow serving bowls and garnish with the kaffir lime leaves.

SPICED LAMB CURRY PUFFS
WITH MINT YOGHURT

SPICED LAMB BRAISE

1 tablespoon vegetable oil
600 g lamb shoulder
2 litres (8 cups) Asian chicken
　stock (see page 232)
1 tablespoon coriander seeds,
　lightly toasted
5 whole star anise, lightly toasted
250 g yellow rock sugar, grated
1 tablespoon white peppercorns

CURRY PUFFS

5 garlic cloves, finely chopped
25 g (approx 5 cm) fresh ginger,
　peeled and finely chopped
6 spring onions, white part only,
　thinly sliced
1 lemongrass stem, white part
　only, finely chopped
3 tablespoons Chinese black
　vinegar
4 red bird's eye chillies,
　finely chopped
2 teaspoons salt and pepper mix
　(see page 241)
5 sheets of frozen butter puff
　pastry, thawed, cut into twelve
　9 cm discs and covered with
　a clean damp tea towel
2 egg yolks, lightly beaten
750 ml (3 cups) vegetable oil
1 tablespoon sea salt

MINT YOGHURT

250 g plain yoghurt
2 garlic cloves, finely chopped
20 ml lime juice
1 pinch of sea salt
1 handful of mint leaves,
　finely chopped

* **To make a cartouche**, cut
out a circle of greaseproof
paper slightly larger than your
casserole dish.

METHOD

Spiced lamb braise Preheat the oven to 160°C.

Heat a large frying pan over medium heat, add the oil and seal the lamb on all sides until golden brown. (This adds a caramelised flavour to the meat and stock.)

Combine the stock, coriander seeds, star anise, sugar and peppercorns in a saucepan and bring to a simmer. Place the lamb in a 4-litre casserole dish and cover with the stock. Place a cartouche* over the meat and stock, cover with the lid and place in the oven for 2 hours until a skewer inserted into the meat goes straight through, without any resistance. Remove from the oven, take out the meat and place on a wire rack with a tray underneath to catch the juices. Allow to cool. Strain the stock into a saucepan, place over low–medium heat and reduce by three-quarters until thick and gelatinous.

Curry puffs Shred the lamb into a bowl, add 75 ml of the reduced stock, the garlic, ginger, spring onion, lemongrass, black vinegar, chilli and salt and pepper mix and mix well. Cover with plastic wrap and place in the refrigerator for 30 minutes to chill and make the mixture easier to work with. Using three puff pastry discs at a time, place 1 heaped tablespoon of the lamb mixture in the middle of each disc, brush one side of the pastry with the egg yolk and fold over to form a half moon shape. Tightly press the edges together to seal. Place on a tray, cover with a clean damp cloth and transfer to the refrigerator for 15 minutes or until completely chilled.

Mint yoghurt Spoon the yoghurt into the middle of a 30 x 30 cm piece of muslin cloth, bring the edges together and tie up with kitchen twine. Hang over a bowl for 1 hour to drain and get rid of excess moisture. Place the drained yoghurt into a bowl, add the garlic, lime juice and salt and mix well. Just before serving, stir in the mint and transfer to a ramekin.

TO SERVE

Place a wok over high heat and heat the oil to 180°C (you can test if the oil is the right temperature by dropping in a cube of bread; if the bread browns in 30 seconds, the oil is ready). Deep-fry the curry puffs for 5–6 minutes until golden. Drain on paper towel and lightly season with the salt. Serve with the mint yoghurt.

STEAMED TARO, CORN AND SPRING ONION DUMPLINGS
WITH PLUM, CHILLI AND LIME DRESSING

Serves four to share

PLUM, CHILLI AND LIME DRESSING

150 g light palm sugar, grated
50 ml water
300 g blood plums, roughly
    chopped
2 green bird's eye chillies,
    finely chopped
30 g (approx 6 cm) fresh ginger,
    peeled and finely chopped
4 garlic cloves, finely chopped
80 ml lime juice
2 tablespoons fish sauce
6 spring onions, white part only,
    thinly sliced

STEAMED TARO, CORN AND SPRING ONION DUMPLINGS

200 g taro, peeled and cut into
    2.5 cm dice
kernels cut from 1 corn cob
6 spring onions, white part only,
    thinly sliced
4 garlic cloves, finely chopped
8 cherry tomatoes, cut into
    quarters
3 tablespoons kecap manis
1 red bird's eye chilli, thinly sliced
1 teaspoon sea salt
12 gyoza skins

METHOD

Plum, chilli and lime dressing Combine the sugar and water in a large saucepan over medium heat and bring to the boil, stirring to dissolve the sugar. Reduce to a simmer and cook until the sugar has dissolved and the syrup is pale golden. Add the plums, chilli, ginger and garlic and cook, stirring constantly to stop the mixture sticking to the base of the pan, for 45 minutes until a thin jam forms. Take off the heat and set aside to cool. Transfer to the bowl of a food processor and blitz to form a smooth paste. Add the lime juice, fish sauce and spring onion and blitz again. Set aside.

Steamed taro, corn and spring onion dumplings Place the taro in a bamboo steamer, cover and steam over a wok of simmering water for 25 minutes until the taro is tender when pierced with the tip of a knife. Transfer to a large bowl and mash with a potato masher. Add the corn, spring onion, garlic, cherry tomatoes, kecap manis, chilli and salt and mix to combine, making sure you don't overwork the mixture. Set aside to cool for 20 minutes.

Using one gyoza skin at a time, put 1 heaped tablespoon of the taro mixture in the middle, brush the edge of the skin with water and fold over, pinching the edges together to seal. Tap the base on the bench to flatten it slightly so the dumpling can sit upright.

TO SERVE

Place a perforated stainless steel disc insert in a steamer basket, spray with cooking spray and add the dumplings in a single layer, leaving a 2 cm space around each one so they don't stick together. Cover and steam over a wok of simmering water for 4–5 minutes, or until cooked through.

Place three dumplings on each serving plate and serve with the plum, chilli and lime dressing.

SWORDFISH TATAKI
WITH KOREAN BLACK BEAN DRESSING AND PICKLED CUCUMBER

Serves four to share

PICKLED CUCUMBER

250 ml (1 cup) rice wine vinegar

110 g (½ cup) caster sugar

3 tablespoons sichuan pepper, lightly toasted

1 telegraph (long) cucumber, peeled, deseeded and cut into 2 mm thick slices

1 small handful of coriander leaves

2 large red chillies, deseeded and thinly sliced lengthways

KOREAN BLACK BEAN DRESSING

3 red shallots, finely chopped

4 garlic cloves, finely chopped

15 g (approx 3 cm) fresh ginger, peeled and finely chopped

50 g dehydrated salted black beans

2 tablespoons freshly ground black pepper

150 ml light soy sauce

2 tablespoons gula melaka (see page 238)

80 ml lime juice

2½ tablespoons Chinese black vinegar

SWORDFISH

500 g mid-loin swordfish, skin removed, cut in half lengthways

1 tablespoon prickly ash (see page 240)

2 tablespoons vegetable oil

GARNISH

½ cup fried garlic (see page 236)

50 g shiso cress

METHOD

Pickled cucumber Place the vinegar, sugar and pepper in a small saucepan and bring to the boil. Set aside to cool. Place in the refrigerator for 20 minutes to cool completely, then add the cucumber and allow to pickle for 15 minutes. Drain and discard the pickling liquid and set the pickled cucumber aside.

Korean black bean dressing Combine all of the ingredients in a large bowl, taste for seasoning and adjust if required. Set aside.

Swordfish Season the swordfish with the prickly ash. Heat the oil in a large frying pan over high heat and, when it starts to smoke, add the swordfish and sear quickly on each side for 10 seconds. Set aside to rest for 5 minutes, then cut into 2 mm thick slices.

TO SERVE

Arrange the sliced swordfish on each serving plate and spoon on the black bean dressing. Mix the coriander and chilli into the pickled cucumber, place on top of the swordfish and garnish with the fried garlic and shiso cress.

Fresh bamboo is available from specialised Asian markets in springtime.
When roasted whole, with the skin on, you get a great nutty flavour.

ROASTED BAMBOO SHOOT
WITH RED CAPSICUM AND BLACK BEAN SOY SAUCE

Serves four to share

BLACK BEAN SOY SAUCE

3 red shallots, finely chopped

4 garlic cloves, finely chopped

15 g (approx 3 cm) fresh ginger,
   peeled and finely chopped

50 g dehydrated salted black
   beans

½ tablespoon freshly ground
   black pepper

150 ml light soy sauce

2 tablespoons gula melaka
   (see page 238)

80 ml lime juice

2½ tablespoons Chinese
   black vinegar

ROASTED BAMBOO SHOOT
WITH RED CAPSICUM

500 g fresh bamboo shoots

16 garlic cloves, peeled

300 ml vegetable oil

1 white onion, thinly sliced

300 g red capsicums, cut into
   1 cm thick strips

200 g zucchini, halved lengthways
   and cut into 2–3 mm thick slices

1 bunch of kangkong, leafy part
   only, thinly sliced

2 tablespoons shaoxing rice wine

1 cup crispy fried taro
   (see page 235)

1 handful of mint leaves

METHOD

Black bean soy sauce Place all of the ingredients in a large bowl and combine well. Taste for seasoning and adjust if required. Set aside.

Roasted bamboo shoot with red capsicum Preheat the oven to 180˚C.

Place the bamboo on a baking tray and roast for 45 minutes until tender. Cut off the outside of the bamboo and discard. Cut the bamboo in half lengthways, then cut into quarters and finally into 1 cm thick slices.

Combine the garlic and oil in a small saucepan over low heat and cook for 1 hour until soft. Remove from the heat and set aside to cool.

Place a wok over high heat, pour 3 tablespoons of the garlic cooking oil into the wok, add the onion and fry for 1 minute. Next add the bamboo, capsicum and zucchini and cook for 2 minutes. Once you have colour on the zucchini, add the kangkong and confit garlic and gently toss, trying not to break up the garlic. Add the shaoxing wine and the black bean soy and cook for 2 minutes. Take the wok off the heat.

TO SERVE

Pour the contents of the wok straight into a deep serving bowl and garnish with the crispy fried taro and mint.

You can get edamame beans – baby soy beans in the pod – from any Asian supermarket. They are very nutritious and have a nice texture when cooked properly.

SCALLOP AND GARLIC CHIVE SIU MAI
WITH SOY AND RED VINEGAR

SOY AND RED VINEGAR

150 ml red vinegar

100 ml soy sauce

2 tablespoons gula melaka (see page 238)

1 teaspoon freshly ground white pepper

SCALLOP AND GARLIC CHIVE SIU MAI

150 g bream fillets, skin removed and pin-boned, roughly chopped

200 g scallops, roughly chopped

4 garlic cloves, finely chopped

2 green bird's eye chillies, thinly sliced

30 g (approx 6 cm) fresh ginger, peeled and finely chopped

½ bunch of garlic chives, finely chopped

4 spring onions, white part only, thinly sliced

3 coriander roots, washed and finely chopped

1 tablespoon light soy sauce

1 teaspoon freshly ground white pepper

1 teaspoon sea salt

300 g frozen edamame beans

12 square yellow won ton skins, cut into rounds with a 9 cm cutter

METHOD

Soy and red vinegar Combine all of the ingredients in a bowl and set aside.

Scallop and garlic chive siu mai Place the fish in the bowl of a chilled food processor and pulse for 30 seconds, or until a smooth paste forms. Transfer to a large bowl and add the scallops, garlic, chilli, ginger, chives, spring onion, coriander root, soy sauce, pepper and salt and mix thoroughly.

Bring a saucepan of water to the boil, add the edamame and cook until the beans float to the surface. Drain and refresh in iced water for 2 minutes. Drain again, take the beans out of the pod and add to the siu mai mixture, combining well.

Place a won ton wrapper in the palm of your hand, spoon 1 heaped tablespoon of the siu mai mixture into the centre and use a crimping motion to fold the edges of the wrapper up around the sides of the filling, leaving the top open. Tap the base on the bench to flatten it slightly so the dumpling can sit upright. Repeat with the remaining wrappers and siu mai mixture.

TO SERVE

Place a perforated stainless steel disc insert in a steamer basket, spray with cooking spray and add the dumplings in a single layer, leaving a 2 cm space around each one so they don't stick together. Cover and steam over a wok of simmering water for 4–5 minutes, or until the base of the dumplings is firm and they are cooked through.

Spoon 2 tablespoons of the soy and red vinegar into four shallow serving bowls then place three dumplings in each bowl.

Serves four to share

These ribs are a great beer snack while sitting out in the sun in the afternoon. They are available from most Asian grocers or large food markets with a poultry shop. If you cannot find them, you can substitute chicken wings. You'll need to start this recipe two days ahead, for best results.

SALT AND PEPPER CHICKEN SPARE RIBS

SALT AND PEPPER CHICKEN SPARE RIBS

1 kg chicken spare ribs
4 tablespoons light soy sauce
4 tablespoons shaoxing rice wine
3 tablespoons sesame oil
2 tablespoons five-spice
2 tablespoons prickly ash
  (see page 240)
225 g (1½ cups) self-raising flour
3 eggs
750 ml (3 cups) vegetable oil
250 ml (1 cup) green chilli soy
  (see page 237)

METHOD

Salt and pepper chicken spare ribs Place the chicken in a deep container with a lid. Add the soy sauce, shaoxing rice wine, oil, five-spice and 1 teaspoon of the prickly ash. Mix until well combined, cover with a lid and leave in the refrigerator for two days for the flavours to infuse.

Place the flour in a shallow bowl and the eggs in a separate bowl and lightly beat. Dip the ribs in the egg wash, then coat with the flour, shaking off any excess. Heat the oil in a wok to 180˚C (you can test if the oil is the right temperature by dropping in a cube of bread; if the bread browns in 30 seconds, the oil is ready). Fry the ribs for 5–6 minutes until golden. Drain on paper towel.

TO SERVE

Season the ribs with the remaining prickly ash and place them in a large serving bowl. Pour the green chilli soy into a large ramekin and serve on the side for dipping.

MUSHROOM SAN CHOI BAO

MUSHROOM SAN CHOI BAO

3 tablespoons vegetable oil
100 g enoki mushrooms, trimmed
100 g wood ear fungus, thinly
  sliced
100 g shiitake mushrooms,
  trimmed and thickly sliced
100 g Swiss brown mushrooms,
  trimmed and thickly sliced
3 garlic cloves, finely chopped
15 g (approx 3 cm) fresh ginger,
  peeled and finely chopped
6 red shallots, peeled and finely
  chopped
3 tablespoons shaoxing rice wine
2½ tablespoons hoisin sauce
40 ml lime juice
1 teaspoon prickly ash
  (see page 240)
100 g water chestnuts, thickly
  sliced
12 iceberg lettuce cups
  (see page 238)
1 tablespoon white sesame seeds,
  lightly toasted
5 spring onions, white part only,
  thinly sliced

METHOD

Mushroom san choi bao Heat a wok over medium–high heat, add the oil and mushrooms and sauté for 2 minutes until the mushrooms lightly colour. Stir in the garlic, ginger and shallots and cook for 1 minute. Pour in the shaoxing rice wine and the hoisin sauce and gently move the mushrooms around for a couple of minutes until caramelised. Now add the lime juice, prickly ash, water chestnuts and sauté for 1 minute until well combined. Transfer to a bowl.

TO SERVE

Place three lettuce cups on each serving plate, then spoon 2 tablespoons of the mushroom mixture into each cup, lightly sprinkle with the sesame seeds and spring onion to finish.

RICE FLOUR-BATTERED OYSTERS
WITH SOY AND GINGER DRESSING

Serves four to share

SOY AND GINGER DRESSING

3½ tablespoons light soy sauce
1 tablespoon rice wine vinegar
1 tablespoon yellow rock sugar
1 tablespoon mirin
3 tablespoons water
1 tablespoon Chinese black vinegar
15 g (approx 3 cm) fresh ginger, peeled and finely chopped
1 garlic clove, finely chopped
2 dried shiitake mushrooms

RICE FLOUR-BATTERED OYSTERS

750 ml (3 cups) vegetable oil
12 freshly shucked oysters
250 ml (1 cup) rice flour batter (see page 240)
1 tablespoon prickly ash (see page 240)
1 egg white
50 g table salt

GARNISH

1 tablespoon white sesame seeds, lightly toasted
1 small handful of coriander cress

METHOD

Soy and ginger dressing Place all of the ingredients in a small saucepan over medium heat and bring to a gentle simmer. Remove from the heat and set aside for 15 minutes to allow the flavours to infuse. Strain into a clean saucepan and reheat.

Rice flour-battered oysters Heat the oil in a wok to 180°C (you can test if the oil is the right temperature by dropping in a cube of bread; if the bread browns in 30 seconds, the oil is ready). Dip the oysters in the rice flour batter, coating them completely, then shake off excess batter and deep-fry the oysters for 1–2 minutes until pale golden. Drain on paper towel. Season lightly with the prickly ash and place the oysters in the shells.

Whisk the egg white and table salt in a bowl until light and fluffy.

TO SERVE

To hold each oyster shell in place, spoon 3 tablespoons of the egg white and salt mixture on each serving plate and place an oyster shell on top of each. Spoon 1 tablespoon of the dressing over the top of each oyster and garnish with a small pinch of sesame seeds and a little coriander cress.

Wagyu beef bresaola with hot and sour salad and crispy fish

Quail and scallops wrapped in spring onion pancakes

Wagyu beef bresaola, a fantastic product, is available at some fine food stores. If you can't get any, you can substitute it with the oven-dried beef on page 136.

WAGYU BEEF BRESAOLA
WITH HOT AND SOUR SALAD AND CRISPY FISH

Serves four to share

CRISPY FISH

300 g ocean trout fillet, skin
 removed, pin-boned and thinly
 cut into 10 cm-long slices
1 teaspoon sea salt
750 ml (3 cups) vegetable oil

HOT AND SOUR SALAD

1 large handful of coriander leaves
1 large handful of mint leaves
1 large handful of Thai basil leaves
20 g (approx 4 cm) fresh ginger,
 peeled and thinly sliced
5 red shallots, thinly sliced
1 teaspoon dried shrimp powder
3 tablespoons hot and sour
 dressing (see page 238)
3 betel leaves, wiped with damp
 paper towel and thinly sliced
½ red onion, thinly sliced
50 g salmon roe
½ cup baby coconut
 (see page 232)

WAGYU BEEF BRESAOLA

300 g wagyu beef bresaola,
 thinly sliced

METHOD

Crispy fish Preheat the oven to 170°C.

Season the trout with the salt, place it on a baking tray and bake for 1 hour until golden and well cooked. Drain the fish on paper towel and set aside to cool. Transfer to the bowl of a food processor and pulse for 15 seconds.

Heat the oil in a wok to 180°C (you can test if the oil is the right temperature by dropping in a cube of bread; if the bread browns in 30 seconds, the oil is ready), add the trout and fry for 1 minute until golden brown and crispy. (You may have to stir constantly and reduce the heat of the oil to prevent burning.) Drain on paper towel.

Hot and sour salad Combine all of the ingredients in a large bowl and gently toss.

TO SERVE

Arrange the bresaola on serving plates, top with the salad and scatter on the crispy fish.

QUAIL AND SCALLOPS
WRAPPED IN SPRING ONION PANCAKES

Serves four to share

MARINATED QUAIL

4 large whole quails, butterflied and de-boned
250 ml (1 cup) spiced hoisin (see page 241)

SPRING ONION PANCAKES

150 g (1 cup) self-raising flour
1 egg
250 ml (1 cup) milk
6 spring onions, white part only, thinly sliced
10 g (approx 3 cm) fresh ginger, peeled and finely chopped
2 garlic cloves, finely chopped
2 pinches of sea salt
2 tablespoons water
2 tablespoons vegetable oil

QUAIL AND SCALLOPS

2 tablespoons vegetable oil
1 red onion, thinly sliced
80 g bean shoots, trimmed
3½ tablespoons shaoxing rice wine
12 large scallops, cleaned
1 large handful of coriander leaves

METHOD

Marinated quail Cut each quail in half between the breasts, then cut into quarters between the breasts and the leg. Place the quail pieces in a large shallow bowl, pour on one-third of the spiced hoisin and massage it into the meat. Cover with plastic wrap and leave in the refrigerator for one hour.

Spring onion pancakes Combine the flour, egg, milk, spring onion, ginger, garlic, salt and water in a large bowl and whisk well. Cover with plastic wrap and rest in the refrigerator for 20 minutes.

Heat a non-stick frying pan over medium heat, add 1 teaspoon of the oil and ladle in 70 ml of the pancake batter, tilting the pan to spread the batter to the edge. Cook for 1 minute, then flip over and cook for a further minute until lightly golden on both sides. Place on a wire rack to cool. Repeat with remaining batter until you have four pancakes in total. Place a perforated stainless steel disc insert in a bamboo steamer, spray with cooking spray then layer the pancakes in the steamer with a small sheet of baking paper between each one. Place a lid on the steamer, then place it over a saucepan filled with 750 ml of simmering water.

Quail and scallops While the pancakes are being steamed, heat a wok over high heat. Add the vegetable oil to the wok, then stir-fry the red onion and marinated quail for 1 minute. Deglaze with the shaoxing rice wine and cook for a further minute. Add the scallops and the remaining spiced hoisin and cook for 2 minutes until lightly caramelised. Transfer to a large bowl and add the bean shoots.

TO SERVE

Place a pancake on each serving plate and spoon one-quarter of the quail and scallop mixture into the middle. Then garnish with coriander. Fold pancake over to enclose filling.

Serves four to share

SPICED PORK NECK
WITH FRIED STICKY RICE BALLS AND GREEN CHILLI SAMBAL

SPICED PORK NECK

1.5 litres master stock
  (see page 239)
600 g pork neck, cut into
  3 cm dice

GREEN CHILLI SAMBAL

3 garlic cloves, roughly chopped
3 red shallots, roughly chopped
20 g (approx 4 cm) fresh ginger,
  peeled and roughly chopped
5 large green chillies, roughly
  chopped
80 g light palm sugar, grated
1 handful of coriander leaves
6 tablespoons fish sauce
130 ml lime juice
3 tablespoons gula melaka
  (see page 238)

BEAN SHOOT SALAD

150 g bean shoots, trimmed
3½ tablespoons green chilli pickle
  dressing (see page 237)
1 cup baby coconut
  (see page 232)
4 red shallots, thinly sliced
1 ruby grapefruit, segmented
1 avocado, cut into 1 cm dice
1 handful of Thai basil leaves
3 cups fried sticky rice balls
  (see page 237)

METHOD

Spiced pork neck Preheat the oven to 160°C.

Pour the stock into a stockpot and bring to the boil over medium heat. Place the pork neck in a 4-litre casserole dish and pour on the hot stock to completely cover, place a cartouche* over the top and cover with the lid. Braise for 2 to 3 hours until the pork is tender and falling apart. Remove the pork from the stock, spread out on a wire rack with a tray underneath to catch the juices and set aside to cool. Strain the stock into an airtight container, cover and place in the refrigerator until ready to serve.

Green chilli sambal Pound the garlic, shallots, ginger and chilli to a fine paste in a mortar and pestle. Transfer to a saucepan and cook over medium heat for 3–4 minutes until fragrant and lightly coloured. Add the palm sugar and cook for a further 4 minutes until aromatic and pale golden. Set aside to cool.

Combine the coriander and paste in the bowl of a food processor and blitz to form a smooth paste. You may need to add half of the fish sauce, lime juice and gula melaka if the paste is too dry to process. Spoon into a bowl and mix in the fish sauce, lime juice and gula melaka.

Bean shoot salad Mix the bean shoots and chilli pickle in a bowl and set aside for 5 minutes to allow the bean shoots to pickle. Drain and discard the pickling liquid, then add the remaining ingredients to the bean shoots, mix well and set aside until needed.

TO SERVE

Bring half of the stock to the boil in a saucepan over medium heat. Add the pork and simmer for 5 minutes.

Spoon 3 tablespoons of the green chilli sambal into shallow serving bowls, place six to seven pieces of pork on top and finish with a large handful of salad and 4–5 fried sticky rice balls.

*_To make a cartouche_, cut out a circle of greaseproof paper slightly larger than your casserole dish.

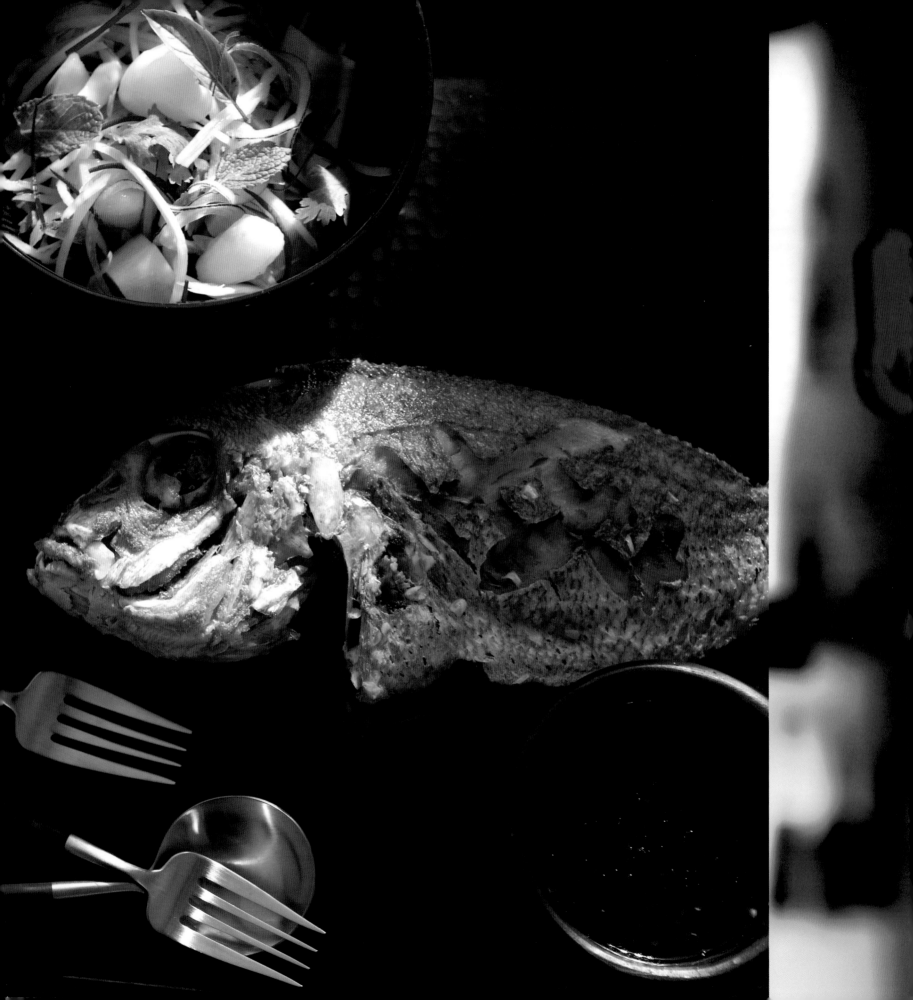

This great summer dish is one of gingerboy's favourites: the depth of flavour in the dressing works so well with the sweetness of the snapper and the freshness of the mango and lychee.

WHOLE BABY SNAPPER
WITH MANGO AND LYCHEE SALAD

Serves four to share

MANGO AND LYCHEE SALAD

1 mango, cut into 1 cm dice
½ red onion, thinly sliced
1 telegraph (long) cucumber, peeled and thinly sliced
10 lychees, peeled and cut in half
½ cup baby coconut (see page 232)
1 long red chilli, deseeded and thinly sliced
2 spring onions, white part only, thinly sliced on an angle
1 small handful of coriander leaves
1 small handful of Thai basil leaves
1 small handful of mint leaves
3 tablespoons hot and sour dressing (see page 238)

WHOLE BABY SNAPPER

750 ml (3 cups) vegetable oil
2 whole baby snapper, about 600 g each, cleaned and scored to the bone on both sides
roasted chilli dressing (see page 110)

METHOD

Mango and lychee salad Combine the mango, onion, cucumber, lychees, coconut, chilli, spring onion, coriander, basil and mint in a large bowl, lightly dress with the hot and sour dressing and toss gently, trying not to break up the mango.

Whole baby snapper Heat the oil in a wok to 180°C (you can test if the oil is the right temperature by dropping in a cube of bread; if the bread browns in 30 seconds, the oil is ready) and deep-fry the snapper for 5 minutes until cooked through. Drain on paper towel.

TO SERVE

Divide the mango and lychee salad between two serving bowls. Divide roasted chilli dressing between two small serving dishes. Place the snapper in the middle of each serving plate and serve with the dressing and salad.

Eel is great for this dish as the flesh is sweet, meaty and has a good amount of fat in it. You can substitute king george whiting, garfish or baby stingray for the eel.

TAMARIND CARAMELISED EEL
WITH NASHI PEAR

TAMARIND CARAMELISED EEL WITH NASHI PEAR

1 nashi pear, peeled and cut into 1 cm dice
40 ml lemon juice
1 pinch of sea salt
3 spring onions, white part only, thinly sliced on an angle
2 tablespoons vegetable oil
500 g freshwater eel fillets, pin-boned, and cut into 2.5 cm lengths
4 red shallots, thinly sliced
4 garlic cloves, finely chopped
125 g snow peas, topped and tailed, cut in half
100 ml tamarind paste (see page 242)
1 tablespoon grated light palm sugar
2 red bird's eye chillies, thinly sliced
2 tablespoons fish sauce
40 ml lime juice

GARNISH

1 nashi pear, extra, peeled and cut into a 1 cm dice
1 handful of Thai basil leaves
2 large red chillies, deseeded and finely sliced
4 spring onions, white part only, finely sliced on an angle

METHOD

Tamarind caramelised eel with nashi pear Place the nashi pear, lemon juice and salt in a bowl and mix well. Add the spring onion and reserve.

Place a wok over high heat, add the oil and eel and fry for 2 minutes. Stir in the shallots, garlic, snow peas and tamarind paste and cook for a further 30 seconds. Add the palm sugar and stir-fry for 1 minute. Turn off the heat, add the chilli, fish sauce and lime juice and taste for a balance of hot, sweet, salty and sour, adjust if necessary.

TO SERVE

Spoon the eel on to serving plates and garnish with the extra nashi pear, basil, chilli and spring onion.

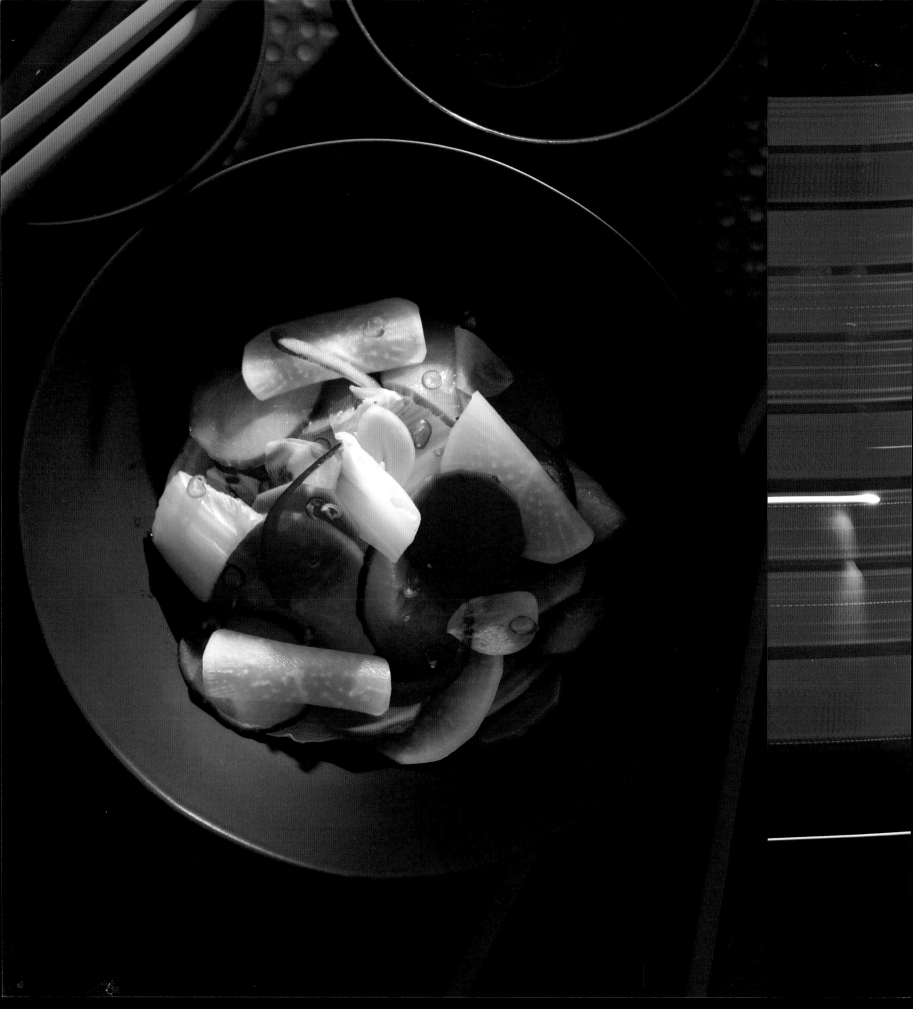

This is a very simple but great accompaniment to go in the middle of the table when you serve curries or any rich dishes that need something to help cleanse the palate. You can change the vegetables around to suit what is in season.

SICHUAN-PICKLED VEGETABLE SALAD

SICHUAN-PICKLED VEGETABLE SALAD

2 cups green chilli pickle dressing (see page 237)

1 telegraph (long) cucumber, peeled and cut into 2 mm thick rounds

½ small Chinese cabbage (wong bok), cut into 2.5 cm squares

1 red onion, cut in half and thinly sliced

1 large carrot, peeled and cut into 2 mm thick rounds

2 cups sichuan pepper pickling liquid (see page 241)

1 daikon, peeled and cut into 2 mm thick rounds

2 green bird's eye chillies, thinly sliced

1 teaspoon sea salt

METHOD

Sichuan-pickled vegetable salad Place ½ cup of the green chilli pickle in a small saucepan and bring to a simmer. Put the cucumber in a small airtight container, pour on the chilli pickle, cover and set aside for 1 hour. Repeat this process with the Chinese cabbage, using 1 cup of the green chilli pickle.

Place the onion in a small airtight container, pour the remaining green chilli pickle over the top, cover with a lid and set aside for 30 minutes.

Bring a saucepan of water to the boil. Add the carrot and cook for 1 minute. Drain and refresh in iced water. Place the carrot in a small airtight container and pour on 1 cup of the sichuan pickling liquid, cover with a lid and set aside for 30 minutes. Repeat this process for the daikon.

TO SERVE

Drain all the vegetables and place them in a large serving bowl, add the chilli and salt and toss well.

These scallops are lightly cured, so you need to get fresh live scallops. They should be available from your local fish market. Fuji apples are fresh, light red apples that are sweet and crunchy.

SOY AND SAKE SCALLOPS
WITH FUJI APPLE AND TARO CHIPS

SOY AND SAKE SCALLOPS

180 ml cooking sake
150 ml light soy sauce
80 ml lime juice
12 fresh scallops, on the half shell

FUJI APPLE AND TARO CHIPS

250 g taro, peeled and cut into
    1 mm thick slices
750 ml (3 cups) vegetable oil
1 pinch of sea salt
1 large fuji apple, cut into 2 mm
    thick batons
3 tablespoons green ginger wine
    dressing (see page 238)
4 spring onions, white part only,
    finely sliced on an angle
2 red shallots, thinly sliced
green chilli mayonnaise
    (see page 118)

METHOD

Soy and sake scallops Bring the sake to the boil in a small saucepan over high heat, flame and allow the alcohol to burn off. Once the flame has died down, remove from heat and set aside to cool slightly. Add the soy sauce and lime juice, mix well and transfer to the refrigerator to cool.

Place the scallops in a single layer in a small deep tray and pour on the chilled soy and sake mixture. Set aside for 30 minutes to allow the scallops to cure.

Fuji apple and taro chips Place the taro slices in a bowl of cold water for 5 minutes. Drain well.

Place a wok over medium heat, add the oil and heat to 180°C (you can test if the oil is the right temperature by dropping in a cube of bread; if the bread browns in 30 seconds, the oil is ready). Deep-fry the taro for 25 seconds on one side, then flip over and cook for a further 10 seconds. Drain on paper towel. Season with the salt.

Place the apple in a bowl and mix in the green ginger wine.

TO SERVE

Remove the scallops from the soy and sake marinade, pat dry with paper towel and cut in half.

Place three taro chips on each serving plate and put two scallop halves on top. Mix the spring onion and shallots into the apple, spoon a small neat pile over the scallops and finish with 1 teaspoon of the green chilli mayonnaise.

Red claw crayfish are great eating, as the meat is nice and sweet. They can be found at fish markets, if not, you can substitute yabbies.

RED CLAW CRAYFISH,
YUZU KOSHO AIOLI, SANSHO CHILLI SALT WITH NASHI PEAR SALAD

Serves four to share

YUZU KOSHO AIOLI

1 egg yolk
2 garlic cloves, pounded in a
   mortar and pestle
1 tablespoon dijon mustard
1 tablespoon yuzu kosho
2½ tablespoons rice wine vinegar
300 ml vegetable oil

SANSHO CHILLI SALT

1 teaspoon sansho pepper
1 teaspoon shichimi togarashi
1 teaspoon sugar
1 tablespoon sea salt

NASHI PEAR SALAD

2 nashi pears, cut into 2 mm thick
   batons
2 large red chillies, deseeded and
   thinly sliced
6 spring onions, white part only,
   thinly sliced
1 large handful of coriander leaves
1 handful of Thai basil leaves
250 ml (1 cup) green ginger wine
   dressing (see page 238)
2 banana leaves

RED CLAW CRAYFISH

6 fresh king-sized red claw
   crayfish (each weighing approx
   100–110 g)
1 lemon, cut in half

METHOD

Yuzu kosho aioli Place the egg yolk, garlic, mustard, yuzu kosho and vinegar in the bowl of a food processor and blitz to combine. With the motor running, slowly pour in the oil in a thin steady stream until smooth and creamy. Taste for seasoning; it should not need any salt as the yuzu kosho is quite sour and salty and has a nice amount of kick to it. Transfer to an airtight container and set aside.

Sansho chilli salt Combine all of the ingredients in a bowl and rub between your hands to mix well, breaking the salt flakes down a little.

Nashi pear salad Put the nashi pear in a bowl, add the chilli, spring onion, coriander and basil, toss well and set aside.

Spread the banana leaves out on a chopping board and, using a sharp paring knife, cut four rounds approx 10 cm in diameter, using a small plate as a guide.

Red claw crayfish Place the crayfish in the freezer for 20 minutes so they go to sleep.

Bring a large saucepan of water to the boil. Fill a large bucket with iced water. Plunge the crayfish into the boiling water and cook for 30 seconds. Transfer to the iced water for 3 minutes. Cut in half lengthways down the middle.

TO SERVE

Spoon a line of sansho chilli salt down one side of each serving plate and a line of the aioli on the opposite side. Place a banana leaf round in the middle of each plate.

Heat the barbecue to hot. Lightly season the crayfish and place, flesh side down, on the barbecue for 1–2 minutes, being careful not to overcook as the flesh loses it sweet freshness. Squeeze the lemon over the top while cooking. Arrange three crayfish halves on each banana leaf round.

Dress the salad with the green ginger wine dressing, toss well and place on the crayfish.

STEAMED SCALLOPS
WITH SMOKED CHILLI AND BLACK BEAN DRESSING

SMOKED CHILLI AND BLACK BEAN DRESSING

3 large green chillies, thinly sliced

3 garlic cloves, thinly sliced

100 g woodchips (manuka is the best but any from your local barbecue store will work)

3 red shallots, finely chopped

20 g (approx 4 cm) fresh ginger, peeled and finely chopped

30 g dehydrated salted black beans

1 teaspoon freshly ground black pepper

100 ml light soy sauce

3 tablespoons gula melaka (see page 238)

120 ml lime juice

3 tablespoons Chinese black vinegar

SCALLOPS

12 large scallops, on the half shell, cleaned

GARNISH

½ cup crispy fried taro (see page 235)

1 handful of mustard cress leaves, washed

METHOD

Smoked chilli and black bean dressing Line the base of a bamboo steamer with muslin cloth, then add the chilli and garlic in a single layer.

Line a wok with a sheet of foil, place over high heat and add the woodchips, spreading them out evenly. Once the woodchips start to smoke, move them around with a spoon to evenly distribute the heat and place the steamer on top. Cover and smoke for 8 minutes. Turn off the heat and leave the steamer in the wok for 5 minutes the smoky flavour to infuse the chilli and garlic. Remove the steamer, move the woodchips around again and place over medium heat until smoking. Place the steamer back on the woodchips, cover and smoke for 5 minute. Turn off the heat and leave for 5 minutes, then remove the steamer from the wok.

Combine the smoked chilli and garlic with the shallots, ginger, black beans, pepper, soy sauce, gula melaka, lime juice and vinegar in a bowl and set aside for 15 minutes to allow the flavours to infuse. Reserve.

Scallops Place the scallop shells in a single layer in the steamer, cover and place in a wok of simmering water and steam for 1 minute until firm but still a little transparent.

TO SERVE

Arrange the scallops on a plate and spoon 1 teaspoon of the dressing over the top of each one, making sure to get some chilli, garlic and black beans. Garnish with a small amount of the crispy fried taro and a few mustard cress leaves.

These prawn dumplings are very tasty. We use fresh raw Crystal Bay prawns from Queensland as they are sweet and have a fine texture. The peanut chilli soy balances the flavours of the dumpling.

STEAMED PRAWN AND GINGER DUMPLINGS
WITH PEANUT CHILLI SOY

Serves four to share

PEANUT CHILLI SOY

2 tablespoons fried chilli peanuts (see page 236)
100 ml light soy sauce
2 tablespoons kecap manis
3 tablespoons mirin
1 large red chilli, finely chopped
2 garlic cloves, finely chopped
½ teaspoon chilli powder
1 teaspoon freshly ground white pepper
2 tablespoons gula melaka (see page 238)
120 ml lime juice

PRAWN AND GINGER DUMPLINGS

200 g raw banana prawns, peeled, deveined and roughly chopped
200 g bream fillets, skin removed, pin-boned
8 spring onions, white part only, thinly sliced
4 garlic cloves, finely chopped
30 g (approx 6 cm) fresh ginger, peeled and finely chopped
2 red bird's eye chillies, finely chopped
1 tablespoon caster sugar
2 pinches of salt
3 tablespoons fish sauce
12 square yellow won ton wrappers, cut into 9 cm rounds

GARNISH

2 red shallots, thinly sliced

METHOD

Peanut chilli soy Pound the peanuts to a coarse paste in a mortar and pestle. Transfer to a bowl, add the remaining ingredients and mix well. Set aside.

Prawn and ginger dumplings Place the prawns in a large bowl.

Puree the bream in the chilled bowl of a food processor, add to the prawns and combine well. Mix in the spring onion, garlic, ginger and chilli. Add the sugar, salt and fish sauce and stir to combine. Cover with plastic wrap and leave in the refrigerator for 1 hour.

Using one won ton wrapper at a time, put 1 large tablespoon of the prawn mixture in the middle, brush some water around the edge and fold in half. Press firmly to seal the edges and expel the air. Tap the base on the bench to flatten it slightly so the dumpling can sit upright.

TO SERVE

Place a perforated stainless steel disc insert in a steamer basket, spray with cooking spray and add the dumplings, in a single layer, leaving a 2 cm space around each one so they don't stick together. Cover and steam over a wok of simmering water for 4–5 minutes, or until cooked through. Check the underside of a dumpling to make sure it is completely cooked and there are no raw patches.

Spoon the peanut chilli soy into a ramekin for dipping, then place a mound of the shallots on a platter and arrange the dumplings on top.

Green peppercorns are available in Australia from April–September.
Try to use them in season as the green peppercorns in brine are not as good.
When they're in season, you will be able to buy them fresh from an Asian market.

GREEN PEPPERCORN AND GARLIC SQUID

GREEN PEPPERCORN AND GARLIC SQUID

2 tablespoons sesame oil
600 g cleaned squid tubes,
   opened up, scored and cut into
   2 cm thick slices
3 garlic cloves, finely chopped
100 g fresh green peppercorns
4 spring onions, white part only,
   thinly sliced
100 ml shaoxing rice wine
3½ tablespoons light soy sauce
½ cup finely chopped garlic chives
80 ml lime juice
1 pinch of sea salt
1 pinch of prickly ash
   (see page 240)
½ cup fried garlic (see page 236)
2 lemons, cut into wedges

METHOD

Green peppercorn and garlic squid Place a wok over high heat, add the sesame oil and squid and stir-fry for 1 minute. Add the garlic, peppercorns and spring onion and stir-fry for a further minute. Pour in the shaoxing rice wine and soy sauce and stir-fry for a further minute, then add the garlic chives, lime juice, salt and prickly ash and stir until well combined. Remove from heat.

TO SERVE

Place 3 heaped tablespoons of the green peppercorn and garlic squid in shallow serving bowls and garnish with the fried garlic and lemon wedges.

You can buy fresh rice noodle sheets, a widely used Asian ingredient, from any Asian grocer. They have a great texture and are great for stir-fries, soups and noodle rolls and many more dishes.

RICE NOODLE ROLLS
WITH DUCK AND ENOKI MUSHROOMS

Serves four to share

RICE NOODLE ROLLS

400 g fresh rice noodle sheets
75 ml spiced hoisin (see page 241)
2 boneless duck breasts
½ telegraph (long) cucumber, core removed, cut into 5 cm batons
4 spring onions, white part only, cut into quarters lengthways
20 g (approx 4 cm) fresh ginger, peeled and finely chopped
60 g enoki mushrooms, stalks removed
1 tablespoon prickly ash (see page 240)

GARNISH

75 ml spiced hoisin (see page 241)
2 limes, peeled and segmented
2 cups crispy fried sweet potato (see page 235)
50 g enoki mushrooms

METHOD

Rice noodle rolls Open out the rice noodle sheets and gently pull apart into four lots of three sheets. Place a perforated stainless steel disc insert in a steamer basket, then spray with cooking spray and line with one lot of noodle sheets. Place another portion on top at a 45 degree angle, cover and steam over a wok of simmering water for 5 minutes. Remove from the heat and cool for 5 minutes as they will be extremely hot. Repeat with the remaining noodle sheets.

Place a frying pan over medium heat. Add duck breasts, skin side down, and cook for 4 minutes. Turn over and cook for a further 2 minutes. Remove the duck from the pan, set aside to rest, then slice.

Spread the spiced hoisin over one long side of each portion of rice noodle sheets. Top with the duck, then lay the cucumber the length of the rice noodle sheet. Scatter on some spring onion, ginger, enoki mushrooms and sprinkle on a little prickly ash. Tightly roll the rice noodle sheets around the filling. Cover each noodle roll tightly with two layers of plastic wrap.

TO SERVE

Add the noodle rolls to the steamer. Cover, place over a wok of simmering water and steam for 10 minutes. Unwrap from the plastic when cool enough to handle.

Dot spots of spiced hoisin on each serving plate. Cut the noodle rolls into six evenly sized pieces and arrange on plate. Garnish with lime segments, crispy fried sweet potato and raw enoki mushrooms.

Cold-smoked ocean trout can be substituted with cold-smoked salmon, but make sure it is cold-smoked not hot-smoked as the texture is completely different.

COLD-SMOKED OCEAN TROUT TARTARE
ON BETEL LEAVES WITH RED CHILLI MAYONNAISE

Serves four to share

TROUT TARTARE

300 g cold-smoked ocean trout, skin removed and finely chopped

1 small white onion, finely chopped

4 spring onions, white part only thinly sliced

2 kaffir lime leaves, thinly sliced

3 green bird's eye chillies, thinly sliced

3 garlic cloves, finely chopped

1 tablespoon kecap manis

RED CHILLI MAYONNAISE

2 garlic cloves, finely chopped

1 large red chilli, finely chopped

2 coriander roots, washed and finely chopped

2 tablespoons dijon mustard

1 egg yolk

2 tablespoons coconut vinegar

200 ml vegetable oil

1 pinch of sea salt

20 ml lime juice

GARNISH

12 betel leaves, wiped with damp paper towel (betel leaves can be purchased at Asian grocers or fresh food markets)

1 cup fried shallots (see page 237)

METHOD

Trout tartare Combine the trout, onion, spring onion, lime leaves, chilli, garlic and kecap manis in a bowl and, using your hands, knead the mixture, so it will take on the flavour of the other ingredients. Cover with plastic wrap and leave in the refrigerator for 30 minutes.

Red chilli mayonnaise Place the garlic, chilli, coriander, mustard and egg yolks in the chilled bowl of a food processor and blitz until well combined. Pour in the vinegar and blitz, then, with the motor running, slowly pour in the oil in a thin, steady stream. Process until all the oil has been added and the mayonnaise is a creamy consistency. Season with the salt and lime juice. Transfer to a bowl and store in the refrigerator.

TO SERVE

Arrange three betel leaves, shiny side up, on each serving plate, then, using 2 tablespoons, spoon a quenelle of the tartare onto each leaf. Place 1 teaspoon of the red chilli mayonnaise over the middle of the trout and sprinkle a small amount of the fried shallots over the top.

Hunan-style pork is a great, well-balanced dish that is seasoned with black vinegar and roasted shrimp paste. Hunan, a province in China, is located to the south.

HUNAN-STYLE PORK
AND GREEN BEANS IN LETTUCE CUPS

Serves four to share

HUNAN-STYLE PORK

2 tablespoons sesame oil

400 g minced pork

3 garlic cloves, finely chopped

20 g (approx 4 cm) fresh ginger, peeled and finely chopped

4 red shallots, finely chopped

120 ml shaoxing rice wine

100 g green beans, trimmed and cut into 2 cm lengths

1 red bird's eye chilli, thinly sliced

1 teaspoon belacan shrimp paste, roasted

1 tablespoon dried shrimp

3 tablespoons gula melaka (see page 238)

3 tablespoons Chinese black vinegar

40 ml lime juice

1 pinch of sea salt

1 pinch of freshly ground white pepper

12 baby cos lettuce leaves

METHOD

Hunan-style pork Heat a wok over high heat, add the oil and stir-fry the pork for 2 minutes until brown. Add the garlic, ginger and shallots and stir-fry for a further 2 minutes. Pour in the shaoxing rice wine and cook for 1 minute until evaporated and the pork is crumbly in texture. Next add the green beans, chilli, shrimp paste and dried shrimp and cook for 1 minute. Stir in the gula melaka and cook for 1 minute. Season with the vinegar, lime juice, salt and pepper and mix well.

TO SERVE

Transfer the pork to a large serving bowl and serve with the lettuce leaves.

Fresh sugarcane is available from Asian markets or grocers.
It adds a great sweetness to this dish.

SPICED PRAWN ON SUGARCANE
WITH CHILLI CARAMEL

Serves four to share

SPICED PRAWN

300 g raw tiger prawns, peeled
and deveined

100 g sea bream or whiting fillet,
skin removed, pin-boned

1 lemongrass stem, white part
only, finely chopped

2 green bird's eye chillies

6 spring onions, white part only,
thinly sliced

4 garlic cloves, finely chopped

3 kaffir lime leaves, thinly sliced

2 pinches of sea salt

1 tablespoon fish sauce

30 cm length of fresh sugarcane,
chopped into three 10 cm
lengths

150 g (1 cup) plain flour

750 ml (3 cups) vegetable oil

GARNISH

1 telegraph (long) cucumber,
peeled and thinly sliced into
ribbons using a vegetable
peeler

1 handful of Vietnamese mint
leaves

leaves of 2 butter lettuces,
trimmed

1 cup chilli caramel (see page 233)

METHOD

Spiced prawn Place the prawns and bream in the chilled bowl of a food processor and blitz to a puree. Process for a further 30 seconds to work the proteins in the prawns and fish.

Transfer the prawn mixture to a bowl, add the lemongrass, chilli, spring onion, garlic and lime leaves and mix well. Season with the salt and fish sauce.

Now, using a chef's knife, trim and remove the outside layer of the sugarcane lengths, then quarter each piece lengthways, so you have 12 pieces. Using the back of your knife, gently tap the middle of each piece of sugarcane. This will bruise the sugarcane, allowing its sweetness to be released. Divide the prawn mixture into 12 equal portions and wrap each portion around a sugarcane length, so that the prawn covers about two-thirds of the sugarcane (the end result will look like a large lollipop).

Place the flour in a shallow bowl. Roll the prawn mixture in the flour and gently tap to remove any excess flour.

Heat the oil in a wok to 180°C (you can test if the oil is the right temperature by dropping in a cube of bread; if the bread browns in 30 seconds, the oil is ready). Reduce the heat to low–medium and deep-fry the sugarcane prawn for 4 minutes until golden brown. Drain on paper towel for 2 minutes.

TO SERVE

Place a small pile of cucumber and mint in each lettuce leaf, drizzle with a small amount of the chilli carmel and rest a sugarcane prawn on top. Spoon the remaining chilli caramel into a small bowl and serve alongside.

Soft shell crabs are perfect for frying, their meat is sweet and juicy.
They are readily available from Thailand and Vietnam and are now farmed in
Australia. Sawtooth coriander originates from South America and has the same
flavour as coriander. It has a saw-like edge to the leaf and a great texture.

SALT AND PEPPER SOFT SHELL CRAB
WITH CHILLI, LIME AND PALM SUGAR DRESSING

Serves four to share

CHILLI, LIME AND PALM SUGAR DRESSING

170 g light palm sugar, grated

1 tablespoon water

200 ml lime juice

4 tablespoons fish sauce

2 red bird's eye chillies, finely chopped

½ teaspoon chilli powder

3 garlic cloves, finely chopped

3 kaffir lime leaves, finely chopped

SALT AND PEPPER SOFT SHELL CRAB

6 soft shell crabs, quartered and cleaned

3 teaspoons salt and pepper mix (see page 241)

150 g (1 cup) plain flour

750 ml (3 cups) vegetable oil

GARNISH

1 large handful of sawtooth coriander

3 garlic chives, finely chopped

1 red bird's eye chilli, thinly sliced (optional)

1 iceberg lettuce, finely shredded

METHOD

Chilli, lime and palm sugar dressing Place the palm sugar and water in a saucepan over low heat and bring to the boil, stirring until the sugar dissolves. Remove from the heat, add the lime juice, fish sauce, chilli, chilli powder, garlic and kaffir lime leaf. Set aside to allow the flavours to infuse.

Salt and pepper soft shell crab Place the crabs on paper towel for 15 minutes to absorb any excess liquid.

Mix 2 teaspoons of the salt and pepper mix with the flour in a large bowl. Dust the crabs with the seasoned flour until completely coated.

Heat the oil in a wok to 180°C (you can test if the oil is the right temperature by dropping in a cube of bread; if the bread browns in 30 seconds, the oil is ready). Deep-fry the crabs for 1–2 minutes. Drain on paper towel. Lightly season with the remaining salt and pepper mix.

TO SERVE

Combine the sawtooth coriander, garlic chives and chilli, if you like it hot, in a large bowl. Add the crab and gently toss. Drizzle the dressing around the outer edge of four shallow serving bowls, place a neat pile of lettuce in the centre of each plate, and then top with the soft shell crab.

SPANNER CRAB
WITH ASIAN MUSHROOMS, BLACK VINEGAR AND WON TON CHIPS

BLACK VINEGAR

4 red shallots, thinly sliced

30 g (approx 6 cm) fresh ginger,
    peeled and thinly sliced

5 coriander stems and roots,
    washed and finely chopped

3 tablespoons kecap manis

3 tablespoons light soy sauce

3 tablespoons black vinegar

1 tablespoon sesame oil

2 tablespoons gula melaka
    (see page 238)

80 ml lime juice

WON TON CHIPS

700 ml vegetable oil

20 yellow won ton wrappers

1 teaspoon sea salt

SPANNER CRAB

3 litres water

1 garlic bulb, cut in half

150 g fresh ginger, roughly
    chopped

1 red onion, roughly chopped

1 tablespoon salt

10 white peppercorns

2 x 500 g spanner crabs, cleaned

ASIAN MUSHROOMS

2½ tablespoons vegetable oil

50 g shiitake mushrooms,
    stems removed, cut into
    2 mm thick slices

50 g oyster mushrooms,
    torn into 2 mm thick pieces

50 g shimeji mushrooms,
    stems removed, torn

50 g enoki mushrooms,
    stems removed

3½ tablespoons shaoxing
    rice wine

3 spring onions, white part only,
    thinly sliced on an angle

METHOD

Black vinegar Combine all of the ingredients in a bowl and mix well. Set aside.

Won ton chips Place a wok over high heat, pour in the oil and heat to 170°C (you can test if the oil is the right temperature by dropping in a cube of bread; if the bread browns in 40 seconds, the oil is ready). Deep-fry the won ton wrappers, in four batches, for 10 seconds, then flip over and fry for a further 10 seconds. Drain on paper towel. Season lightly with salt.

Spanner crab Place a large stockpot over medium–high heat and add the water, garlic, ginger, onion, salt and peppercorns and bring to the boil. Add the crabs and cook for 8 minutes. Transfer crabs to a bowl of iced water to stop the cooking process, and set aside for 5–10 minutes. Drain well. Prise off the main shell and cut the body in half. Twist off the legs and break open with the back of a knife. Extract the crabmeat, using a crab fork or the handle of a long, thin teaspoon, scraping into all the cracks and crevices, and place in a bowl. Gently rub your fingers through the crabmeat and pick out any little bits of shell.

Asian mushrooms Place a wok over high heat, add the oil and shiitake, oyster and shimeji mushrooms and stir-fry for 2 minutes. Add the enoki mushrooms and shaoxing rice wine and stir continuously until all the liquid has evaporated. Stir in the crabmeat, then mix in half of the black vinegar and immediately remove from the heat.

TO SERVE

Place five won ton chips on each serving plate, divide the crab and mushroom mixture between each plate, drizzle 1 teaspoon of the remaining black vinegar over the top, and then dot the plate with a little more black vinegar. Garnish with the spring onion.

CRISPY CHICKEN
AND CHINESE BROCCOLI DUMPLINGS

CRISPY CHICKEN AND CHINESE BROCCOLI DUMPLINGS

1 cup finely shredded Chinese broccoli (gai larn)

300 g minced chicken thighs

3 garlic cloves, finely chopped

1 teaspoon freshly ground black pepper

3 green bird's eye chillies, thinly sliced

4 red shallots, finely chopped

1 tablespoon light soy sauce

1 tablespoon sea salt, plus extra to serve

12 square yellow won ton wrappers

750 ml (3 cups) vegetable oil

125 ml (½ cup) mustard soy sauce (see page 239)

METHOD

Crispy chicken and Chinese broccoli dumplings Heat a wok over high heat, add the broccoli and stir-fry for 30 seconds until wilted. Remove and set aside to cool.

Combine the chicken, garlic, pepper, chilli, shallots, soy sauce and salt in a large bowl. Add the broccoli and knead for 3 minutes to work the proteins in the meat. Cover with plastic wrap and store in the refrigerator for 2 hours.

Using one won ton wrapper at a time, place 1 tablespoon of the chicken mixture in the centre, brush around the edges with a little water, then pick up and pinch each corner together. Press firmly to seal the edges and expel the air. To give each dumpling a nice flat base, hold the pinched edge in your fingers and press down on the bench.

Heat the oil in a wok to 180°C (you can test if the oil is the right temperature by dropping in a cube of bread; if the bread browns in 30 seconds, the oil is ready), gently add the dumplings, in two batches, and fry for 3 minutes until nice and golden brown all over. Remove with a slotted spoon and drain on paper towel.

TO SERVE

Season the dumplings with a small pinch of salt, place three on each serving plate and serve with a ramekin of the mustard soy sauce.

Eel is great because the flavour is not intense and the texture is gelatinous when cooked. If you can't find fresh eel, you can get a product called unagi (ready-to-use soy-glazed eel) from Asian supermarkets.

TEMPURA-FRIED EEL
WITH CORIANDER, MINT AND LIME SALAD

TEMPURA-FRIED EEL

700 g freshwater eel fillets, pin-boned
2 tablespoons apple juice
2 tablespoons light soy sauce
200 ml kecap manis
1 Pink Lady apple, peeled and roughly chopped
750 ml (3 cups) vegetable oil
2 cups tempura batter (see page 242)
1 tablespoon prickly ash (see page 240)
185 g (¾ cup) green chilli mayonnaise (see page 118)

CORIANDER, MINT AND LIME SALAD

1 large handful of coriander leaves
1 large handful of mint leaves
1 red onion, thinly sliced
150 g bean shoots, trimmed
1 green bird's eye chilli, thinly sliced
2 limes, segmented
4 tablespoons lime juice
3½ tablespoons fish sauce

METHOD

Tempura-fried eel Bring a large saucepan of water to the boil. Blanch the eel for 30 seconds, then plunge into a bowl of iced water to cool completely. Drain well. Place the eel, flesh side down, on a chopping board and scrape all of the goo from the skin with the back of a knife. Cut in half and place on a wire rack with a tray underneath.

Combine the apple juice, soy sauce, kecap manis and apple in a small saucepan, slowly bring to the boil and simmer for 5 minutes. Remove from the heat, transfer to a blender and blend to make a smooth glaze.

Heat the grill to medium. Brush the apple soy glaze over the eel and place under the grill, skin side down, for 3 minutes. Brush on another coat of apple soy glaze and grill for 2 minutes. Flip the eel over and grill for 4 minutes, then flip back onto the other side, brush on another coat of apple soy glaze and grill for a further 2–3 minutes until caramelised all over. Set aside to cool.

Cut the eel in half lengthways, then cut into 2.5 cm lengths. Place the eel in a bowl, cover with plastic wrap and place in the refrigerator for 30 minutes to cool completely.

Coriander, mint and lime salad Combine the coriander, mint, onion, bean shoots, chilli and lime segments in a bowl.

TO SERVE

Heat the oil in a wok to 180°C. To test if the oil is hot enough, dip a teaspoon in the tempura batter, then hold it about 2.5 cm above the oil and let a little bit drip in. If the batter sinks and then comes back to the top, the oil is ready; if the batter stays at the bottom, you need to let the oil heat up for longer. Coat the eel in the batter, shake off excess and fry, in three batches, in the hot oil for 2 minutes until golden brown. Drain on paper towel and lightly season with a sprinkle of prickly ash.

Dress the salad with the lime juice and fish sauce and gently toss. Divide the eel between four serving plates and add 2 tablespoons of the green chilli mayonnaise and some salad.

Hainan chicken rice, a very tasty dish from China, is great to serve as part of a banquet.

HAINAN CHICKEN RICE
WITH CHILLI, GARLIC AND GINGER SAUCE

HAINAN CHICKEN RICE

2 litres (8 cups) Asian chicken stock (see page 232)

30 g (approx 6 cm) fresh ginger, peeled and sliced

2 garlic cloves, thinly sliced

4 boneless chicken breasts, skin on

300 g jasmine rice

1 teaspoon sesame oil

1 telegraph (long) cucumber, peeled and cut into 1 mm thick slices

4 spring onions, white part only, thinly sliced

CHILLI, GARLIC AND GINGER SAUCE

3 long red chillies, finely chopped

2 garlic cloves, finely grated

20 g (approx 4 cm) fresh ginger, peeled and finely grated

1 pinch of sea salt

2 tablespoons grated light palm sugar

2 tablespoons Asian chicken stock (see page 232)

80 ml lime juice

1 tablespoon fish sauce

METHOD

Hainan chicken rice Pour 1.5 litres of the stock into a large saucepan, add the ginger and garlic and bring to the boil. Add the chicken breasts, turn off the heat, cover the pan with the lid and leave the chicken to poach for 40 minutes.

Rinse the rice in cold water until the water runs clear. Place in a saucepan and cover with 500 ml (2 cups) of the remaining stock. Bring to the boil, reduce the heat to low, cover with a tight-fitting lid and simmer for 20 minutes. Remove from the heat and set aside for 5 minutes.

Chilli, garlic and ginger sauce Place the chilli, garlic, ginger, salt and sugar in a mortar and pound into a thick, even paste. Transfer to a large bowl and add the stock, lime juice and fish sauce and mix until well combined. Reserve on the side until needed.

TO SERVE

Remove the chicken from the poaching liquid, coat the skin with the sesame oil and thinly slice against the grain. Reheat the chicken stock. Add the cucumber and spring onion to the rice, mix well and spoon into a large serving bowl. Place the sliced chicken on top, pour on enough warm stock to cover the rice and spoon on the chilli, garlic and ginger sauce.

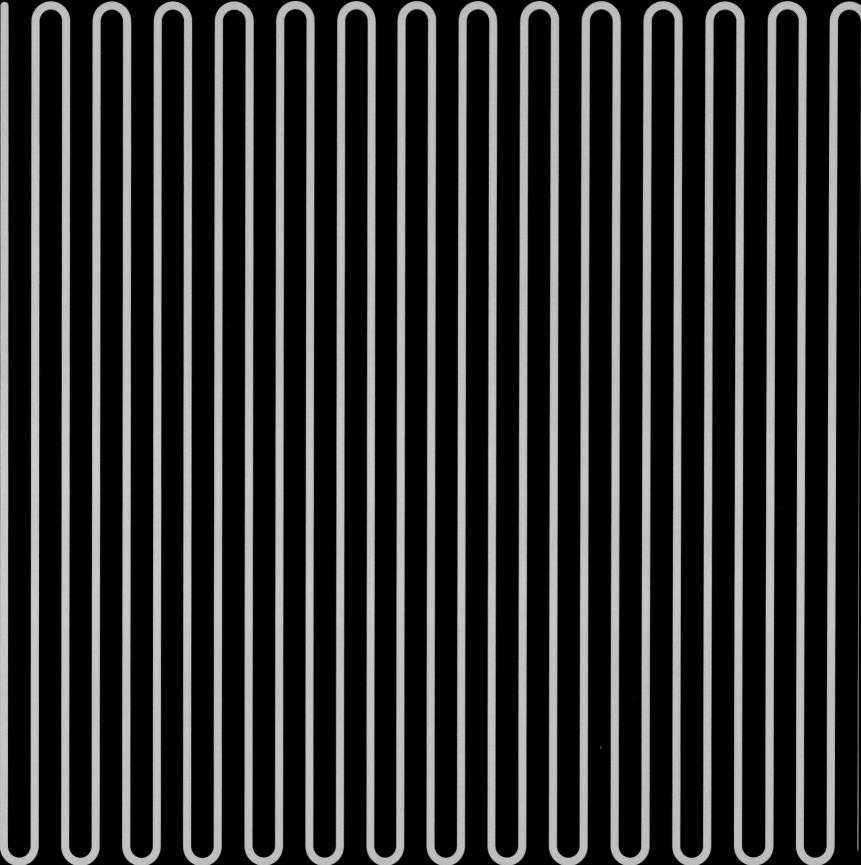

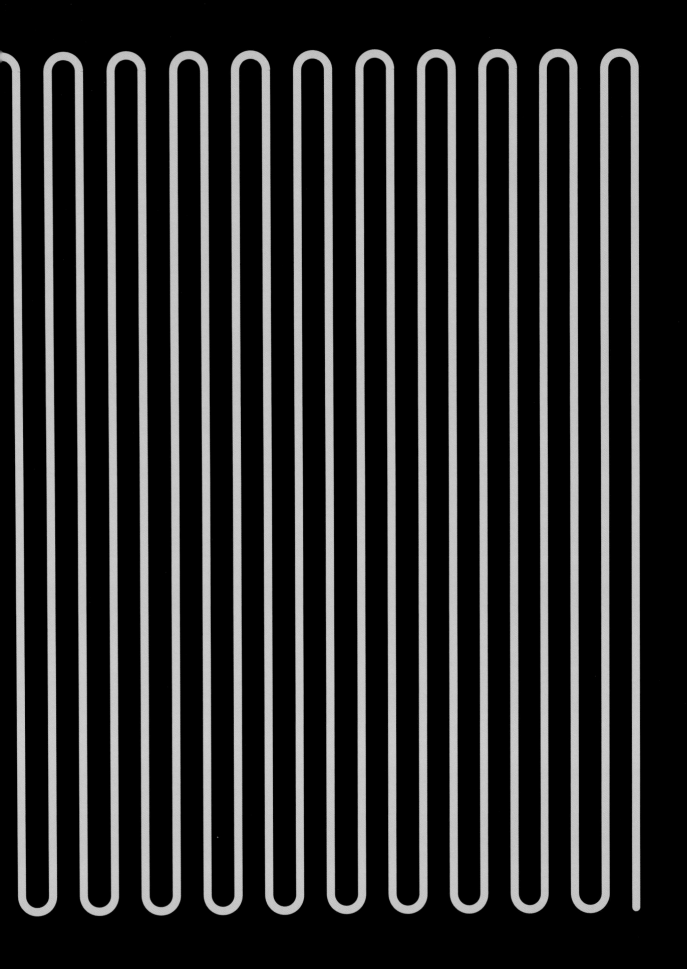

DESSERTS

This dish is a spin on the old coconut jelly you have at dim sum lunches. With vibrant colours and a great aroma, it is the perfect balance of sweet and sour. You'll need to make the jelly the day before so that it has time to set.

TOASTED COCONUT JELLY
WITH STRAWBERRY, LYCHEE AND CRISPY RICE NOODLES

TOASTED COCONUT JELLY

90 g (1 cup) desiccated coconut
600 ml coconut cream
150 ml sugar syrup
    (see page 242)
5 gelatine sheets
250 ml (1 cup) cold water

SPICED STRAWBERRY SOUP

500 g ripe strawberries
300 g caster sugar
700 ml water
2½ tablespoons Chinese black
    vinegar
3 whole star anise, lightly toasted
2 cinnamon sticks, lightly toasted
4 cardamom pods, lightly toasted

CRISPY RICE NOODLES

500 ml (2 cups) vegetable oil
100 g vermicelli rice noodles
1 tablespoon chilli rock sugar
    (see page 234)

GARNISH

200 g lychees, peeled and halved
250 g strawberries, hulled and
    halved
zest of 2 limes, if desired

METHOD

Toasted coconut jelly Preheat the oven to 170°C.

Spread the desiccated coconut on a baking tray and toast for 5 minutes. Remove the tray from the oven, move the coconut around and place back in the oven for a further 4–5 minutes until pale golden brown. Transfer to a large saucepan, pour in the coconut cream and cook over low heat for 15 minutes to slowly infuse the toasted coconut flavour through the coconut cream. Add the sugar syrup and mix well. Strain through a fine strainer, using a ladle to push the liquid through.

Soak the gelatine in the water for 2 minutes until soft, then squeeze to get rid of the excess water. Add the gelatine to the coconut cream and stir until dissolved. Spray a deep 10 x 20 cm tray with cooking spray and pour in the coconut jelly liquid. Leave in the refrigerator overnight to set.

Spiced strawberry soup Place the strawberries, sugar, water, vinegar and the toasted spices in a large heatproof bowl and cover with plastic wrap. Place the bowl over a saucepan of gently simmering water and steam for 25 minutes. You want to heat the liquid in the bowl to a low heat (about 65°C) as this will extract all the flavour from the strawberries and will keep the liquid clear; if it gets much hotter the syrup will turn brown. Strain the strawberry soup through a fine strainer and store in an airtight container in the refrigerator until needed.

Crispy rice noodles Heat the oil in a wok to 180°C (you can test if the oil is the right temperature by dropping a noodle into the oil; if the noodle puffs up straight away, the oil is ready).

Add the rice noodles, cook for 5 seconds, then flip over and cook for a further 5 seconds until puffed and crispy. Drain on paper towel and sprinkle the chilli rock sugar over the noodles.

TO SERVE

Invert the toasted coconut jelly onto a chopping board and cut into four rectangles.

Place the jelly in dessert bowls, pour on 150 ml of the spiced strawberry soup and add five pieces of lychee and five halved strawberries.

Break up the noodles a little, place a neat pile on top of the jelly and sprinkle the lime zest over the top, if desired, for a fresh lime aroma.

MANGO PUDDINGS, SUMMER BERRIES
AND COCONUT CREAM

MANGO PUDDINGS

5 gelatine sheets
250 ml (1 cup) cold water
500 ml (2 cups) full-cream milk
125 g caster sugar
150 ml thickened cream
275 g mango purée
2½ tablespoons mango liqueur

COCONUT CREAM

400 ml coconut milk
40 g caster sugar

RASPBERRY COULIS

300 g frozen raspberries
100 ml sugar syrup
  (see page 242)

GARNISH

150 g raspberries
150 g strawberries

METHOD

Mango puddings Soak the gelatine sheets in the water for 5 minutes.

Combine the milk and sugar in a saucepan over low heat and cook, stirring occasionally, until the sugar has dissolved.

Squeeze out the excess water from the gelatine and add to the milk, stirring until the gelatine dissolves.

Pour in the cream, mango purée and liqueur, and whisk to make sure it is well combined.

Pass through a fine sieve. Pour the mixture into four greased dariole moulds (125 ml capacity) and place in the refrigerator until needed.

Coconut cream Place the coconut milk in a small saucepan and simmer over medium heat, until reduced by half. Remove from the heat, add the sugar and stir until dissolved. Pass the cream through a fine sieve, pour into a squeeze bottle with a nozzle, and place in refrigerator until needed.

Raspberry coulis Blitz the raspberries and sugar syrup in a blender until well combined. Pass through a fine sieve into a saucepan. Cook the raspberry coulis over medium heat for 5 minutes until slightly reduced. Set aside to cool.

TO SERVE

Place the mango puddings left of centre on a serving plate. Squeeze three lines of the coconut cream onto the plate, and then squeeze three lines of raspberry coulis on top of the coconut cream. Arrange three raspberries on the middle line. Repeat the pattern of lines over each mango pudding and place 3–4 strawberries on top.

RASPBERRY AND PASSIONFRUIT SPLICE

PASSIONFRUIT ICE CREAM

220 ml coconut cream
100 ml full-cream milk
5 egg yolks
110 g (½ cup) caster sugar
2½ tablespoons passionfruit pulp

RASPBERRY SORBET

110 g (½ cup) caster sugar
125 ml (½ cup) water
300 g frozen raspberries
40 ml lemon juice
1 egg white

LIME JELLY

125 ml (½ cup) sugar syrup
  (see page 242)
1 gelatine sheet
250 ml (1 cup) cold water
zest and juice of 1 lime
50 g (¼ cup) caster sugar

GARNISH

200 g dried mango cheeks,
  cut into 5 mm thick slices
1 large red chilli, deseeded
  and thinly sliced
1 large handful of mint leaves

METHOD

Passionfruit ice cream Lightly spray an 8 x 20 cm terrine tin with cooking spray and line the base and sides with baking paper or plastic wrap.

Combine the coconut cream and milk in a saucepan over low heat and bring to a gentle simmer.

Beat the egg yolks and sugar in a bowl until pale and thick. Whisk in the coconut cream mixture, then pour the combined mixtures into a clean saucepan and cook over medium heat, stirring constantly, until the custard coats the back of a wooden spoon. Remove from the heat and plunge into a bowl of iced water to stop the cooking process and allow the custard to cool. Once cool, stir in the passionfruit pulp, then pour the custard into an ice-cream machine and churn, according to the manufacturer's instructions. Transfer to an airtight container and place in the freezer to set for 30 minutes. Remove the ice cream from the freezer and spoon into the prepared tin until about 2 cm from the top, to allow room for the raspberry sorbet. Cover the tin and return to the freezer to set.

Raspberry sorbet Combine the sugar and water in a small saucepan and stir over low heat, without boiling, until the sugar has dissolved. Bring to the boil and simmer, without stirring, for 5 minutes.

Place the raspberries in the bowl of a food processor, add the lemon juice and hot sugar syrup and process until smooth. Use a ladle to push the raspberry purée through a fine sieve into a large bowl and allow to cool.

Add the egg white and mix well. Pour into an ice-cream machine and churn according to the manufacturer's instructions. Transfer to an airtight container and place in the freezer for 40 minutes.

Take the raspberry sorbet out of the freezer and, using a palette knife, spread a 2 cm thick layer on top of the passionfruit ice cream in the terrine tin. Return to the freezer to set.

Lime jelly Pour the sugar syrup into a small saucepan, place over medium heat until the syrup is tepid (about 50°C). Soak the gelatine sheets in cold water for 5 minutes until soft. Squeeze out the excess water, add the gelatine to the hot sugar syrup and stir until dissolved. Set aside to cool slightly. Then stir in the lime zest, lime juice and sugar. Stir until the sugar has dissolved. Lightly spray a 4 cm deep 10 x 15 cm plastic tray with cooking spray and pour in the jelly mixture. Refrigerate for 3–4 hours until set.

TO SERVE

Combine the dried mango, chilli and mint in a bowl and mix well.

Take the jelly out of the refrigerator and, using 3 cm round cutters, cut out 8 jelly discs. Place two jelly discs slightly to the left on each serving plate.

Remove the splice from the freezer, unmould onto a chopping board and cut into four 2.5 cm thick slices. Place a slice in the centre of each plate and top with a small amount of the dried mango salad.

SPICED PEAR AND TAPIOCA DUMPLINGS
WITH BABY COCONUT SOUP

SPICED PEAR AND TAPIOCA DUMPLINGS

150 g (1 cup) grated palm sugar
2½ tablespoons water
8 brown pears, peeled and diced
3 whole cloves, lightly toasted
3 cinnamon sticks, lightly toasted
3 whole star anise, lightly toasted
zest and juice of 3 lemons
65 g tapioca pearls
24 yellow won ton wrappers
(available from Asian
supermarkets)

BABY COCONUT SOUP

500 ml (2 cups) baby coconut
liquid (see page 232)
85 g caster sugar
20 g (approx 4 cm) fresh ginger,
peeled
2 cinnamon sticks
40 ml lime juice

GARNISH

4 slices baby coconut
(see page 232)

METHOD

Spiced pear and tapioca dumplings Combine the sugar and water in a saucepan and stir over medium heat, without boiling, until the sugar has dissolved. Add the diced pear and cook for 5 minutes.

Place the cloves, cinnamon, star anise and lemon zest in a piece of muslin cloth and tie up with kitchen twine. Add the spice bag to the pan and cook, stirring constantly to stop the mixture from sticking to the pan, for 6 minutes, until the liquid has evaporated and the pears are aromatic, a little sticky and a lovely golden brown. Turn off the heat and add the lemon juice. Transfer the caramelised pear to a bowl and set aside to cool for 25 minutes. Open the spice bag and set the spices aside to be used later as garnish.

Bring a saucepan of water to the boil, add the tapioca and simmer, stirring gently, for 5 minutes or until the tapioca pearls have a small white spot in the centre. Pour the tapioca into a fine strainer and run under cold water to cool completely. Drain well and mix into the caramelised pear. Place in the refrigerator and chill for 20 minutes to make the pear mixture easier to work with.

Place 12 won ton wrappers on a clean work surface and spoon 1 heaped tablespoon of the pear mixture into the centre of each one. Lightly brush the edges of each wrapper with a little water and place one of the remaining wrappers on top. Press around the edges to seal. Cup your hand around the filling and gently curl in your fingers to squeeze out all the air. Gently place the blunt side of a 4 cm round cutter over the filling to shape it into a round, then press a 6 cm cutter around the edge of dumpling to cut it into a disc. Set aside.

Baby coconut soup Strain the coconut juice through a fine sieve into a saucepan to remove any small pieces of husk. Add the sugar, ginger, cinnamon and lime juice and bring to a gentle simmer over low heat. Stir to dissolve the sugar.

Remove from the heat, set aside for 15 minutes to allow the flavours to infuse, then strain through a fine sieve. Set the cinnamon sticks aside to be used later as garnish. Gently reheat the soup.

TO SERVE

Place a perforated stainless steel disc insert in a steamer basket, spray with cooking spray and add the dumplings, leaving space around each one so they don't stick together. Cover and steam in a wok of simmering water for 5 minutes, until the underside of each dumpling is cooked and the skin is transparent.

Place three dumplings in each serving bowl and pour on enough coconut soup to just cover the base of each dumpling. Garnish with the reserved spices and a slice of baby coconut.

This is one of the simplest dishes, yet the flavour speaks for itself. It brings out the best of all the ingredients you use, as long you purchase firm but ripe mangoes.

CARAMELISED MANGO
WITH CHILLI ROCK SUGAR AND LIME

CARAMELISED MANGO

2 firm ripe mangoes
8 tablespoons demerara sugar
4 teaspoons chilli rock sugar
  (see page 234)
8 lime cheeks

METHOD

Caramelised mango Heat the grill to a high heat. Line a baking tray with baking paper.

Place the mangoes on a chopping board and slice off both cheeks. Making sure you do not slice all the way through to the skin, use a small, sharp knife to cut three evenly spaced lines across one mango cheek. Turn 90 degrees and cut three more evenly spaced lines, to create a criss-cross shape. Repeat with the remaining mango cheeks.

Transfer the mango cheeks, skin side down, to the prepared tray. Sprinkle 2 tablespoons of the demerara sugar over each mango cheek. Place under the grill for 5 minutes or until the top of the mango is golden brown. To test if the mango cheeks are ready, stick a teaspoon into one. It should be really soft and smooth.

TO SERVE

Place a mango cheek on each serving plate. Serve with two lime cheeks and a small pile of the chilli rock sugar.

CHILLED WHITE CHOCOLATE PUDDINGS
WITH POACHED PINEAPPLE AND SESAME TUILES

WHITE CHOCOLATE PUDDINGS

500 ml (2 cups) pouring cream
10 cardamom pods
3 cinnamon sticks
4 whole star anise
1 vanilla bean, split lengthways
   and seeds scraped
10 g (approx 2 cm) fresh ginger,
   peeled and roughly chopped
3 gelatine sheets
210 g white chocolate, chopped
170 ml (⅔ cup) milk

POACHED PINEAPPLE

150 g (⅔ cup) caster sugar
400 ml water
5 whole star anise
5 cinnamon sticks
15 sichuan peppercorns
½ pineapple, peeled, cored
   and cut into 1 cm thick slices

SESAME TUILES

125 g icing sugar, sifted
2½ tablespoons orange juice
65 g clarified butter, melted
50 g (⅓ cup) white sesame seeds
40 g plain flour, sifted

GARNISH

2 tablespoons chilli rock sugar
   (see page 234)

METHOD

Puddings Spray four 125 ml (½ cup) plastic dariole moulds with cooking spray. Combine the cream, spices, vanilla and ginger in a saucepan over medium heat and bring to a gentle simmer. Remove from heat and set aside for 30 minutes to allow the flavours to infuse.

Place the gelatine sheets in a small bowl of cold water and set aside for 5 minutes to soften up. Remove the gelatine and squeeze out the excess water.

Place chocolate in a large heatproof mixing bowl over a saucepan of simmering water then pour the cream mixture over the chocolate and stir until melted and mixed through. Add the gelatine, then stir in the milk. Pass through a fine sieve so the mixture is nice and silky.

Pour the chocolate mixture into the prepared dariole moulds and place in the refrigerator for 4–6 hours, or until set.

Poached pineapple Combine the sugar, water and spices in a small saucepan over medium heat and bring to a gentle simmer. Add the pineapple and gently simmer for 15 minutes or until the pineapple is beginning to turn transparent. Remove from the heat and set aside for 20 minutes to allow the pineapple to cool in the poaching liquid. Remove the pineapple slices from the poaching liquid and place them in a container.

Return the pan to the stovetop, pour in the poaching liquid and cook over a medium heat until the poaching liquid is reduced by two-thirds. Set aside to cool.

Sesame tuiles Preheat the oven to 160°C. Line a baking tray with baking paper.

Whisk the sugar and orange juice in a bowl, add the clarified butter, sesame seeds and flour, and beat till smooth. Spoon 1 teaspoon of the sesame mixture onto the prepared tray and spread out to form a 7–10 cm disc. Repeat with the remaining mixture. (Although this will make more tuiles than required, some will break.) Bake for 3–5 minutes, or until a nice golden colour. Set aside to cool on the tray.

TO SERVE

Run a paring knife around the moulds and slide the puddings onto serving plates. Place each pudding just off centre, then add three or four pieces of pineapple to one side of the plate.

Remove a cooled tuile from the baking tray by sliding a thin spatula underneath it and place it beside the chocolate pudding.

Sprinkle ½ tablespoon of chilli rock sugar over and around each pudding. Pour the reserved pineapple poaching syrup into a small serving jug and serve alongside.

This is the gingerboy spin on your standard banana fritter – here it is complemented with silky smooth Baileys ice cream.

PANDANUS BATTERED BANANA FRITTERS
WITH BAILEYS ICE CREAM

BAILEYS ICE CREAM

8 egg yolks
160 g caster sugar
750 ml (3 cups) thickened cream
100 ml Baileys Irish Cream liqueur

PANDANUS BATTERED BANANA FRITTERS

225 g (1½ cups) self-raising flour
330 ml (1⅓ cups) lager
½ teaspoon green pandan essence
2 tablespoons coconut cream
750 ml (3 cups) vegetable oil
4 large ripe bananas, peeled and left whole

CHILLI CITRUS SUGAR

zest of 2 limes
zest of 2 oranges
zest of 2 lemons
½ cup chilli rock sugar (see page 234)

METHOD

Baileys ice cream Whisk the egg yolks and sugar in a heatproof bowl until pale and thick. Whisk in the cream and continue to whisk until well combined.

Place the bowl over a saucepan of simmering water and, whisking constantly, cook for 5–10 minutes until the custard coats the back of a wooden spoon. Remove the bowl from the heat and plunge into a bowl of iced water to stop the cooking process and to allow the custard to cool. Once cool, add the Baileys and stir to combine. Strain the mixture into an ice-cream machine and churn, according to the manufacturer's instructions.

Transfer the ice cream to an airtight container and store in the freezer until needed. Alternatively, pour the custard into a shallow dish or container, cover and place in the freezer for 30–40 minutes, until frozen at the edge; scrape into a bowl and beat with electric beaters, then return to the dish and place back in the freezer; repeat this process three or four times, until the ice cream has set.

Pandanus battered banana fritters Whisk the flour, lager, pandan essence and coconut cream in a bowl and place in the refrigerator to chill – the batter works much better when cold.

Chilli citrus sugar Spread the zests on a tray lined with baking paper and set aside in a warm place for 2 hours to dry out.

Lightly pound the zests using a mortar and pestle, add the chilli rock sugar and mix through. Set aside.

TO SERVE

Heat the oil in a wok to around 180°C (you can test if the oil is the right temperature by dropping in a few drops of batter; if the batter floats up straight away and turns golden in 1 minute, the oil is ready).

Dip a banana in the batter, making sure it is completely covered, and carefully lower into the oil using a slotted spoon. Deep-fry for 2–3 minutes, until the batter is nice and crispy. Drain on paper towel. Repeat with the remaining bananas.

While the bananas are still warm, pile them on a large serving plate and dust them with the chilli citrus sugar.

Spoon two scoops of Baileys ice cream into a ramekin and serve alongside the banana fritters.

CHINESE RED DATE PUDDINGS
WITH BANANA AND PALM SUGAR ICE CREAM AND COCONUT BUTTERSCOTCH SAUCE

Serves four

BANANA AND PALM SUGAR ICE CREAM

10 g unsalted butter

2 ripe bananas (about 200 g), roughly chopped

2 tablespoons caster sugar

6 egg yolks

125 g finely grated dark palm sugar

250 ml (1 cup) milk

250 ml (1 cup) pouring cream

CHINESE RED DATE PUDDINGS

180 g deseeded and chopped Chinese red dates

240 ml sugar syrup (see page 242)

25 ml mandarin liqueur

90 g unsalted butter

180 g brown sugar

1 vanilla bean, split in half lengthways and seeds scraped

2 eggs

325 g self-raising flour, sifted

750 ml (3 cups) water

COCONUT BUTTERSCOTCH SAUCE

50 g unsalted butter

80 g brown sugar

200 ml coconut cream

METHOD

Banana and palm sugar ice cream Heat a saucepan over high heat, add the butter and banana and cook for 1 minute. Sprinkle on the sugar and cook for 2 minutes until caramelised. Transfer to the bowl of a food processor and blitz to a purée.

Whisk the egg yolks and sugar in a heatproof bowl until pale and thick.

Combine the milk and cream in a saucepan over medium heat and bring to the boil. Strain into the egg yolk mixture, whisking briskly.

Add the banana purée to the egg yolk mixture and mix well. Place the bowl over a saucepan of simmering water and cook, stirring constantly, until the custard coats the back of a wooden spoon. Remove the bowl from the heat and plunge into a bowl of iced water to stop the cooking process and to allow the custard to cool. Once cool, strain the mixture into an ice-cream machine and churn, following the manufacturer's instructions. Transfer the ice cream to an airtight container and store in the freezer.

Chinese red date puddings Preheat the oven to 170°C. Place the dates, sugar syrup and mandarin liqueur in a container and refrigerate overnight.

The next day, place the butter, brown sugar and vanilla in the bowl of an electric mixer and beat until pale and fluffy. Turn the mixer down to low and add the eggs one at a time, mixing well after each addition. Add the sifted flour and stir to combine. Add the chopped date mix and stir to combine. Lightly spray four dariole moulds with cooking spray then fill the moulds with the batter, stopping 1 cm from the top. Place the moulds on a baking tray and place in the oven. Bake for 24 minutes or until cooked through when tested with a skewer. Remove the puddings from the oven and cool for 10 minutes. Gently run a knife around the edges of the puddings to loosen before turning out onto a cooling rack.

Coconut butterscotch sauce Melt the butter in a small saucepan over medium heat. Add the sugar and cook for 2–3 minutes until the sugar starts to caramelise. Pour in the coconut cream and whisk until well combined. Bring to the boil, remove from the heat and set aside until needed.

TO SERVE

Transfer the puddings to a bamboo steamer, leaving about 2 cm of space around each pudding so they reheat evenly. Cover and steam over a wok of simmering water for 5 minutes. Insert a metal skewer into the middle of the puddings; the puddings are ready when the metal skewer is hot when it is pulled out.

Place the puddings off centre on each serving plate. Pour 2 tablespoons of the coconut butterscotch sauce over the top, then add a large scoop of banana and palm sugar ice cream.

COCONUT AND PANDAN JELLY

COCONUT JELLY

500 ml (2 cups) coconut cream
125 g caster sugar
4 gelatine sheets
250 ml (1 cup) cold water

PANDAN JELLY

500 ml (2 cups) water
250 g caster sugar
1 tablespoon green pandan
    essence
2 pandan leaves, roughly chopped
5 gelatine sheets
250 ml (1 cup) cold water, extra

METHOD

Coconut jelly Combine the coconut cream and sugar in a small saucepan over medium heat and simmer, stirring continuously, for 5 minutes.

Soak the gelatine in the water for 2 minutes until soft. Remove the gelatine and squeeze out the excess liquid. Add the softened gelatine to the hot coconut cream and whisk until the gelatine is dissolved.

Lightly spray a 15-cm square container with cooking spray and pour in the coconut mixture. Cover and place in the refrigerator for 4 hours to set.

Pandan jelly Combine the water, sugar, pandan essence and leaves in a small saucepan over medium heat and bring to a gentle simmer. Soak the gelatine in the extra cold water for 2 minutes until soft, then squeeze out the excess water. Stir the gelatine into the hot pandan liquid until dissolved. Strain the pandan liquid through a fine strainer into a lightly greased 15-cm square container. Cover and place in the refrigerator for 4 hours to set.

TO SERVE

Cut each jelly into eight cubes and place two cubes of each flavour onto small serving plates.

This is a great all-year-round dessert as the pudding is nice and light and the small kick of chilli warms the creamy white chocolate ice cream.

LEMONGRASS PUDDINGS
WITH WHITE CHOCOLATE AND CHILLI ICE CREAM

Serves four

WHITE CHOCOLATE AND CHILLI ICE CREAM

250 ml (1 cup) milk
½ vanilla bean, seeds scraped
7 egg yolks
335 g white chocolate, chopped
375 ml (1½ cups) thickened cream
15 ml Cointreau
1 teaspoon dried chilli flakes, finely ground

LEMONGRASS PUDDINGS

165 ml milk
60 g unsalted butter
3 lemongrass stems, white part only, bruised in a mortar and pestle
90 g self-raising flour
155 g caster sugar
zest of 1 lemon
2 tablespoons lemon juice
2 eggs, separated
750 ml (3 cups) water

LEMONGRASS SYRUP

250 g caster sugar
350 ml water
2 lemongrass stems, white part only, bruised in a mortar and pestle
4 kaffir lime leaves
40 ml lime juice
½ lemongrass stem, white part only, thinly sliced

METHOD

White chocolate and chilli ice cream Place the milk and vanilla in a saucepan over medium heat and bring to a gentle simmer.

Whisk the egg yolks in a heatproof bowl until pale and thick. Slowly pour in the hot milk, whisking continuously so the egg yolks don't scramble. Place the bowl over a saucepan of simmering water and cook, stirring constantly, for 10 minutes, until the custard coats the back of a spoon.

Remove from the heat, add the white chocolate and stir until melted.

Strain through a fine sieve into a clean bowl. Cool for 5 minutes.

Stir in the cream, add the Cointreau and chilli, and place in the refrigerator for 1 hour.

Churn in an ice-cream machine according to the manufacturer's instructions, then transfer the ice cream to an airtight container and leave in the freezer until needed. Alternatively, pour the custard into a glass bowl, cover and place in the freezer for 30 minutes; take the bowl out and whisk the ice-cream mixture for 10 seconds, then place back in the freezer; repeat this process every 20 minutes until the ice cream has set. Pull out 2 minutes before needed, to allow the ice cream to soften.

Lemongrass puddings Preheat the oven to 180°C. Spray four non-stick metal dariole moulds (125 ml capacity) with cooking spray.

Place the milk, butter and lemongrass in a large saucepan over low heat and cook until the butter has melted. Remove from the heat and set aside for 25 minutes to allow the lemongrass flavour to infuse.

Combine the flour, sugar and lemon zest in a large bowl.

Strain the infused milk into another large bowl, discard the lemongrass. Add the lemon juice and egg yolks and whisk until smooth. Fold in the dry ingredients and zest.

Whisk the egg whites in a separate bowl until firm peaks form. Fold the lemon mixture into the egg white in two batches.

Pour the batter into the prepared moulds until about 1 cm below the rim.

Transfer the moulds to a roasting tin. Pour enough water into the tin to come halfway up the sides of the moulds and bake for 14 minutes, then spin the tray around and cook for a further 12 minutes, or until a skewer inserted in the centre of a pudding comes out clean. Set aside to cool in the moulds for 20 minutes.

Trim the top of the pudding so that it is level with the rim of the mould. Turn the puddings out onto a tray lined with baking paper.

Lemongrass syrup Place all of the ingredients in a small saucepan over medium heat and simmer until reduced by two-thirds. Set aside for 10 minutes to cool and allow the flavours to infuse. Strain and reserve until needed.

TO SERVE

Place a perforated stainless steel disc insert into a steamer basket, then add the puddings and place the basket above a wok of simmering water. Cover and steam for 5 minutes until the centres are really hot (check with a skewer). Place a pudding in the centre of each serving plate, pour 2 tablespoons of the lemongrass syrup over the top, then add 1 large scoop of the ice cream.

This dish is a great summer parfait. Mango, when it is in season, is sublime and goes so well in ice creams and sorbets.

MANGO, CHILLI AND LIME PARFAIT
WITH FRIED STICKY RICE AND BLACKBERRY CARAMEL

MANGO, CHILLI AND LIME PARFAIT

500 ml (2 cups) pouring cream
350 ml mango purée
200 g sugar
7 egg yolks
2½ tablespoons water
3 large red chillies, deseeded and finely chopped
½ teaspoon dried chilli flakes
4 kaffir lime leaves, finely chopped
1 cup fried sticky rice balls (see page 237)

BLACKBERRY CARAMEL

150 g sugar
150 ml water
250 g blackberries
3 red bird's eye chillies, deseeded and finely chopped

GARNISH

2 mangoes, cut into 8 wedges
4 Vietnamese mint leaves

METHOD

Mango, chilli and lime parfait Spray a 8 x 25 cm terrine tin with cooking spray and line the base and sides with baking paper or plastic wrap.

Whip the cream to soft peaks in a bowl. Place the mango purée and half of the sugar in a small saucepan over medium heat and simmer, stirring constantly, until reduced to 250 ml (1 cup). Set aside.

Beat the egg yolks in a large heatproof bowl of an electric mixture, until pale and thick.

Combine the remaining sugar and the water in saucepan and bring to the boil, stirring until the sugar has dissolved. Simmer, without stirring, for 8–10 minutes, until the syrup reaches 118°C on a sugar thermometer. Take off the heat and slowly pour into the electric mixing bowl containing the egg yolks, beating the whole time. Beat the syrup and egg yolk mixture for 10 minutes, or until the bottom of the mixing bowl is at room temperature.

Fold in the mango mixture, chopped chilli, dried chilli flakes and lime leaves, then gently fold in the whipped cream in two stages. Pour into the prepared tin and place in the freezer overnight to set.

Blackberry caramel Combine the sugar and water in a saucepan and bring to the boil, stirring until the sugar has dissolved. Simmer for 5 minutes, until the syrup turns golden brown, then immediately add the blackberries and chilli.

Continue to simmer for 10 minutes, or until the blackberries and chilli are soft and the liquid has reduced to a jam-like consistency.

Remove from the heat and allow to cool for 15 minutes. Transfer to a blender and purée, then push through a sieve to remove the seeds and chilli.

TO SERVE

Place the fried sticky rice balls in a mortar and pestle and lightly pound until they are finely ground. Transfer to a shallow dish.

Using a pastry brush, paint the blackberry caramel onto each serving plate and place two mango wedges and a mint leaf alongside. Cut the parfait into four slices and roll the edges in the ground rice. Place a slice of parfait on the caramel.

CHINESE DOUGHNUTS
WITH RASPBERRY CHILLI JAM

Serves six to share

CHINESE DOUGHNUTS

75 ml warm water
30 g (1½ tablespoons) dried yeast
375 ml (1½ cups) milk
75 g unsalted butter
1 egg
650 g bakers' flour (available
   from supermarkets)
75 g caster sugar
750 ml (3 cups) vegetable oil
1 pinch of salt

CINNAMON SUGAR

1 teaspoon ground cinnamon
50 g caster sugar

RASPBERRY CHILLI JAM

250 g frozen raspberries
150 g (⅔ cup) caster sugar
150 ml water
1 red bird's eye chilli,
   roughly chopped

METHOD

Chinese doughnuts Combine the warm water and yeast in a small bowl and set aside for 3–4 minutes to allow the yeast to become active (frothy).

Heat the milk and butter in a small saucepan over low heat until the butter has melted.

Place the egg, yeast mixture, milk and butter in a large bowl, sift in the dry ingredients and mix until well combined. Turn out onto a lightly floured work surface and knead for 2 minutes until smooth in texture and pale in colour. Return to the bowl, cover with plastic wrap and set aside to prove in a warm spot for 30 minutes, or until doubled in size.

'Knock back' the dough by picking it up and hitting it down, then roll it into a long sausage and cut into 24 portions.

Transfer to a tray lined with plastic wrap and again set aside in a warm place for 20 minutes, until doubled in size. Be sure to leave a 2 cm gap around each doughnut, as they will expand.

Cinnamon sugar Mix the sugar and cinnamon in a bowl and set aside.

Raspberry chilli jam Place the raspberries in a colander to drain as they thaw. Discard the liquid.

Combine the sugar and water in a saucepan over medium–high heat and cook for 5 minutes, until a nice golden colour. Add the raspberries and chilli and continue to simmer for a few minutes until the raspberries break down and the mixture begins to thicken up like a jam.

Remove from the heat and pass through a fine sieve, using a small ladle to push the jam through. Discard the seeds.

Pour the jam into a squeeze bottle with a nozzle and place in the refrigerator to chill completely.

TO SERVE

Heat the oil in a wok to 160°C (you can test if the oil is the right temperature by dropping in a small piece of the dough; if it turns golden in 1 minute, the oil is ready).

Use a slotted spoon to carefully lower the doughnuts into the oil, in batches of four, and deep-fry for 2 minutes on one side, then turn and cook for a further 1 minute until golden brown. Remove with a slotted spoon and drain, moving them around a little bit, on paper towel.

Toss the doughnuts in the cinnamon sugar, then stick the squeeze bottle nozzle into the base of each doughnut and gently squeeze in some raspberry chilli jam.

Place the filled and sugared doughnuts, jam holes facing up, in serving bowls.

This dessert is a nice, rich, silky smooth-textured chocolate cheesecake with a sour cherry jelly on top. The jelly complements the cheesecake really well, making this is a great way to finish a meal if you're a fan of chocolate.

DARK CHOCOLATE TOFU CHEESECAKE
WITH CHILLI CHERRY JELLY

Serves four

BISCUIT BASE

85 g marie biscuit crumbs
55 g butter, melted
110 g (½ cup, firmly packed) brown sugar
1 pinch of ground cinnamon
1 pinch of ground ginger
1 pinch of sea salt
1 teaspoon black sesame seeds

DARK CHOCOLATE TOFU CHEESECAKE

200 g silken tofu
200 g dark chocolate, chopped
200 ml thickened cream
150 g cream cheese, at room temperature
110 g (½ cup) caster sugar
1 gelatine sheet
250 ml (1 cup) cold water
½ tablespoon Cointreau

CHILLI CHERRY JELLY

270 ml sour cherry purée (available from fine foods stores)
70 g caster sugar
1 red bird's eye chilli, roughly chopped
2 tablespoons water
2 gelatine sheets
250 ml (1 cup) cold water

POACHED RHUBARB

600 ml water
350 g caster sugar
7 cardamom pods
3 cinnamon sticks
4 whole star anise
zest and juice of 1 orange
zest and juice of 1 mandarin
500 g rhubarb, cut into 2.5 cm lengths

METHOD

Biscuit base Grease a 15 cm springform cake tin, line the base and side with baking paper and grease again.

Combine the biscuit crumbs, butter, sugar, ground spices, salt and sesame seeds in a large bowl and mix well with your hands. Transfer the biscuit mixture to the prepared tin, spread evenly over the base and press down with the back of your hand or a large kitchen spoon until about 1 cm thick. Place in the refrigerator for 30 minutes.

Dark chocolate tofu cheesecake Line a strainer with a piece of muslin cloth and place over a large bowl. Place the tofu in the centre of the muslin and set aside for 2 hours for the excess liquid to drain.

Bring a saucepan of water to the boil and turn off the heat. Combine the chocolate and cream in a heatproof bowl and place on the pan, making sure the water does not touch the base of the bowl. Stir until smooth and the chocolate has melted.

Place the cream cheese in the bowl of a food processor and blitz until smooth. Add the sugar, blitz again until smooth, then add the drained tofu and process until well combined.

Soak the gelatine in the cold water for 3 minutes, then squeeze out the excess water.

Stir the gelatine into the chocolate mixture until dissolved. Add the cream cheese mixture and Cointreau and mix well.

Pull the cake tin out of the refrigerator and pour the chocolate mixture over the biscuit base. Lightly tap the tin on the bench, then place in the refrigerator for 1 hour.

Chilli cherry jelly Combine the sour cherry purée, sugar, chilli and the 2 tablespoons of water in a small saucepan over low heat. Bring to a gentle simmer and cook, constantly stirring so it doesn't stick to the base of the pan, for 5 minutes. Strain through a fine sieve into a bowl.

Soak the gelatine in the 250 ml of cold water for 5 minutes until softened. Squeeze out the excess water and add the gelatine sheet to the purée, stirring until dissolved.

Slowly pour the chilli cherry jelly over the top of the cheesecake, then return to the refrigerator to set for 4 hours.

Poached rhubarb Combine the water, sugar, spices and zests in a saucepan over low heat. Bring to a gentle simmer, turn off the heat and set aside for 20 minutes to allow the flavours to infuse.

Add the rhubarb to the syrup, cover with a cartouche*, and place over low heat with the saucepan lid on. Simmer for 5 minutes, turn off the heat and stand for 5 minutes to cook through. If the pan comes to the boil at any time, you risk overcooking the rhubarb.

Remove the rhubarb, reserving the syrup, and spread on a tray. Cover the tray with plastic wrap and place in the refrigerator until needed.

Return the pan to the stovetop and cook over medium heat until the syrup is reduced by two-thirds. Allow to cool.

TO SERVE

Remove the side of the tin. Place a large knife in a jug of hot water for 1 minute to heat up, then wipe the knife dry before cutting into the cheesecake. Cut the cheesecake in half, slowly cutting through the jelly layer so it doesn't rip and break. Reheat the knife, then cut the cheesecake into quarters. Slide the knife under each portion of cheesecake and lift onto a serving plate. Pile a few pieces of the rhubarb next to the cheesecake and dot 1 tablespoon of the poaching syrup alongside.

* *To make a cartouche*, cut out a circle of greaseproof paper slightly larger than your saucepan.

COCONUT TAPIOCA
WITH PAPAYA SALAD AND FIVE-SPICE ICE CREAM

FIVE-SPICE ICE CREAM

600 ml pouring cream
1 vanilla bean, split lengthways
   and seeds scraped
1½ teaspoons five-spice
7 egg yolks
175 g caster sugar
zest of 1 orange

COCONUT TAPIOCA

500 ml (2 cups) coconut cream
250 g grated light palm sugar
250 g tapioca pearls
cold water

PAPAYA SALAD

300 g papaya, diced
2 limes, segmented
4 kaffir lime leaves, thinly sliced
80 ml (⅓ cup) gula melaka
   (see page 238), to serve

METHOD

Five-spice ice cream Combine the cream, vanilla and five-spice in a saucepan over medium heat and bring to the boil. Remove from the heat.

Whisk the egg yolks and sugar in a heatproof bowl until pale and thick. Slowly whisk in the infused cream, then place the bowl over a saucepan of simmering water and cook, stirring continuously, for 10–15 minutes, until the custard coats the back of a wooden spoon. Remove the bowl from the heat and plunge into a bowl of iced water to stop the cooking process and to allow the custard to cool. Once cool, strain the mixture into an ice-cream machine and churn, following the manufacturer's instructions.

Transfer the ice cream to an airtight container and place in the freezer until ready to serve. Alternatively, spoon the custard into a glass bowl, cover and place in the freezer; pull out every 30 minutes and whisk the custard until it starts to freeze and turn into ice cream; repeat this process until the ice cream has set. Remove from the freezer to soften 2 minutes before needed.

Coconut tapioca Place the coconut cream and palm sugar in a saucepan over low heat and simmer until reduced by half. Set aside.

Pour 1.5 litres of water into a saucepan, bring to the boil, add the tapioca and let it come back to the boil. Add 2½ tablespoons of cold water and bring to the boil for 1 minute, then add 2 tablespoons more cold water and simmer for 5 minutes, until there is just a tiny little bit of white in the centre of each tapioca pearl. Drain the tapioca, refresh under cold running water and drain again.

Combine the tapioca and sweetened coconut cream in a clean saucepan and place over low heat to bring up to a gentle simmer.

Papaya salad Place the papaya, lime segments and lime leaves in a bowl and gently toss.

TO SERVE

Spoon the tapioca into serving dishes, place some papaya salad on top, add a nice scoop of the five-spice ice cream and drizzle 1 teaspoon of the gula melaka over the top.

PANDAN PANCAKE AND POACHED QUINCES

POACHED QUINCES

3 large quinces
80 ml lemon juice
2 cinnamon sticks
3 whole star anise
400 g caster sugar
600 ml water
zest of 1 orange

PANDAN PANCAKES

60 g plain flour
1 teaspoon caster sugar
1 egg
350 ml coconut milk
½ teaspoon pandan essence
12 g unsalted butter

METHOD

Poached quinces Peel, core and cut the quinces into quarters. Add the lemon juice to a bowl of water and place the quince pieces in the acidulated water to prevent discoloration. Collect all the peelings and seeds from the quinces and put them in a piece of muslin 30 cm x 30 cm, add the cinnamon sticks and star anise and tie up with kitchen twine to form a bundle.

Combine the sugar, water and orange zest in a large saucepan and bring to a simmer. Reduce the heat to low, add the spice bag and quinces and poach gently for 3 hours, until the quinces are tender. Remove from the heat and allow the quinces to cool in the poaching syrup for 30 minutes. Remove the orange zest and spice bag from the poaching liquid. Set the zest, cinnamon and star anise aside to be used later as garnish.

Pandan pancakes Place the flour and sugar in a bowl and mix well. Gradually add the egg and coconut milk and whisk to form a smooth and lump-free batter. Stir in the pandan essence and refrigerate for 1 hour.

Heat a non-stick frying pan or crêpe pan over medium heat. Melt a little of the butter in the pan, ladle in 125 ml (½ cup) of the batter and swirl to spread it evenly over the base (tip any excess back into the bowl). Cook for 1–2 minutes, until small bubbles appear on the surface. Use a spatula to turn the pancake over carefully and cook the other side for another minute or so. Transfer the cooked pancake to a plate lined with baking paper.

Repeat with the remaining batter.

TO SERVE

Place the pancakes in a bamboo steamer and steam for 2 minutes over a wok of simmering water. Reheat the poaching syrup.

Place two pancakes in the centre of each serving plate, top with a neat pile of the quinces and spoon a little of the reserved poaching liquid over the top. Garnish with the reserved zest and spices.

TOFU CHEESECAKE
WITH PANDAN JELLY AND ROASTED PEACHES

Serves four to share

TOFU

500 g silken tofu

BISCUIT BASE

85 g granita biscuits, crumbled
60 g melted butter
110 g brown sugar
1 pinch of ground cinnamon
1 pinch of ground ginger
1 pinch of sea salt
1 tablespoon black sesame seeds

CHEESECAKE FILLING

340 g cream cheese, at room
    temperature
155 g caster sugar
1½ tablespoons green ginger wine
zest and juice of 2 oranges
zest and juice of 1½ lemons
5 gelatine sheets
250 ml (1 cup) cold water
200 ml thickened cream
40 ml lemon juice, extra

PANDAN JELLY

200 ml water
¼ teaspoon green pandan
    essence
150 ml sugar syrup
    (see page 242)
3 gelatine sheets
250 ml (1 cup) cold water, extra

ROASTED PEACHES

60 g butter
6 peaches, cut into wedges
60 g caster sugar
1 vanilla bean, split in half
    lengthways and seeds scraped

METHOD

Tofu Line a strainer with a piece of muslin cloth and place over a large bowl. Place the tofu in the centre of the muslin and set aside overnight for the excess liquid to drain.

Biscuit base Grease a 15 cm springform cake tin, line the base and side with baking paper and grease again.

Place the biscuits crumbs in the bowl of a food processor and blitz until they resemble fine breadcrumbs.

Combine the biscuit crumbs, butter, sugar, ground spices, salt and sesame seeds in a large bowl and mix well with your hands.

Transfer the biscuit mixture to the prepared tin, spread evenly over the base and press down with the back of your hand or a large kitchen spoon until about 1 cm thick. Place in the refrigerator for 30 minutes.

Cheesecake filling Combine the cream cheese and sugar in the bowl of a food processor and blitz until smooth. Add the drained tofu, ginger wine and orange and lemon zests and blitz again until smooth.

Soak the gelatine in the cold water for 5 minutes until soft. Squeeze out excess water.

Place the cream in a small saucepan and heat up. Bring just to the boil. Add the gelatine and stir until dissolved.

Add the orange juice and the juice from 1½ lemons to the tofu mixture, then gently stir in the cream mixture. Pour over the biscuit base until 1.5 cm from the top. (You need to leave some room for the jelly layer.) Place in the refrigerator for 4 hours to set.

Pandan jelly Place the water, pandan essence and sugar syrup in a saucepan over medium heat and bring to 80°C, or until it's almost at a gentle simmer. Remove from the heat.

Soak the gelatine in the cold water for 5 minutes to soften. Squeeze out excess water. Add the gelatine to the pandan syrup and stir until dissolved. Cool to room temperature (otherwise it will melt the cheesecake mix), then pour over the tofu layer of the cheesecake. Refrigerate until set.

Roasted peaches Melt the butter in a large saucepan over medium-high heat, add the peaches and cook for 3 minutes, until lightly coloured. Add the sugar and vanilla seeds and stir in. Cook for 4–5 minutes, until the peach wedges are golden and caramelised. Take the peaches out of the pan and cool on a wire rack.

TO SERVE

Remove the cheesecake from the cake tin. Fill a jug with boiling water and place a large knife in the jug for 2 minutes to get really hot. Wipe the knife, then cut the cheesecake in half, dip the knife back in the boiling water, wipe the knife again and cut the cheesecake into quarters.

Place a piece of cheesecake in the centre of each serving plate, then pile five of the roasted peach wedges to the right of the cheesecake.

CRISPY APPLE DUMPLINGS
WITH CINNAMON SUGAR

APPLE DUMPLINGS

1 litre (4 cups) water

550 g (2½ cups) caster sugar

2 cinnamon sticks

4 whole star anise

2 vanilla beans, split in half
   lengthways and seeds scraped

6 large granny smith apples,
   peeled, cored and quartered

24 square yellow won ton
   wrappers (available from Asian
   supermarkets)

750 ml (3 cups) vegetable oil

CINNAMON SUGAR

1 teaspoon ground cinnamon

50 g caster sugar

METHOD

Apple dumplings Combine the water, sugar, cinnamon sticks, star anise and vanilla beans and seeds in a saucepan over medium heat, stirring to dissolve the sugar. Simmer for 5 minutes.

Cut 1 cm off the ends of each apple quarter, then trim to form rectangles about 1.5 cm thick and 3.5 cm long x 2.5 cm wide.

Add the apple to the poaching liquid, place a cartouche* over the top, and cover with a plate to hold the apple down. Reduce the heat to low and simmer for 8 minutes, until the apple is nicely poached but still holding its shape and a little firm. Transfer the poached apple to a wire rack to cool for 15 minutes.

Place the won ton wrappers on a clean work surface and place an apple piece in the centre. Fold over one side, then, using a pastry brush, lightly moisten the edges of the wrapper with a little water. Fold over the edges, making sure the ends are stuck. Transfer the dumplings to a tray and place in the refrigerator for 30 minutes.

Cinnamon sugar Combine the cinnamon and sugar in a bowl.

TO SERVE

Heat the oil in a wok to 180°C (you can test if the oil is the right temperature by dropping in a cube of bread; if the bread browns in 30 seconds, the oil is ready). Carefully add the dumplings, in batches of four, and cook for 2–3 minutes, or until golden brown and crispy. Drain on paper towel and, while still warm, gently toss in the cinnamon sugar to coat evenly.

* To make a cartouche, cut out a circle of greaseproof paper slightly larger than your saucepan.

Sticky black rice is also known as Thai black rice or Thai purple rice. Quinces are available during the winter months and, when cooked correctly, their texture is great with the black rice.

STICKY BLACK RICE
WITH COCONUT-POACHED QUINCE AND JASMINE TEA ICE CREAM

Serves four

JASMINE TEA ICE CREAM

650 ml pouring cream

3 tablespoons jasmine tea leaves

7 egg yolks

200 g caster sugar

100 ml strong jasmine tea

STICKY BLACK RICE

300 g palm sugar

2 tablespoons water

750 ml (3 cups) coconut cream

150 g (¾ cup) glutinous white rice, soaked in 500 ml (2 cups) cold water overnight in the refrigerator

750 ml (3 cups) water

150 g (¾ cup) glutinous black rice, soaked in 500 ml (2 cups) cold water overnight in the refrigerator

500 ml (2 cups) water

COCONUT-POACHED QUINCE

6 quinces

3 cinnamon sticks, lightly toasted

3 whole star anise, lightly toasted

zest of 2 oranges

liquid from 3 baby coconuts (approx 1.4 litres) (see page 232)

500 g caster sugar

METHOD

Jasmine tea ice cream Place the cream and tea leaves in a saucepan over low heat and bring to about 65°C, or until little bubbles appear at the bottom of the saucepan. Set aside 15 minutes to allow flavours to infuse.

Whisk the egg yolks and sugar in a heatproof bowl until pale and thick. Carefully strain in the cooled jasmine-infused cream and jasmine tea and place the bowl over a saucepan of simmering water. Cook, stirring constantly, for 5–10 minutes until the custard coats the back of a wooden spoon. Remove the bowl from the heat and plunge into a bowl of iced water to stop the cooking process and to allow the custard to cool. Once cool, strain the mixture into an ice-cream machine and churn, according to the manufacturer's instructions.

Transfer the ice cream to an airtight container and place in the freezer until ready to serve. Alternatively, pour the custard into a shallow container, cover and place in the freezer for 30–40 minutes, until frozen at the edges. Whisk it for 1 minute then place back in the freezer for 30–40 minutes. Repeat this process until the ice cream is set.

Sticky black rice Combine the sugar, 2 tablespoons of water and the coconut cream in a small saucepan and stir over low heat until the sugar has dissolved. Take off heat and set aside. Drain the white rice and place it with 750 ml (3 cups) water in a wok to steam on a medium heat for 30 minutes, taking care the water doesn't run dry.

Drain the black rice and place it with 500 ml (2 cups) water in a saucepan over a medium heat and bring to the boil. Reduce the heat to low, place the lid on and cook for 30–40 minutes, or until tender.

Combine the cooked white and black rices in a bowl and mix in half of the sweetened coconut cream, then spread out evenly on a tray to cool.

Coconut-poached quince Preheat the oven to 140°C. Peel, quarter and core the quinces, reserving the cores and peeled skin. Place the cinnamon, star anise, orange zest and quince cores and skin in a large piece of muslin cloth and tie up with kitchen twine.

Combine the baby coconut juice and sugar in a large casserole dish, add the spice bag and quince quarters, cover with a cartouche* and a lid, and cook for 5 hours, or until the quince quarters are a little firm but cooked right through and a beautiful ruby red. Place the quince on a chopping board and cut into 1 cm dice.

TO SERVE

Place the cooled rice and the remaining sweetened coconut cream in a saucepan and reheat, gently stirring with a wooden spoon, over low heat. Once the rice is hot enough, gently fold in the quince.

Divide the rice between dessert bowls and place a scoop of the jasmine tea ice cream on the side.

* *To make a cartouche*, cut out a circle of greaseproof paper slightly larger than your casserole dish.

STEAMED APPLE AND VANILLA BUNS
WITH COCONUT CUSTARD

COCONUT CUSTARD

130 ml coconut cream
200 ml full-cream milk
6 egg yolks
130 g caster sugar

CARAMELISED APPLE AND VANILLA

8 green apples, peeled, cored
    and diced
150 g (⅔ cup) caster sugar
1 whole star anise, lightly toasted
1 vanilla bean, split in half
    lengthways and seeds scraped

BUN DOUGH

400 g bun dough flour (available
    from Asian supermarkets)
250 ml (1 cup) full-cream milk
1 tablespoon vegetable oil
125 g caster sugar

METHOD

Coconut custard Combine the coconut cream and milk in a small saucepan over low heat and bring to a simmer.

Whisk the egg yolks and sugar in a heatproof bowl until pale and thick. Whisk in the warm coconut cream mixture and continue to whisk until well combined. Place the bowl over a saucepan of simmering water and, whisking constantly, cook for 5–10 minutes, until the custard coats the back of a wooden spoon. Remove the bowl from the heat and plunge into a bowl of iced water to stop the cooking process and to allow the custard to cool. Once cool, cover with plastic wrap and refrigerate until needed.

Caramelised apple and vanilla Place two-thirds of the diced apple in a large saucepan over medium–high heat, stir in the sugar, star anise and vanilla bean and seeds and cook, stirring constantly, for 5 minutes, until the apple has broken down and is transparent.

Turn the heat down to medium, add the remaining diced apple and cook for a further 10 minutes, or until the mixture is golden brown with some apple chunks for texture. Remove the star anise and vanilla bean.

Transfer the caramelised apple mixture to a tray and set aside for 15 minutes to cool, then refrigerate to chill completely and make it easier to work with.

Buns Place the flour and sugar in a bowl and slowly beat in the milk until the mixture comes together. Add the oil and mix with your hands or with an electric mixer until well combined, then cover with plastic wrap and put in the refrigerator for 20 minutes.

Remove the dough from the refrigerator. Begin making the first of 12 buns by tearing off a piece of dough about the size of a lime, then place on a lightly floured work surface and flatten slightly with the palm of your hand or with a rolling pin. Roll out to form a round about 0.5 cm think and 10 cm in diameter.

Place 1 tablespoon of the caramelised apple mixture in the centre of the dough, bring the edges together and press tightly to seal. Turn the bun over and lightly score the base with an 'X', don't press too hard; you don't want to go all the way through the dough. Repeat with the remaining dough and apple mixture.

TO SERVE

Place a perforated stainless steel disc insert in a steamer basket, spray with cooking spray and add the buns in a single layer, leaving about 2 cm space around each one so they don't stick together. Cover and steam in a wok of simmering water for 5 minutes until light and fluffy. To test if they are ready, stick a wooden skewer in the centre of a bun, then place the skewer on your lip; if it is hot, they are done.

Place three buns on each serving plate and pour about 3 tablespoons of the coconut custard over the top.

STEAMED GINGER PUDDINGS
WITH MANDARIN CHILLI ICE CREAM AND CARAMELISED APPLE

MANDARIN CHILLI ICE CREAM

zest and juice of 8 mandarins
(you will need 200 ml mandarin
juice)
200 g caster sugar
750 ml (3 cups) pouring cream
9 egg yolks
½ teaspoon dried chilli flakes

STEAMED GINGER PUDDINGS

75 g butter
2½ tablespoons golden syrup
90 ml gula melaka (see page 238)
2 eggs
35 g sour cream
90 ml full-cream milk
130 g self-raising flour
½ teaspoon baking powder
1 teaspoon ground ginger
½ teaspoon ground cinnamon

CARAMELISED APPLE

200 g grated light palm sugar
300 ml water
300 g gula melaka (see page 238)
4 green apples, peeled, cored and
quartered

METHOD

Mandarin chilli ice cream Combine the mandarin juice and 100 g of the sugar in a small saucepan over low heat and gently simmer until reduced by half. Set aside for 15 minutes to cool.

Bring the cream to a gentle simmer in a separate small saucepan.

Whisk the egg yolks and the remaining sugar in a heatproof bowl until pale and thick. Slowly whisk in the cream and continue to whisk until well combined. Add the mandarin syrup, place the bowl over a saucepan of simmering water and, whisking constantly, cook for 5–10 minutes until the custard coats the back of a wooden spoon. Remove the bowl from the heat and plunge into a bowl of iced water to stop the cooking process and to allow the custard to cool. Once cool, stir the dried chilli through, pour into an ice-cream machine and churn, according to the manufacturer's instructions.

Transfer the ice cream to an airtight container and leave in the freezer until needed. Alternatively, pour the custard into a glass bowl, cover and place in the freezer for 30–40 minutes. Take the bowl out and whisk the ice-cream mixture for 10 seconds, then place back in the freezer. Repeat this process every 30–40 minutes until the ice cream has set.

Steamed ginger puddings Preheat the oven to 170°C. Spray four aluminium dariole moulds (125 ml capacity) with cooking spray.

Melt the butter, golden syrup and gula melaka in a saucepan over medium heat. Set aside.

Whisk the eggs and sour cream in a large bowl for 2 minutes until well combined, then add the milk and mix through. Pour in the butter mixture and whisk until well combined, then sift in the dry ingredients and stir until well combined. The mixture should be a nice brown wet dough.

Pour the pudding mixture into the prepared moulds to about 1 cm below the rim. Place the moulds in a baking tin and fill the tin with water to come a third of the way up the sides of the moulds. Bake for 25–30 minutes, until the tops of the puddings are dark brown (it doesn't matter if they burn a little, as the tops will be cut off) and a wooden skewer inserted in the centre comes out clean. Leave the puddings to cool in the moulds for 20 minutes.

Cut the top off each pudding, so the pudding is level with the rim of the mould, and turn out onto a plate so that they can later easily be placed in the steamer. Reserve until needed.

Caramelised apple Place the sugar, water and gula melaka in a saucepan over high heat and bring to a simmer, stirring to dissolve the sugar. Reduce the heat to medium and simmer for 10 minutes, or until golden.

Add the apple, reduce the heat to low and simmer, stirring gently, for 10 minutes until the apple is transparent but still holding its shape. Transfer the apple to a bowl.

Return the syrup in the pan to the stovetop and simmer over medium heat until reduced by one-third. Add the apple to the reduced syrup and cook over low heat for a further 10 minutes. Keep warm.

TO SERVE

Place a perforated stainless steel disc insert in a steamer basket, add the puddings, cover and steam in a wok of simmering water for 4–5 minutes. Insert a metal skewer into the middle of the puddings; the puddings are ready when the metal skewer is hot when it is pulled out.

Remove the ice cream from the refrigerator 2 minutes before required, to allow it time to soften.

Arrange six pieces of apple on each serving plate, place a pudding alongside and drizzle on 2 tablespoonfuls of the syrup.

Scoop some mandarin chilli ice cream into four small ramekins and serve on the side.

TOASTED COCONUT PARFAIT
WITH SPICED PINEAPPLE

COCONUT PARFAIT

90 g threaded coconut (available from supermarkets)
500 ml (2 cups) coconut milk
8 egg yolks
210 g caster sugar
75 ml water
250 ml (1 cup) pouring cream, softly whipped

PINEAPPLE AND KAFFIR LIME SYRUP

½ pineapple, peeled
300 g caster sugar
2½ tablespoons water
5 kaffir lime leaves, finely shredded

TOASTED COCONUT

250 g threaded coconut
150 g icing sugar, sifted

SPICED PINEAPPLE

1 pineapple, peeled and cored
1 lemongrass stem, bruised and roughly chopped
50 g (approx 8 cm) fresh ginger, peeled and roughly chopped
800 ml water
300 g sugar
10 g sichuan peppercorns

METHOD

Coconut parfait Lightly spray an 8 x 25 cm bar tin with canola spray before lining it with greaseproof paper. Set aside. Combine the threaded coconut and coconut milk in a saucepan over medium heat and simmer until reduced to 250 ml (1 cup). Strain and set aside.

Whisk the egg yolks in a large heatproof electric mixing bowl until pale and thick.

Combine the sugar and water in a saucepan and boil until the syrup reaches 118°C. Be sure to use a sugar thermometer and be exact. Slowly whisk the sugar syrup into the egg yolks and continue to whisk for 20–30 minutes, or until the mixture is cool. Pour in the coconut milk and whisk for a further 2–3 minutes. The mixture should be light, aerated and well combined.

Fold in the whipped cream and pour into lined moulds. Place in the freezer overnight to set.

Pineapple and kaffir lime syrup Blitz the pineapple in a blender and pass through a fine sieve, reserving the juice.

Place the sugar and water in a saucepan over medium heat and simmer for 5 minutes, or until golden brown. Add the reserved pineapple juice and continue to boil for a further 10 minutes until reduced by one-quarter. Strain and set aside to cool. Once cool, stir through the shredded kaffir lime leaves and set aside for 15 minutes to allow the flavours to infuse.

Toasted coconut Preheat the oven to 160°C.

Place the coconut on a baking tray and toast, checking and stirring every 3 minutes to ensure the coconut colours evenly, for 10–12 minutes until golden brown. Transfer to a large bowl and set aside to cool.

Combine the coconut and icing sugar in the bowl of a food processor and blitz for 3 minutes until it is a coarse powder. Place into a shallow tray.

Spiced pineapple Cut the pineapple into 2 cm slices on an angle to form triangular shapes. Place the lemongrass, ginger, water and sugar in a saucepan and bring to the boil. Add the pepper and pineapple, reduce the heat to low and simmer for 25 minutes until the pineapple is soft and the syrup reduced.

TO SERVE

Remove the parfait from the freezer, cut into eight even slices and then roll the edges of each portion in the toasted coconut. Divide the spiced pineapple between eight serving plates and place a slice of parfait alongside. Top the spiced pineapple with the pineapple and kaffir lime syrup to serve.

TOM KHA CUSTARD BRÛLÉE
WITH TROPICAL FRUIT SALAD

Serves four

COCONUT CREAM INFUSION

50 g (approx 10 cm) fresh ginger, peeled
40 g (approx 8 cm) galangal, peeled
6 kaffir lime leaves
2 lemongrass stems, white part only
750 ml (3 cups) coconut cream
zest of 3 medium or 4 small limes

TOM KHA CUSTARD

8 egg yolks
100 g caster sugar
200 ml thickened cream
200 ml thick (double) cream
150 g demerara sugar

TROPICAL FRUIT SALAD

200 g pineapple, diced
200 g banana, diced
200 g mango, diced
4 kaffir lime leaves, finely chopped
2 tablespoons lime juice

METHOD

Coconut cream infusion Bruise the ginger, galangal, lime leaves and lemongrass in a mortar and pestle. Transfer to a saucepan, add the coconut cream and bring to a simmer, stirring constantly, over low heat. Remove from the heat, add the lime zest and cover the pan with its lid. Set aside for 45 minutes to allow the flavours to infuse.

Strain through a fine sieve into a jug and reserve for the tom kha custard and fruit salad.

Tom kha custard Whisk the egg yolks and caster sugar in a bowl until pale and thick. Fold in 340 ml of the reserved coconut cream infusion, then add the thickened and the thick cream, and very gently mix. Transfer to an airtight container and refrigerate until needed.

Preheat the oven to 160˚C.

Place four (ungreased) brûlée dishes (175–200 ml capacity) in a deep baking tin and slowly pour the tom kha custard into the dishes until 1 cm from the top, to allow for the custards to rise. Pour boiling water into the baking tin to come up the sides of the dishes. Cover the tin with foil and bake for 12 minutes.

Take the tin out of the oven and check the custards; if they are still liquid, cover with the foil again and return to the oven for a further 10 minutes until set. Give one of the moulds a little shake; the custards should wobble slightly in the centre. Remove the custards from the tin and cool completely on a wire rack. Place in the refrigerator to chill for 2–3 hours.

Tropical fruit salad Combine all of the ingredients in a bowl and add 2 tablespoons of the reserved coconut cream infusion. Mix well.

TO SERVE

Sprinkle 2 tablespoons of the demerara sugar in an even layer over the top of each custard. Light a kitchen blow torch, turn it to a low–medium flame and, starting from the centre and working your way out to the edges, caramelise the sugar until golden brown. Alternatively, caramelise under a very hot grill.

Place each brûlée dish on a serving plate, spoon 2 tablespoons of the tropical fruit salad on top of the tom kha custard brûlée, and serve.

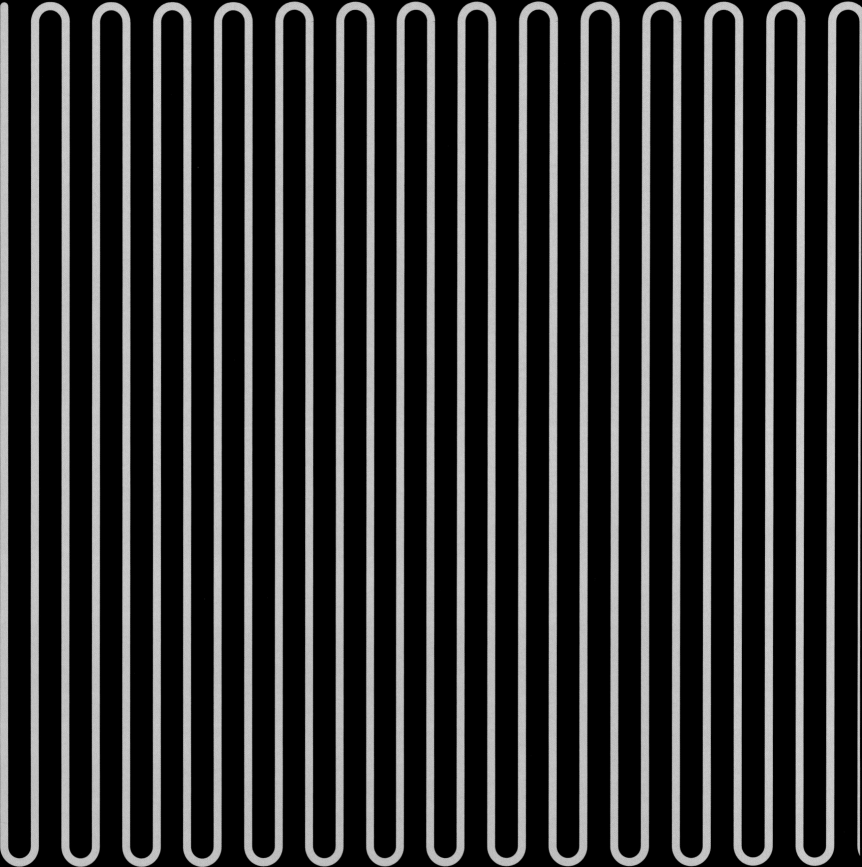

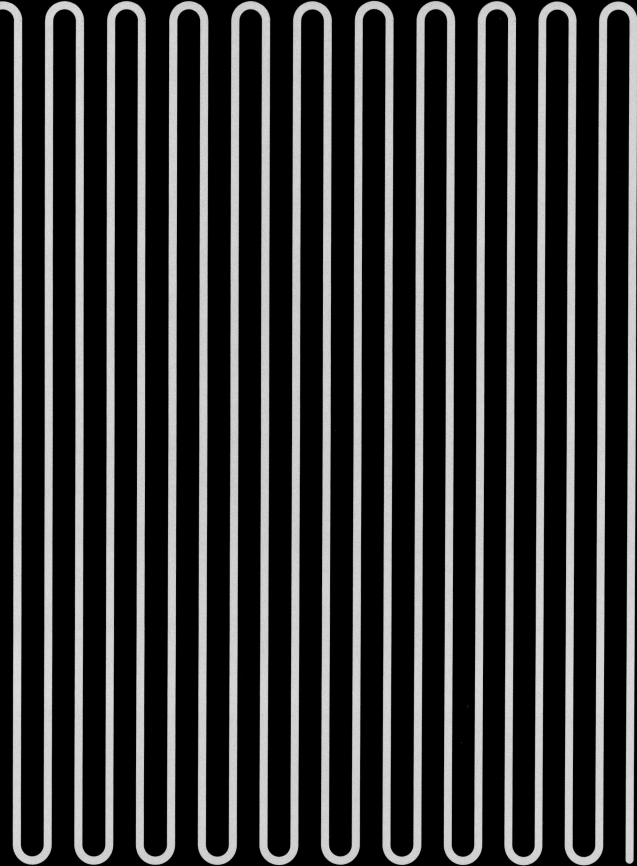

ASIAN CHICKEN STOCK

2 kg chicken carcasses, chopped
2 brown onions, roughly chopped
2 carrots, roughly chopped
1 leek, white part only, roughly chopped
12 cups (3 litres) water
1 handful of coriander leaves
30 ml light soy sauce
200 ml shaoxing rice wine
8 garlic cloves, roughly chopped
125 g fresh ginger, roughly chopped
6 whole star anise, lightly toasted
6 cinnamon sticks, lightly toasted
2 tablespoons coriander seeds, lightly toasted
1 tablespoon black pepper
1 tablespoon sichuan pepper, lightly toasted

METHOD

Preheat the oven to 170°C.

Spread the chicken on a baking tray and roast in the oven for 45 minutes until golden brown.

Saute the onions, carrots and leek in a stockpot or large saucepan over high heat, until golden brown. Add the chicken and water, bring to the boil, reduce the heat to medium–low heat and simmer for 25 minutes, skimming off all the scum and foam that floats to the top.

Add the remaining ingredients, reduce the heat to low and simmer for 2 hours.

Strain the stock through a fine sieve and set aside to cool.

Keep, stored in an airtight container in the refrigerator, for up to 4 or 5 days. It can also be frozen for later use.

MAKES 8 CUPS (2 LITRES)

This stock is great for cooking and braising meat, fish and poultry.

BABY COCONUT

1 young coconut (300–400g)

METHOD

Place the coconut on a chopping board with the flat side down (when you buy a young coconut, the husk will have been cut off and the bottom end will be flat).

Using a meat cleaver, carefully make a cut in the top of the coconut, then remove the cleaver and spin the coconut around at a 45 degree angle. Cut into the top again, being sure to try to connect with the previous cut. Repeat this process twice so you have a square hole in the top.

Tip the liquid out (reserve the liquid for a drink, dessert or curry). Cut the coconut in half and, using a tablespoon, scrape out all of the flesh. Carefully cut away and discard the thin brown skin. Evenly cut the coconut flesh into 2 mm thick slices.

Place the sliced coconut in an airtight container and store in the refrigerator for up to 2 days.

MAKES 1 CUP

BEAN SHOOT PICKLE DRESSING

150 ml mirin
150 ml rice wine vinegar
75 ml light soy sauce
1 tablespoon grated light palm sugar

METHOD

Place the mirin, vinegar, soy sauce and palm sugar in a bowl and whisk until the sugar has dissolved.

Store in an airtight container in the refrigerator for up to a week.

MAKES 1½ CUPS

Use this dressing to pickle bean shoots. Always use the pickled shoots within an hour, so that they retain their crunch.

BLACK VINEGAR CARAMEL

100 g light palm sugar, grated
3 tablespoons water
3½ tablespoons Chinese black vinegar
2 tablespoons rice wine vinegar
2 tablespoons light soy sauce
4 lime cheeks

METHOD

Put the palm sugar and water in a small saucepan over medium heat and bring to the boil, stirring occasionally. Simmer for 8 minutes until the sugar has dissolved and the syrup has thickened and is golden brown. Carefully add the vinegars and soy sauce as the caramel tends to spit and bubble over. Return to the boil and simmer for 3 minutes. Set aside to cool.

BLUE SWIMMER CRABMEAT

12 cups (3 litres) water
6 garlic cloves, roughly chopped
150 g fresh ginger, peeled and roughly chopped
1 red onion, roughly chopped
1 tablespoon salt
10 white peppercorns
2 kg live blue swimmer crabs
1 leek, white part only, roughly chopped
2 carrots, roughly chopped

METHOD

Put the live crabs into the freezer for 20 minutes to put them to sleep.

Place a stockpot or large saucepan over medium–high heat and add the water, garlic, ginger, onion, salt and peppercorns and bring to the boil. Add the crabs and simmer gently for 8 minutes. Transfer the crabs to a bowl of iced water to stop the cooking process. Drain and place each crab on its front on a chopping board. Take the main shell off and cut the crab in half. Twist off all the legs and claws, then break open the body with the back of a knife. Pull the meat out with either a crab fork or the handle of a thin teaspoon, making sure you scrape the meat out of all the cracks and crevices.

Spread the picked crabmeat on a tray and gently rub your fingers through it to find and remove any little bits of shell.

Place the crabmeat in a bowl, cover with plastic wrap and store in the refrigerator for immediate use.

MAKES 1 CUP

CHAR SIU MARINADE

3 tablespoons hoisin sauce
3 tablespoons tomato ketchup
80 ml (⅓ cup) shaoxing rice wine
2 tablespoons kecap manis
2 tablespoons light soy sauce
3 garlic cloves, finely chopped
30 g fresh ginger, peeled and finely chopped

METHOD

Place all of the ingredients in a bowl and whisk together. Set aside for 10 minutes for the flavours to infuse.

Store in an airtight container in the refrigerator for up to a week.

MAKES 1 CUP

CHILLI CARAMEL

300 g light palm sugar, grated
150 ml water
2 large red chillies, thinly sliced
2 large green chillies, thinly sliced
1 red bird's eye chilli, thinly sliced
2 tablespoons fish sauce
3 tablespoons lime juice

METHOD

Place the sugar and water in a saucepan over high heat and bring to the boil, stirring continuously to dissolve the sugar. Turn the heat down to medium and simmer for 8–10 minutes, until the syrup begins to colour and turn golden brown. Leave the caramel on the heat for a further 1 minute, then add the chillies and cook for 30 seconds. Stir in the fish sauce and lime juice, remove the pan from the heat and set aside to cool.

Once cool, check the seasoning: it should be hot, sweet and salty.

Store in an airtight container in a cool, dry place for up to a week.

MAKES 1 CUP

CHILLI JAM

500 g roma tomatoes, roughly chopped (but not peeled
  or seeded)
10 garlic cloves, peeled and roughly chopped
70 g fresh ginger, peeled and roughly chopped
6 large red chillies, roughly chopped
4 red bird's eye chilli, roughly chopped
4 red capsicums, deseeded and roughly chopped
350 g red shallots, roughly chopped
300 g pale palm sugar, grated
7½ tablespoons fish sauce
150 ml lime juice

METHOD

Place the tomatoes, garlic, ginger, chillies, capsicum and shallots in a large saucepan over low heat and cook, stirring frequently, for 45 minutes, until the mixture has broken down.

Cover the pan with a lid and cook for 1 hour.

Remove the lid and continue to cook, stirring occasionally so it doesn't stick, for 1 hour, until reduced and starting to look like a jam. At this stage, add the sugar and cook for a further 20 minutes, until the jam is a smooth, deep, shiny red.

Set aside to cool.

Transfer the jam to the bowl of a food processor and purée until smooth. Stir in the fish sauce and lime juice.

Put the jam into an airtight container and pour in some vegetable oil to keep out the air. Store in the refrigerator for up to a week.

MAKES 2 CUPS

This chilli jam is great with seafood, meat and barbecues, or even egg and bacon sandwiches.

CHILLI ROCK SUGAR

zest of 2 limes (use a microplane or zester)
150 g yellow rock sugar
1 teaspoon dried chilli flakes

METHOD

Preheat the oven to 145°C.

Line a baking tray with baking paper. Spread the lime zest on the prepared tray and place in the oven for 10 minutes to dry out.

Pound the sugar using a mortar and pestle until very fine. Place in a bowl.

Grind the chilli flakes to a very fine powder in the mortar and pestle and combine with the sugar and lime zest.

Transfer to an airtight container and store in a cool dry place for up to 2 weeks.

MAKES ½ CUP

CRISPY FRIED SAMBAL

1 tablespoon belacan shrimp paste, roasted
750 ml (3 cups) vegetable oil
6 red shallots, thinly sliced
3 long red chillies, thinly sliced on the diagonal
6 garlic cloves, thinly sliced
30 g (approx 6 cm) fresh ginger, peeled and finely sliced

METHOD

Using your fingers, crumble the shrimp paste into a bowl and set aside.

Heat the oil in a wok to 160°C (you can test if the oil is the right temperature by dropping in a cube of bread; if the bread browns in 50 seconds, the oil is ready). Fry the shallots until golden brown, remove with a slotted spoon and drain on paper towel. Repeat with the chilli, garlic and ginger.

Add all fried ingredients to the bowl and gently mix with the shrimp paste.

This sambal is best made fresh on the day.

MAKES 1 CUP

CRISPY FRIED SWEET POTATO

300 g sweet potato, cut into 3 mm thick julienne on a mandolin
700 ml vegetable oil
1 teaspoon sea salt
½ teaspoon icing sugar

METHOD

Heat the oil in a wok to 160°C (you can test if the oil is the right temperature by dropping in a cube of bread; if the bread turns golden brown in 50 seconds, the oil is ready).

Add the sweet potato and, using a large slotted spoon, gently move it around the wok until the oil stops bubbling and the sweet potato is golden. Drain on paper towel.

Season the sweet potato with the salt, sift the sugar evenly over the top and set aside to cool completely.

Line an airtight container with paper towel, add the sweet potato and use within 2 days.

MAKES 2 CUPS

CRISPY FRIED TARO

300 g taro, cut into 3 mm thick julienne on a mandolin
700 ml vegetable oil
1 teaspoon sea salt
½ teaspoon icing sugar

METHOD

Place the taro in a bowl filled with cold water to wash the starch out. Drain in a fine sieve.

Heat the oil in a wok to 160°C (you can test if the oil is the right temperature by dropping in a cube of bread; if the bread turns golden in 50 seconds, the oil is ready).

Add the taro and, using a large slotted spoon, gently move it around the wok until the oil stops bubbling and the taro is crispy. Drain on paper towel.

Season the taro lightly with the salt and sift the sugar evenly over the top. Set aside to cool completely.

Line an airtight container with paper towel, add the taro and use within 1 day.

MAKES 2 CUPS

FRESH BAMBOO SHOOT

2 heads of bamboo shoot (about 500 g)

METHOD

Preheat the oven to 180°C.

Place the bamboo on a baking tray and roast for 1 hour, or until a skewer can easily be inserted. Set aside to cool.

Remove the outside layer from the bamboo with a small, sharp knife, then cut into the desired shape.

MAKES 1 CUP

When cutting the outside of the bamboo be sure to wear an apron and gloves as the little spikes on the bamboo will get stuck in your skin and irritate you. Fresh bamboo can be bought from Asian food markets and large fresh food markets.

FRIED CHILLI PEANUTS

500 ml (2 cups) peanut oil
300 g roasted unsalted peanuts, roughly chopped
4 red shallots, finely chopped
6 garlic cloves, finely chopped
30 g fresh ginger, peeled and finely chopped
5 red bird's eye chillies, deseeded and finely chopped
1 tablespoon sea salt

METHOD

Heat the oil in a wok to 160°C (you can test if the oil is the right temperature by dropping in a cube of bread; if the bread turns golden brown after 50 seconds, the oil is ready).

Add the peanuts, shallots, garlic, ginger and chilli and deep-fry until just golden. (The peanuts will continue to cook and deepen in colour when removed from the oil.) Drain on paper towel. Season with the salt and set aside to cool.

Store in an airtight container in the refrigerator for up to a week.

MAKES 2 CUPS

FRIED GARLIC

12 garlic cloves, thinly sliced on a mandolin
200 ml milk
300 ml vegetable oil
1 teaspoon sea salt

METHOD

Place the garlic in a small saucepan, cover with the milk and bring to a simmer over medium heat. (This draws out some of the natural sugars in the garlic and stops it from burning so quickly when you cook it in the oil.) Drain and rinse the garlic under cold running water.

Transfer the garlic to a clean saucepan over high heat, cover with cold oil and fry, stirring frequently, until golden brown. Remove with a slotted spoon and drain on paper towel.

Lightly season with the salt and set aside until needed.

This is best made fresh on the day.

MAKES ⅓ CUP

FRIED ONION

2 white onions, thinly sliced on a mandolin
700 ml vegetable oil
1 teaspoon sea salt

METHOD

Heat the oil in a wok to 160°C (you can test if the oil is the right temperature by dropping in a cube of bread; if the bread turns golden brown after 50 seconds, the oil is ready).

Add the onion and gently move it around the wok with a slotted spoon for 1–2 minutes, or until golden brown and crispy. Drain on paper towel.

Lightly season with the salt and set aside to cool.

This is best made fresh on the day.

MAKES 1 CUP

FRIED SHALLOTS

750 ml (3 cups) vegetable oil
12 red shallots, thinly sliced on a mandolin
1 pinch of sea salt
1 tablespoon icing sugar

METHOD

Heat the oil in a wok to 160°C (you can test if the oil is the right temperature by dropping in a cube of bread; if the bread turns golden brown after 50 seconds, the oil is ready).

Add the shallots and fry for 1–2 minutes until golden brown. Drain on paper towel. Using two forks, gently toss the shallots so they can cool evenly.

Season the shallots with the salt and sift the sugar evenly over the top.

This is best made fresh on the day.

MAKES 1 CUP

FRIED STICKY RICE BALLS

80 g glutinous rice, soaked in 250 ml (1 cup) water
    for 4 hours then drained
500 ml (2 cups) vegetable oil, for deep-frying

METHOD

Line a bamboo steamer with muslin cloth, then add the soaked rice. Cover and steam over a wok of simmering water for 45 minutes, occasionally checking the water in the wok so it doesn't run dry. Set aside to cool, then roll the rice into loose walnut-sized balls.

Wipe out the wok, add the oil and heat to 170°C (you can test if the oil is the right temperature by dropping in a cube of bread; if the bread browns in 40 seconds, the oil is ready). Deep-fry the rice balls for 2 minutes until golden brown. Drain on paper towel.

GREEN CHILLI PICKLE DRESSING

3 large green chillies, deseeded and thickly sliced
3 garlic cloves, thinly sliced
1 tablespoon sea salt
250 ml water
250 ml rice wine vinegar
200 g caster sugar

METHOD

Place the chilli and garlic in a strainer over a bowl, sprinkle the salt over the top and mix well. Set aside for 5 minutes.

Rinse the chilli mixture to wash off the excess salt. Place the chilli mixture in a clean bowl, add the water, vinegar and sugar and whisk until combined.

Store in an airtight container in the refrigerator for up to 2 weeks.

MAKES 2 CUPS

GREEN CHILLI SOY

75 ml light soy sauce
75 ml kecap manis
1 tablespoon lemon juice
4 green bird's eye chillies, deseeded and finely chopped
1 teaspoon freshly ground white pepper

METHOD

Combine all of the ingredients in a small bowl and set aside to allow the flavours to infuse.

Store in an airtight container in the refrigerator for up to a week.

MAKES 150 ML

GREEN GINGER WINE DRESSING

300 ml green ginger wine
125 g light palm sugar, grated
2½ tablespoons rice wine vinegar
100 ml lemon juice

METHOD

Combine the ginger wine and sugar in a small saucepan over low heat and gently whisk until the sugar has dissolved. Remove from the heat.

Let cool, then mix in the vinegar and lemon juice.

Pour into an airtight container and store in the refrigerator for up to 2 weeks.

MAKES 2 CUPS

GULA MELAKA

300 g dark palm sugar, grated
300 ml water
2 large strips of dried mandarin peel
1 cinnamon stick, broken

METHOD

Combine all the ingredients in a saucepan and bring to the boil.

Reduce the heat to low and simmer until reduced by around half and the consistency is syrupy. (The gula melaka will thicken slightly as it cools.)

Set aside to cool.

Pour the gula melaka into a jar or container (mandarin zest and cinnamon included, as their flavours will continue to infuse the syrup) and store in the refrigerator for up to 2 weeks.

MAKES 300 ML

HOT AND SOUR DRESSING

100 ml lime juice
2 tablespoons fish sauce
2 tablespoons tamarind paste (see page 242)
2 red bird's eye chillies, thinly sliced
½ teaspoon chilli powder

METHOD

Combine all the ingredients in a small bowl and stir well. Set aside for 3 minutes, then taste to check the balance of flavours. Add more lime juice or fish sauce if necessary.

Store in an airtight container in the refrigerator for up to 2 days.

MAKES 200 ML

ICEBERG LETTUCE CUPS

1 large iceberg lettuce

METHOD

Place the lettuce on a chopping board with the core facing up. Cut in half and remove the core. Cut each half in half again and pull off the outer leaves. Using a pair of scissors, trim the leaves into circular cups, 10–15 cm in diameter.

Transfer to an airtight container, cover with a damp cloth and store in the refrigerator.

MAKES 8–12 LETTUCE CUPS

MASTER STOCK

3 litres (12 cups) water
500 ml (2 cups) shaoxing rice wine
300 ml light soy sauce
200 g yellow rock sugar
6 garlic cloves, bruised with the back of a knife and peeled
50 g fresh ginger, peeled and roughly chopped
7 whole star anise, lightly toasted
4 cinnamon sticks, lightly toasted
5 cardamom pods, lightly toasted
1 teaspoon fennel seeds, lightly toasted
1 teaspoon sichuan peppercorns, lightly toasted
3 whole cloves, lightly toasted
6 black peppercorns

METHOD

Place all of the ingredients in a stockpot or large saucepan and simmer for 25 minutes. Set aside to cool completely.

Pour the master stock into an airtight container and store in the refrigerator for up to 7 days.

Note: If you are not using the master stock all the time, store it in the freezer, then thaw and bring to the boil when you wish to use it. Every second time you use it, add half of all the dry ingredients (i.e. half of the rock sugar, garlic, ginger, star anise, cinnamon, cardamom pods, fennel, sichuan peppercorns, cloves and peppercorns) and a third of the liquids. You want to retain the balance of flavours in the aromatic, glossy stock. If it starts to get too strong, add more water. It needs to be brought to boil every time you use it, and adding some more shaoxing wine will help to keep it.

MAKES 12 CUPS (3 LITRES)

Master stock is a flavoured aromatic braising liquid used for poaching meat and poultry. It takes on the flavour of the protein, spices and liquids added to it.

MUSTARD SOY SAUCE

150 ml apple juice
100 g light palm sugar, grated
2 teaspoons yellow mustard powder
2 teaspoons yellow mustard seeds, soaked in cold water for 5 minutes
175 ml light soy sauce
100 ml shiso vinegar
75 ml lime juice

METHOD

Place the apple juice and sugar in a small saucepan over medium heat and simmer for 7–8 minutes or until a shiny golden brown 'caramel' forms (when the bubbles start to slow right down, it is ready).

Add the mustard powder and seeds and cook for 10 seconds to allow the heat to bring out their flavour. Pour in the soy sauce and vinegar and simmer, stirring occasionally, for 1–2 minutes, until the sugar dissolves. Set aside to cool.

Add the lime juice to the sauce and store in an airtight container in the refrigerator for up to a week.

MAKES 1 CUP

NUOC CHAM

160 g light palm sugar, grated
2 garlic cloves, finely chopped
4 red bird's eye chillies, finely chopped
140 ml lime juice
7½ tablespoons fish sauce
2½ tablespoons water

METHOD

Pound the palm sugar in a mortar and pestle until it is a smooth paste. Add the garlic, chilli, lime juice, fish sauce and water, and pound until well combined. Store in an airtight container in the refrigerator for up to 1 week.

MAKES 1 CUP

A versatile Vietnamese dipping sauce that is great for dumplings. For extra heat, add more chilli.

PRICKLY ASH

3 tablespoons sichuan peppercorns
2 tablespoons sea salt

METHOD

Toast the peppercorns and salt in a wok over a medium–hot heat for 2 minutes, or until fragrant and the pepper stops popping and crackling. Remove from the heat. Grind to a fine powder using a mortar and pestle, then pass through a fine sieve.

It can be stored in an airtight container for 2–3 weeks (after that, it will lose its intensity).

MAKES ½ CUP

Named for the prickly sensation on the tongue when eaten, this is an essential seasoning for meats and poultry.

PRIK NAM PLA

3 red shallots, finely chopped
2 garlic cloves, finely chopped
2 red bird's eye chillies, finely chopped
4 kaffir lime leaves, thinly sliced
150 ml lime juice
5½ tablespoons fish sauce

METHOD

Combine all of the ingredients in a small bowl and taste. You are after a balanced sour, salty and hot dressing. Set aside.

MAKES 1 CUP

RICE FLOUR BATTER

200 g rice flour
150 g tapioca flour
2 egg yolks
1 cup (250 ml) soda water

METHOD

Combine all of the ingredients in a bowl and whisk well. Cover with plastic wrap and place in the refrigerator for 15 minutes to chill before using.

MAKES 2 CUPS

This light and crispy gluten-free batter works really well with vegetables, tofu and seafood.

ROASTED RICE

200 g (1 cup) jasmine rice

METHOD

Preheat the oven to 200°C.

Spread the rice out on a baking tray and roast for 15 minutes or until golden brown, shaking the rice every few minutes to get an even colour.

Transfer half of the rice to a mortar and pestle and grind to a fine powder. Repeat this process with the remaining rice. Alternatively, you can grind the rice in a spice grinder, which will give an even finer result.

Store in an airtight container for up to 2 days.

MAKES 1 CUP

SALT AND PEPPER MIX

1 tablespoon black peppercorns
1 tablespoon sichuan peppercorns
2 tablespoons white peppercorns
1 cinnamon stick
2 whole star anise
100 g sea salt

METHOD

Toast all of the ingredients in a wok for 2–3 minutes, or until a nice aroma is being released. Set aside to cool.

Transfer the salt and pepper mixture to a mortar and pestle and pound into a fine powder. Pass through a fine sieve.

Store in an airtight container for up to a week.

MAKES 1 CUP

SICHUAN PEPPER PICKLING LIQUID

100 g caster sugar
100 ml rice wine vinegar
100 ml water
2 tablespoons sichuan peppercorns
1 red bird's eye chilli, roughly chopped
1 teaspoon salt

METHOD

Combine all of the ingredients in a small saucepan over low heat and bring to a gentle simmer. Set aside to cool.

Strain into an airtight container and store in the refrigerator for up to 4 weeks.

MAKES 1 CUP

SPICED CHILLI SALT

1 cinnamon stick, broken
1 tablespoon sichuan peppercorns
1 tablespoon coriander seeds
1 teaspoon white peppercorns
2 whole star anise
1 tablespoon dried chilli flakes
2 tablespoons white sesame seeds
6 tablespoons sea salt

METHOD

Toast all of the spices in a wok over medium heat until fragrant. Pound the spice mixture to a fine powder using a mortar and pestle or a spice grinder, then pass through a fine sieve.

Store in an airtight container for up to 2 weeks.

MAKES 1 CUP

SPICED HOISIN

250 ml (1 cup) hoisin sauce
5 spring onions, white part only, thinly sliced
20 g fresh ginger, peeled and finely chopped
2 red bird's eye chillies, thinly sliced
3 garlic cloves, finely chopped
2½ tablespoons lime juice
2½ tablespoons water
1½ tablespoons fish sauce

METHOD

Combine all of the ingredients in a bowl and mix well.

Store in an airtight container in the refrigerator for 2–3 weeks.

MAKES 1½ CUPS

SUGAR SYRUP

500 g caster sugar
500 ml (1 cup) water

METHOD

Put sugar and water into a saucepan, bring to the boil then simmer for 5 minutes. Take it off the heat and let it cool.

Store in an airtight container in the refrigerator for up to a week.

MAKES 2 CUPS

TAMARIND PASTE

375 g tamarind pulp
190 ml boiling water
2 kaffir lime leaves, torn
1 red bird's eye chilli, cut in half lengthways
50 g caster sugar

METHOD

Place the tamarind pulp in a bowl and add the water, lime leaves, chilli and sugar. Cover with plastic wrap and set aside for 10 minutes.

Use your fingers to work the pulp into a smooth paste, then push the paste through a sieve to remove the fibres and seeds.

The paste will keep, stored in an airtight container in the refrigerator, for 7 days.

MAKES 2 CUPS

TEMPURA BATTER

250 g tempura flour
300 ml chilled soda water
2 egg yolks
135 g (1 cup) ice cubes

METHOD

Sift the flour into a bowl and gently whisk in the soda water and egg yolks, breaking up any lumps with your fingers if necessary, until the consistency of a pancake batter. Add the ice cubes. Mix the ice cubes in and let sit for a couple of minutes, then use the batter before they melt.

MAKES 2 CUPS

VEGETABLE STOCK

8 cups (2 litres) water
2 carrots, peeled and roughly chopped
1 brown onion, peeled and roughly chopped
½ cup roughly chopped Asian celery
1 stick lemongrass, bruised in mortar and pestle
5 cloves garlic, peeled and roughly chopped
25 g (approx 5 cm) fresh ginger, peeled and roughly chopped
2 large green chillies, roughly chopped
2 tablespoons kecap manis

METHOD

Place all the ingredients in a stockpot or large saucepan over high heat and bring to the boil. Reduce the heat to medium–low and simmer for 30 minutes. Remove the pot from the heat and strain the stock through a fine sieve into a heatproof bowl or container and set aside to cool for 20 minutes. Once cool, cover with plastic wrap or a lid and store in the refrigerator for up to 2 days. The stock can also be frozen for later use.

MAKES 8 CUPS (2 LITRES)

XO SAUCE

150 g pork belly
200 g dried scallops, soaked overnight in cold water in the refrigerator
200 ml peanut oil
15 red shallots, finely chopped
15 garlic cloves, finely chopped
50 g dried shrimp, soaked for 30 minutes in cold water in the refrigerator
50 g shaved palm sugar
12 dried large red chillies, deseeded and soaked in warm water for
   30 minutes, finely chopped
1 teaspoon freshly ground white pepper
1 tablespoon fish sauce

METHOD

Preheat the oven to 200°C. Place the pork belly on a baking tray and roast for 30 minutes, or until the juices run clear when tested with a skewer. Set aside to cool completely.

Cut the skin from the pork belly and discard, then finely chop the meat and fat.

Drain the scallops, place them in a single layer on a plate and transfer to a bamboo steamer. Cover and steam over a wok of simmering water for 2 hours until tender. Set aside to cool. Roughly chop the scallops, reserving any juices that have pooled in the dish.

Heat the oil in a wok to 130°C (you can test if the oil is the right temperature by dropping in a cube of bread; if the bread browns in 1 minute and 40 seconds, the oil is ready).

Fry the shallots, garlic, dried shrimp and sugar for 10 minutes, until the sugar starts to caramelise.

Add the chilli, chopped pork and scallops and the reserved steaming juices and simmer, stirring frequently, for 1 hour, topping up with water from time to time if the mixture begins to stick on the base of the wok.

Remove from the heat and add the pepper and fish sauce. Set aside to cool. Keep, stored in an airtight container, in the refrigerator for up to 2 weeks.

MAKES 2 CUPS

YELLOW CURRY PASTE

1 tablespoon coriander seeds, lightly toasted
1 teaspoon sea salt
2 tablespoons roasted belacan shrimp paste
8 red shallots, roughly chopped
5 garlic cloves, roughly chopped
30 g fresh ginger, peeled and roughly chopped
30 g galangal, roughly chopped
40 g fresh turmeric, roughly chopped
1 lemongrass stem, white part only, roughly chopped
5 kaffir lime leaves, finely shredded
3 green bird's eye chillies, roughly chopped
5 coriander roots, washed and roughly chopped

METHOD

Grind the coriander seeds and salt in a mortar and pestle to a fine powder. Transfer to a bowl and set aside.

Pound the shrimp paste in the mortar and pestle to form a fine paste.

Place the shallots, garlic, ginger, galangal, turmeric, lemongrass, lime leaves, chilli and coriander root in the bowl of a food processor and blitz to a fine paste. Add the ground spices and the shrimp paste and combine well.

Store in an airtight container in the refrigerator for up to 6 days.

MAKES 1 CUP

XO sauce, referred to as the 'caviar of the Orient', originated in Hong Kong in the 1970s. Its creators considered it the equivalent in quality of XO (extra old) brandy, the best brandy on the market, hence the name. The sauce is a spicy combination of dried seafood and pork, and while you can buy it in jars, I prefer to make my own. Use it with meat dishes, stir-fries, tofu and vegetable dishes.

GLOSSARY

Aperol   A rhubarb-flavoured aperitif made in Italy. It has a crisp, dry taste with hints of orange and citrus on the nose and palate.

atari goma   This is a Japanese white sesame paste used for sauces and dressings.

Bamboo shoots   A common ingredient used all around China for its great texture and unusual flavour.

banana blossom   The dark outer layers of the banana blossom are peeled away to reveal the pale-coloured leaves, which are sliced and used in salads or curries. Be sure to store sliced leaves in citrus water as they will oxidise quickly.

betel leaves   The betel leaf is from a vine belonging to the Piperaceae family, which includes pepper and kava. It is used for its medicinal properties all over Asia.

Campari   A strong aperitif from Italy. Hints of grapefruit on the nose and palate.

Chinese black vinegar   A dark, strong-flavoured vinegar usually made from glutinous rice. It is particularly popular in northern China.

Chinese chives   This herb is narrow and flat with a light garlic flavour. They originate from Southeast Asia and are used commonly in many Chinese dishes. They are available from any Asian food market.

coconut cream   Kara is our preferred brand of coconut cream. Any other type of good, thick, creamy coconut cream will do.

coconut vinegar   This is made from fermented coconut water, high in potassium and great for digestion. It is a cloudy white colour.

cooking sake   A Japanese wine made from fermented rice. Sake has a high alcohol content (about 16 per cent).

coriander cress   Coriander cress is baby coriander and is very aromatic and citrusy in flavour. It is available from fresh fruit and vegetable markets; or you can speak to your local green grocer and ask them to source it for you.

demerera sugar   A form of raw sugar. It is golden and has a rich, distinctive sugarcane flavour.

dried bonito flakes   Steamed bonito fish are dried and flaked. They are used in Japanese cooking and are often mixed with konbu seaweed to form the all-purpose stock, dashi.

dried jellyfish   The jellyfish are salted and dried as soon as they are pulled out of the water as fresh jellyfish spoil within a matter of hours. Heavily salted, they need to be washed well before use. They are available from most Asian grocers.

dried shrimp   These are shrimps that have been dried in the sun. They have a nice clean flavour and are used in many dishes throughout the whole of Southeast Asia.

edamame beans   These are immature soybeans still in the pod. They are found in the freezer in most Asian grocers.

flat rice noodle sheets   Known as ho fun in Cantonese cuisine, these are a slippery, smooth noodle with a slight bite to them.

galangal   An essential ingredient in Southeast Asian cuisines. Galangal is a rhizome, and a member of the ginger family.

Its distinctive flavour is quite different to ginger, and ginger will not do as a substitute. It is best used fresh.

glass noodles   These are clear noodles and have a great texture. They are made from either yam, potato, sweet potato, mung bean or cassava starch. They should not be confused with vermicelli noodles, which are made from rice starch.

glutinous rice   Also known as sticky rice, this is a short-grained rice that when cooked is especially sticky. It is used in a wide variety of sweets, but can also be used in savoury dishes. The black variety has not been polished, so the bran will still be on the grain.

green ginger wine   Stone's green ginger wine is a fortified wine made from raisins and ground ginger. It works really well in dressings or marinades.

green pandan essence   This is the essence of the pandan leaf. It is very green and very strong in flavour so you will only need a drop or two for colouring and flavouring. It can be added to cakes, pancakes or batters, and even coconut dressings. Commonly referred to as 'the vanilla of the east'.

Gula melaka The unrefined form of palm sugar and is available as hard blocks of dark brown sugar.

gyoza skins   These are a Japanese dumpling skin made from plain flour, water and salt.

holy basil   Also known as Thai holy basil, this is one of three basil varieties commonly used in Thai cuisine along with Thai basil and Thai lemon basil. Holy basil has a bit more of a clove flavour to it, and can be harder to get.

jinhua ham   Jinhua ham is salted and dry cured and is used in many stews and braised dishes, and is used to flavour stocks. It has been produced in the Zhejiang Province of eastern China for more than twelve hundred years. It is available from some Asian grocers, but if you cannot find it you can substitute prosciutto for it.

Kaluha   A coffee-flavored liqueur with a really definitive rich flavour – found in most bottle shops.

kang kong   Also known as Chinese water spinach, or water morning glory, this is grown in a sub-tropical climate and is used all over Southeast Asia.

ketjap manis (sweet soy sauce)   This is soy sauce thickened into a molasses-type product. It is made from soy sauce, water and palm sugar.

lup cheong sausage   This is a Chinese-style pork sausage used in many dishes, particularly in Cantonese cuisine. It can be found in all Asian food stores.

Massenez crème de gingembre   A sweet style ginger liqueur from France, this has a unique, subtle spice on the nose with a warm, long-lasting palate.

Massenez lychee liqueur   An aromatic, light style liqueur with a soft lychee flavour.

Matusalem platino rum   Made by a distillery established in the Dominican republic since 1872, this is a dry, crystal-clear rum with a slight taste of sweetness and a subtle fruity array of flavours.

mirin A sweet rice wine used in Japanese cooking. It is made from sugar and glutinous rice.

mustard cress This herb is a native of western Asia and is grown with the sprouts of white mustard seeds and garden cress. It has a spicy peppery taste and a nice baby green leaf so they looks great as a garnish. It is available from most large fruit and vegetable markets, or you can speak to your local green grocer and ask them to source it for you.

nuoc cham This is a common name given to a few different types of Vietnamese dipping sauces.

palm sugar/dark palm sugar Palm sugar is made from the sugary sap of the Palmyra palm or the date palm tree, made by first extracting the sap from the flower bud of a Palmyra tree. Several slits are cut into the bud and a pot is tied underneath the bud to collect the sap. Then the sap is boiled until it thickens and poured into bamboo tubes 3–5 inches in length, and left to solidify to form cylindrical cake blocks.

PAMA pomegranate liqueur Made in Kentucky in the US, PAMA is made with all-natural pomegranate juice to capture the fruit's complex, sweet yet tart flavor. Found in good wine stores.

pandan leaves Also known as 'screwpine' leaves, these are used in Thailand, Malaysia and Indonesia for their distinctive flavour and also for their green colour. They are particularly suited to desserts, but are also used to scent boiled rice and curries. Also referred to as 'the vanilla of the east'.

panko breadcrumbs These are a larger, flakey breadcrumb used in Japanese food. Available from any Asian food store, they are a great substitute in any crumbed dish.

pat chun (sweetened chinese vinegar) This is a vinegar made from glutinous rice, ginger, orange peels, clove and sugar caramels. It is great in salad dressing and also sauces for stir-fries.

ponzu vinegar This is a vinegar made from mirin, rice wine vinegar, konbu and smoked skipjack tuna flakes. It can also be bought from most Asian grocers.

popcorn shoots These are the tender young shoots produced from sprouting popcorn. They turn a great yellow color and are sweet in flavor.

prickly ash Also known as Sichuan peppercorns, these are the seeds from the peppery ash tree (fagara) and are not related to ordinary black pepper. They are most commonly used in Chinese cooking and have a prickly, tingly flavor.

Chinese red dates The texture and flavour of this fruit resembles more an apple then a date. They can be processed as candy, diced fruits, jam, pulp and wine. The Chinese red date is classed with the raisin, date and fig as a pectoral fruit.

red shallots These look similar to golden shallots but are red in colour and are sweeter and more subtle in flavour.

rice wine vinegar This is made from fermented rice and is a very common ingredient in Asian cuisines.

salmon roe This is salmon eggs harvested shortly before the salmon spawn, when they have a large and very well-developed egg mass. It is available from most fish markets. Use fresh wherever possible.

salted black beans These are soy beans that have been fermented in a salty, briny liquid then dried, giving its own unique flavour and aroma. They are small and black and you do not need to wash them before use. A very common ingredient in Chinese and Korean cuisines.

sansho pepper This is Japanese and is related to the Sichuan pepper tree. It gives a numbing sensation on the palate.

sawtooth coriander This is native to central America but is from the same family that coriander comes from. It is a long leaf with saw-like edges all the way along it. Most commonly found during the months of summer; you can speak to your local green grocer and ask them to source it for you.

Shaoxing Chinese wine A strong flavoured Chinese rice wine, mainly used in cooking. It is made in the north of China and has an unfiltered, earthy character. At a pinch, you can substitute sherry.

shiso cress This is baby shiso perilla leaves, and can be found at some large fresh produce markets.

shiso vinegar This vinegar is infused with shiso leaves. Also known as perilla, there are green and red varieties.

shrimp paste Belacan is our preferred variety of shrimp paste. It is made in Malaysia

sichuan peppercorns These are a spice that leaves a numbing sensation on the palate. They are what gives the food of Hunan and Szechuan provinces their bite. It is not actually a pepper as it is not related to any of the pepper families.

small round rice paper sheets Used for fresh rice paper rolls. They are made from rice flour, tapioca flour, water and salt. Soak them lightly in cold water before use, then fill with your ingredients, roll up and eat.

smoke salt You can smoke salt yourself at home using manuka woodchips and salt. It is a shortcut to add a smoke flavour to foods without smoking them.

spring roll wrappers These are thin wrappers made from flour, water, rice flour and eggs. They are used in every Asian country.

sugar cane This is a subtropical and tropical crop that loves lots of sun and water. They grow from 2 to 6 metres tall and are harvested for their fibrous stalks that are rich in sugar. Indigenous to Southeast Asia.

tapioca flour This is made from cassava root. Tapioca flour is a thickening agent used in soups, but is also used in making types of dumpling skins, and cassava bread.

tapioca pearls Also made from the cassava root, these are used for savoury and sweet dishes. They are different from sago pearls but are commonly mistaken for them.

taro This is native to Southeast Asia and is a starchy root vegetable. The leaves are also edible and used commonly in Asian cooking,

MEASURES

tempura flour This is available from all Asian supermarkets and contains low-gluten flour and baking powder. Be sure not to work the batter too hard when you mix it otherwise it can become chewy and tough.

Thai basil This is a stronger basil compared to the other basils. The leaves are usually smaller and the plant has purple stems. It has an anise flavour and is served commonly with soups in Thai and Vietnamese cuisines.

threaded coconut This is coconut dried in a thread-like shape. Toast it off to a nice golden brown and use it to flavour coconut milk or cream, add it to curry pastes or use it in salads.

togarashi (shichimi pepper) This is a Japanese seven-spice blend. It is used for soups, noodles and yakitori. It is usually made from red chilli flakes, seaweed, dried orange peel, poppy seeds, black sesame seeds, golden sesame seeds and ginger.

vermicelli noodles Dried, semi-translucent noodles made from rice flour. They range in size, but are typically about 5 mm (1/4 in) wide and need to be boiled or soaked before use. They are particularly popular in Thailand and Vietnam.

Vietnamese mint Also known as Vietnamese coriander or hot mint, this is a herb which is commonly used in soups, stews and salads. It is not in the mint family but the smell and appearance are very similar.

water chestnuts These are native to Southeast Asia but have been grown in China since ancient times. A vegetable grown in marshes, they are a staple in many Chinese dishes and are used for their great texture.

wing beans This is a bean that is 15–22 cm long with four frilly wings that run its length. They are very seasonal and are available during the months of summer, but they need consistent weather to grow well. They are a very good source of vitamins and minerals.

woodchips Manuka is the best, but any from your local barbecue store will work.

woodear fungus Also known as black fungus, black Chinese fungus, this is found in most Asian markets in the dried form. Try to use fresh if you can get them. They have a slightly rubbery feeling and are slightly crunchy. They are used in a lot of Japanese and Chinese cuisine.

yellow rock sugar Large crystals of yellow-tinged sugar used in Chinese cooking. Readily available from Asian grocers.

yellow won ton wrappers Small, square-shaped sheets of fresh dough used to make won ton dumplings and some yum cha dumplings.

yuzu kosho This is a spicy Japanese condiment, made from yuzu zest, green or red chilli, and salt.

LIQUIDS

CUP	METRIC	IMPERIAL
1/8 cup	30 ml	1 fl oz
1/4 cup	60 ml	2 fl oz
1/3 cup	80 ml	2 1/2 fl oz
1/2 cup	125 ml	4 fl oz
2/3 cup	160 ml	5 fl oz
3/4 cup	180 ml	6 fl oz
1 cup	250 ml	8 fl oz
2 cups	500 ml	16 fl oz
4 cups	1 litre	32 fl oz

SOLIDS

METRIC	IMPERIAL
30 g	1 oz
60 g	2 oz
125 g	4 oz
180 g	6 oz
250 g	8 oz
500 g	16 oz (1 lb)
1 kg	32 oz (2 lb)

CELSIUS TO FAHRENHEIT

CELSIUS	FAHRENHEIT
100°C	210°F
120°C	250°F
140°C	280°F
150°C	300°F
160°C	320°F
170°C	340°F
180°C	355°F
190°C	375°F
200°C	400°F
210°C	410°F
220°C	425°F

A cup is 250 ml
A tablespoon is 20 ml
A teaspoon is 5 ml
Eggs are free-range, organic and size 65
Garlic, ginger, onions and shallots are always peeled
Pork is grain-fed
Sea salt is flaked
Non-reactive bowls, saucepans and woks are used
  with any acidic ingredients

WOK The wok is a crucial part of Asian cooking. It has a large surface area and is ideal for steaming, frying and stir-frying. They are available with a round bottom or flat bottom; the flat-bottom wok is best for cooking on a electric stove top where the wok will sit flat and you can get the most surface area touching the element. The round-bottom wok is great for a gas stove where the flames can go up the sides, but you need to make sure it is stable as you don't want the wok to roll around.

Woks are available in different materials such as stainless steel, cast iron and aluminium, and they can also have a non-stick coating. You need to make sure to use the correct cooking equipment so as not scratch or scrape the non-stick coating. We use non-reactive carbon steel or pressed steel woks at gingerboy; you can purchase these from an Asian grocer. If you use a carbon steel wok you need to make sure that you season and clean it correctly as it will rust.

To season your wok you need to place it on a high heat and once it is really hot, use a pair of tongs to rub some pork fat into the wok until it is well coated. Scrunch up some garlic chives in a couple of pieces of paper towel, place in the tongs and wipe the wok clean. Repeat this process three times and then the wok will be ready to use. Never scrub the wok; to clean you only need wipe it out once you have finished cooking.

CLEAVER A heavy cleaver is great for chopping through bones when making stocks. You can use a smaller one for chopping and slicing vegetables but you need to keep it sharp.

CLAY POT Clay pots are great for braising they are glazed on the inside, and are available from most Asian supermarkets. They come in a range of sizes so purchase the one that best suits your cooking needs.

MORTAR AND PESTLE Mortar and pestle is an important part of Asian cooking. They are used for grinding spices, and making curry and spice pastes. There are a few different types of mortar and pestles. Small deep ones are used for spices and the large deep ones are multipurpose. The Indonesian type is the shape of a shallow bowl and is designed for curry pastes only.

STEAMER We use bamboo steamer baskets with perforated stainless steel disc inserts for all of our steaming at gingerboy. They are available in many different sizes and you can purchase them from any Asian grocer.

We steam over the woks and we also have a large domestic steamer but at home you can use a saucepan with a rim the same size as your bamboo steamer. We also use a three-layer aluminium Chinese steamer, in which we place our bamboo baskets. These are also available from most Asian grocers.

MANDOLIN SLICER If you know how to, you can use a sharp knife to finely slice and shred items. If not, there is a piece of Japanese equipment on the market called a mandolin slicer that is great for stronger items such as green mango and green papaya. The blades on these slicers produce consistently sized slices. Take care when using a mandolin slicer as the blade is extremely sharp.

BAR EQUIPMENT FOR COCKTAIL MAKING

SPIRIT MEASURE Spirit measures are available from any good hospitality supply store. We prefer to use the clear plastic ones as they have both 30ml and 15ml measures.

BOSTON SHAKER AND MIXING GLASS Boston shakers and mixing glasses are pieces of bar equipment used for mixing beverages. You add your ingredients, then a whole lot of ice and the Boston shaker chills it right down as you shake and mix the drink. They are available from any good hospitality supply store.

LONG BAR SPOON A long bar spoon is used for stirring or layering cocktails. The Vietnamese espresso (on page 15 in the cocktail section) is the perfect example of a layered cocktail.

MUDDLING STICK The muddling stick is a flat-ended length of wood that is used for pounding ingredients like ginger, lime segments, lemongrass etc, and helping them to release their full flavour.

HAWTHORN STRAINER The hawthorn strainer is the piece of equipment that goes over the top of the shaker and has small holes in it to allow the liquid to run through. They are used when pouring into a serving glass for removing any ingredients from ice to aromatics. They are available from hospitality supply stores.

FINE TEA STRAINER Flecks of ice are an undesirable quality in cocktails served straight up in martini glass, so they are double strained through a fine tea strainer to remove impurities.

ACKNOWLEDGMENTS

There are many special people we would like to thank for putting this book together.

We need to thank Sandy Weir, Roz Hopkins, Natalie Winter, Helen Biles and the team at HarperCollins for giving us this great opportunity to write our book.

Thank you to Earl Carter and his assistant Fraser Marsden for the wonderful photography that has truly brought the pages of this book to life.

Thank you to Indianna Foord, our props stylist, for all the long hours sourcing a huge amount of props, plates and all sorts of weird and wacky bits and pieces. Thanks also to Potier Handmade Objects.

Special thanks to Chris's mum, Bev Donnellan, for her support testing the recipes, and to Teage's wife, Tina.

Paul Scott from Cricketers Arms Lager and Sundance Brewing International for letting us use his head office as a photography studio and supplying the much needed after-work drinks.

The past and present kitchen staff at gingerboy are vital to the success of the restaurant. We would particularly like to thank Leigh Power for putting in long hours and an enormous effort at the restaurant while we were writing this book.

Thank you to Chef De Partie and good friend Paul Jones, who has been with us from day one. His back-of-house support for the photo shoot was much appreciated.

And thank you to Chef Sam for preparing each and every recipe for the book's photography.

Thanks to Ben Thompson and Greg Jacob and the bar team at gingerboy for the beautifully fresh Asian-inspired cocktails that they continue to create.

A big thank you to the front-of-house team for their efforts and their love and passion for the food. Without them, nothing that happens at gingerboy would be possible.

Lastly, thank you to all of the suppliers we use at gingerboy; without their support and great produce we wouldn't be here today. Their continuing efforts in keeping up with menu changes and demand for the best quality produce are very much appreciated. In particular, Euro Fruit who continue to supply us with first-class produce every day and for their enormous effort with supply for the cookbook photography.

HarperCollins_Publishers_

First published in Australia in 2011
by HarperCollins_Publishers_ Australia Pty Limited
ABN 36 009 913 517
harpercollins.com.au

Copyright © Gingerboy Pty Ltd 2011

The rights of Teage Ezard and Chris Donnellan to be identified
as the authors of this work have been asserted by them in accordance
with the _Copyright Amendment (Moral Rights) Act 2000_.

This work is copyright. Apart from any use as permitted under the _Copyright_
Act 1968, no part may be reproduced, copied, scanned, stored in a retrieval system,
recorded, or transmitted, in any form or by any means, without the prior written
permission of the publisher.

HarperCollins_Publishers_
Level 13, 201 Elizabeth Street, Sydney, NSW 2000, Australia
31 View Road, Glenfield, Auckland 0627, New Zealand
A 53, Sector 57, Noida, UP, India
77–85 Fulham Palace Road, London W6 8JB, United Kingdom
2 Bloor Street East, 20th floor, Toronto, Ontario M4W 1A8, Canada
10 East 53rd Street, New York NY 10022, USA

National Library of Australia Cataloguing-in-Publication entry:

Ezard, Teage.
    Gingerboy / Teage Ezard and Chris Donnellan.
    ISBN: 978 0 7322 9347 5 (hbk.)
    Includes index.
    Cooking, Asian.
    Donnellan, Chris.
641.595

Cover and internal design by Natalie Winter
Cover photographs, author photograph and all food photography by Earl Carter
Asian street photography: pages 208 and 217 by Jerry Alexander / Lonely Planet Images;
pages 116–117 by Austin Bush / Lonely Planet Images; pages 108 and 202
by Richard l'Anson / Lonely Planet Images
Typeset in Charter 9/12 by Kirby Jones
Colour reproduction by Graphic Print Group, Adelaide
Printed in China by RR Donnelley on 157gsm Matt Art

5 4 3 2 1   11 12 13 14